Inclusive Primary Teaching

A Critical Approach to Equality and Special Educational Needs

Janet Goepel, Helen Childerhouse & Sheila Sharpe

CRITICAL
TEACHING

First published in 2014 by Critical Publishing Ltd
Reprinted in 2014

British Library Cataloguing in Publication Data
A CIP record for this book is available from the British Library

ISBN: 978-1-909330-29-0

This book is also available in the following e-book formats:

MOBI ISBN: 978-1-909330-30-6
EPUB ISBN: 978-1-909330-31-3
Adobe e-book ISBN: 978-1-909330-32-0

Cover design by Greensplash Limited
Project Management by Out of House Publishing
Printed and bound in Great Britain by Bell and Bain, Glasgow

Critical Publishing
152 Chester Road
Northwich
CW8 4AL
www.criticalpublishing.com

MIX
Paper from
responsible sources
FSC
www.fsc.org   FSC® C007785

Inclusive Primary

Teac

ary

CRITICAL
TEACHING

You might also like the following books in our *Critical Teaching* series

Beyond Early Reading
Edited by David Waugh and Sally Neaum
978-1-909330-41-2
Published September 2013

Primary School Placements: A Critical Guide to Outstanding Teaching
Catriona Robinson, Branwen Bingle and Colin Howard
978-1-909330-45-0
Published June 2013

Reflective Primary Teaching
Tony Ewens
978-1-909682-17-7
Published May 2014

Teaching and Learning Early Years Mathematics: Subject and Pedagogic Knowledge
Mary Briggs
978-1-909330-37-5
Published September 2013

Teaching Systematic Synthetic Phonics and Early English
By Jonathan Glazzard and Jane Stokoe
978-1-909330-09-2
Published March 2013

Most of our titles are also available in a range of electronic formats. To order please go to our website www.criticalpublishing.com or contact our distributor, NBN International, 10 Thornbury Road, Plymouth PL6 7PP, telephone 01752 202301 or email orders@nbninternational.com.

Contents

Acknowledgements

The diagrams on pages 169 and 172 in Chapter 11 are Crown Copyright and are gratefully reproduced free of charge under the terms of the Open Government Licence.

Page 169 Diagram taken from *Working Together to Safeguard Children* (HM Gov. 2013, p 20). Crown Copyright / Department for Education

Page 172 Diagram showing the Common Assessment Framework process, taken from the Department for Education website (2012). Crown Copyright / Department for Education.

Meet the authors

Janet Goepel was a teacher for many years and developed an interest in special educational needs through having children with additional needs in her classes. She has taught children with profound and multiple learning difficulties who otherwise would have had to attend a special school, as well as those with dyslexia, dyspraxia, ADHD and social difficulties. She is now a senior lecturer teaching inclusion at Sheffield Hallam University and hopes to pass on her passion for inclusive practice to trainee teachers as well as SENCos.

Helen Childerhouse is a senior lecturer in primary and Early Years teacher education at Sheffield Hallam University. She teaches on undergraduate modules that involve professional practice and supports trainees while they are on placement. She also teaches on the modules which focus on educational enquiry and research, inclusive practice, child development, partnerships with parents and professionals and the way in which policy influences teaching practice.

Sheila Sharpe was until very recently a senior lecturer at Sheffield Hallam University with roles including course leader for the PG Cert SENCo award and inclusion co-ordinator for the undergraduate and postgraduate primary and Early Years teacher education programme. She has taught children from a wide range of backgrounds and cultures with a range of learning and emotional needs. In addition, she has been a SENCo in a primary school and has worked in an advisory capacity in a local authority supporting teachers in meeting the language and literacy needs of children.

Introduction

The Conservative/Liberal Democrat coalition government which came to power in 2010 archived much of the previous Labour government's education policy and initiatives, including Every Child Matters (DfES, 2004), which was a strong element of many schools' working practice and ethos. New guidance has been slow to be introduced, leaving schools feeling rudderless and uncertain as to the direction they should be taking. In the interim, many schools have continued with previous policies while waiting to understand what new initiatives will be introduced and what this will mean for them in practice. The new National Curriculum is a good example of how the current government has halted the previous government's preparation for a new curriculum and instead has published its own, to be formally introduced in 2014. This new National Curriculum naturally reflects the ideals and beliefs of the coalition government. The introduction of the new Standards for Teachers (DfE, 2013) and SEN initiative (DfE, 2012) provides two other examples of how teachers' professional lives are subject to political influence and expectation, which is monitored by assessment regimes such as Ofsted.

With the frequency of such changes, the need to achieve higher grades in the Ofsted inspection process and the busyness of the day-to-day work of the classroom, it is not easy for teachers to carve out time to think, to reflect and to gather relevant information to inform their professional decisions. It is therefore important that teachers take time away from the classroom situation to consider their own values and beliefs, to think about the underpinning principles of practice and to work through the implications of these in practice.

It is tempting for all teachers, but particularly trainee teachers, just to take on the practices of the school where they are working, a kind of apprentice model, where you see what other teachers do and then do the same. However, it is also important to know what good practice is and why that is so. Taking on the good practice you see modelled by other teachers is a good start, but in time you will need to develop your own practice, and understanding the values which underpin good practice will be important in judging how you want your practice to develop. It will also give you confidence in making decisions which need a quick response as you will have previously thought through your own position on important professional matters.

How to read the book

Teachers are faced with change throughout their careers. There is the imperative to keep up to date with the changing educational landscape as well as constantly working to high standards of teaching and professional practice. Slavishly following requirements, whether new government initiatives, new inspection regimes, managing children with new and more complex difficulties or taking on new roles and responsibilities, without understanding the underpinning principles involved, can be dispiriting. A critical approach which evaluates the rationale for teaching methods and practices provides an anchor in an ever-changing educational world. While teachers will and should be constantly challenged in their values and practice, knowing what you believe, why you believe it and the evidence for your beliefs provides a good foundation for considering change and will enable you to make informed choices about the changes you make.

Smyth (1989) argues that *our experiences as teachers give meaning and significance to events* (p 4) and that teachers play *an interactive part ... in the creation of those events* (p 5). He further states that *the people who do the work of teaching should be the same people who reflect on it* (p 7). However, theory, research, and perspectives from a range of stakeholders, as well as a teacher's previous experiences, all inform how professional practice is executed and help shape values and beliefs. Knowing your own values and beliefs will also help you in dealing with the changes imposed by new government policy and initiatives during your teaching career. The Special Educational Needs (SEN) Green Paper *Support and Aspiration* (DfE, 2012) will undoubtedly bring changes to how SEN is managed in our schools. However, having an understanding of the underlying principles of inclusion and the requirements of legislation such as the Equality Duty, and evaluating the findings of current research and theory will provide a compass to direct you through the complexity of change that each new initiative brings.

Critical thinking and reflection

The notion of being critical is often seen as a negative thing. It is commonly perceived as finding fault or judging harshly. It is usually considered that it is better to be positive, to think about what has gone well or is useful or fit for purpose and then to offer suggestions as to how something might be improved. Being critical is sometimes thought to be hurtful or confrontational and to be avoided. However, thinking critically in an educational sense and in the context of this book is different. Opie (2004, pp 36–37) cites the understanding of criticality as defined by some of his academic colleagues and students. The elements of criticality include:

- analysing and synthesising points of view;

- having the ability to understand, analyse and appraise the ideas, views and findings expressed in a variety of source materials;

- comparing and contrasting, and supporting or not a particular argument or line of thinking;

- making things explicit and open to scrutiny and challengeable;

- having a *vigorously questioning attitude*, a spirit of open-minded enquiry.

Wellington et al. develop these ideas further, stating that

> *being critical is about having the confidence to make informed judgements ... it is about finding your own voice, your own values and building your own standpoint in*

the face of numerous other, often apparently stronger voices (from the literature and elsewhere) and many other view points. (2005, p 84)

This book is not a 'how-to' guide, nor will it provide tick lists of good practice for you to check your practice against. It will, however, provide the means whereby you can *exercise … careful, deliberate and well informed judgement* (Wellington et al., 2005, p 84). However, being critical alone will not result in a change of professional practice. Only by engaging in reflection about your own professional conduct within the context of relevant sources will you be able to develop your practice further.

Moon (2008) promotes the activity of reflecting on an event from the past in order to reprocess or reorganise the way that event has been understood, with a view to improving future performance (p 157). Furthermore, she suggests that reflection can bring about empowerment. She outlines how, in considering how you think about things, who you are as a person and practitioner, along with the social and political context within which you are working, new situations can be created. In the context of this book, these situations may be related to how a child's barriers to learning can be removed and how your classroom practice can include all learners.

Getting the best out of the book

Each of the chapters in this book contains a number of scenarios that outline particular situations that you could meet as a trainee teacher or later in your professional practice. Some of these scenarios are accompanied by spidergrams which detail the range of considerations in managing children's barriers to learning. The scenarios are followed by critical questions that are deliberately designed to provoke you into thinking critically about the scenario and looking more deeply into the situation described. Some of the critical questions will lead you into reflection on your own practice and support you in developing your own values and beliefs in relation to SENs and equality. Giving attention to the scenarios and the following critical questions at a deep level will enable you to get the most out of the book, resulting in greater understanding of the issues and bringing most impact in your practice.

The structure of the book

The book is divided into three parts, each dealing with an important aspect of inclusive practice:

Part 1: Making reasonable adjustments

Part 2: Developing partnerships

Part 3: Developing inclusive environments.

Each of the chapters within these three parts includes an outline of the legislative context within which the theme of the chapter is placed, and in some cases a historical overview is also provided. Each chapter also includes a summary of the most relevant theory and research. These elements of theory, legislation and research provide the background for the discussion of the scenarios and the critical questions. Some chapters include an international perspective which helps to provide a global understanding of education and matters of equality worldwide. While the government guidance, policy and legislation are deemed to be up to date at the time of publishing, it is important for you to be aware that new initiatives are being introduced constantly and new research is coming to the fore. You should therefore make sure you keep up to date with new developments as they will surely impact on your professional practice.

Part 1: Making reasonable adjustments

The Equality Duty (2010) requires that where a disabled person is placed at a substantial disadvantage relative to a non-disabled person, *reasonable adjustments* should be made in order to relieve the disadvantage. This is also the same for any of the nine protected characteristics, including race, religion and sex, identified in this Act.

Part 1 of the book considers a range of barriers to learning and outlines how some of these barriers may be overcome. The approach is about equality for all children, regardless of their needs or circumstances.

Chapter 1, Understanding policy, provides an overview of relevant government education legislation and policy, including a historical perspective since the 1944 Education Act. The Equality Act (UK Government, 2010) and implications for practice are considered and the discussion of terms and concepts relating to inclusion are outlined. This chapter provides a foundation for many of the ideas and constructs outlined in further chapters.

The notion of identity is unpicked in Chapter 2, Understanding identity and gender. The chapter explores how identity is constructed and whether it is something we are born with or whether it is socially constructed. The impact of a child's identity on their ability to learn is discussed and the implications of gender identity for classroom practice are identified. Furthermore, gender inequality in education worldwide is considered, along with the wider perspective of gender inequality in employment and government.

Chapter 3, Understanding behaviour, considers the government's recent emphasis on behaviour management and discipline and examines pupil and teacher behaviour through a scenario featuring a disruptive incident in the classroom. The well-being of the teacher is recognised as an important element in creating a positive classroom. Additionally, some theories of behaviour are discussed, along with practical strategies for positive behaviour management.

One of the Equality Duty's protected characteristics is featured in Chapter 4, Understanding race. Factors which inhibit a fully integrated society, including individual opinion, structural oppression and institutional racism, are identified and the influences on children with regard to their perception of race are discussed, together with concerns of ethnic identity, achievement and performance levels of children from different ethnic backgrounds. A scenario of a racial incident outlines the implications for the class teacher in dealing with such a situation, and notions of anti-discrimination and multiculturalism are explored.

In Chapter 5, Understanding learners in poverty, social class and the class system in the UK is examined. Absolute and relative poverty are defined, along with some of the causes of poverty. The impact of poverty on educational achievement is discussed, including the cost of schooling on parents. This chapter also considers how teachers can support children in poverty.

Understanding learners with English as an additional language (EAL), Chapter 6, raises issues about the different learning requirements of children whose first language is other than English. It details Cummins' theory of language acquisition and shows how teachers need to take into account the length of time it takes to develop academic language proficiency. An awareness of different cultures, traditions and customs is given, along with the importance for teachers to take such matters into account in their provision for children with EAL. This chapter also includes ways in which a positive classroom ethos as well as a positive physical environment can be developed.

The final chapter in Part 1 is called Understanding children with special educational needs and disabilities (SEND). This chapter further develops the medical and social models and considers implications for practice. It discusses the use of terminology and labelling and identifies barriers to learning and how they may be overcome. Processes and systems for the support of children with SEN are outlined, including the Education, Health and Care Plan (EHCP). Consideration is also given to how children with SEN are managed in a range of countries.

Part 2: Developing partnerships

This part of the book recognises that the days when the teacher would work behind a closed classroom door with her class of children are long gone. Increasingly, teachers are expected to work with a wide range of partners, including the children in their class, their parents, other education professionals and professionals from other agencies, such as health and social services. While much of the teacher's roles and responsibilities lie within the classroom, there is also much to be done in developing effective learning partnerships with children and their parents. Engaging colleagues such as other teachers, including the Special Educational Needs Co-ordinator (SENCo) and teaching assistants (TAs), will bring opportunities to gain new knowledge and understanding in order to develop your professional practice; while working with other education professionals such as education psychologists and learning support teachers will provide you with colleagues with specialist skills in assessment as well as advice to support children with specific learning difficulties. It is also important to develop effective partnerships with professionals from other agencies, such as those in health or the social services. All of this is discussed in more detail in this section of the book.

Chapter 8, Working with children, considers the children who need you, as the teacher, to be specially aware of them. It outlines the different ways in which children can communicate with the teacher and how you can create space and opportunity for children's voices to be heard. This chapter considers the teacher/child talk ratio and the need for teachers to be aware of the power imbalance when encouraging children to talk. The importance of understanding children holistically is discussed and safeguarding procedures are detailed.

Chapter 9, Working with parents, considers a range of different kinds of parents and discusses how positive relationships can be built between them and yourself as the teacher of their children. The influence of different cultural experiences and expectations is raised. The chapter also describes how parents can offer valuable insights about their children to support their learning. Ways in which the teacher can build bridges through effective communication are discussed and support for parents, such as Parent Partnership Support Groups, is identified.

In Chapter 10, Working with colleagues, the rise of additional support for teachers within the classroom is described, along with the range of different roles and tasks such support workers might undertake and the qualifications each different role requires. Pitfalls in different expectations of practice are outlined with suggested strategies to support better working practices. This chapter also includes an examination of the effectiveness of TAs' work on the achievement of pupils and considers how beneficial working partnerships can be developed.

Chapter 11, Working with outside agencies, considers the range of professionals working in other services, such as health, social services or the police, who may be involved in supporting children with SEN or who are at risk. The tensions between the different agencies in terms of their expectations and outcomes are identified as well as the importance of being able to work as a team. This chapter examines the nature of multi-agency meetings, the roles and responsibilities of the various professionals involved and implications for practice. It also recognises the need for the teacher to be an advocate for the child who is at the centre of the multi-agency meeting.

Part 3: Developing inclusive environments

The final part of the book looks at the twin aspects of inclusion, the inclusive classroom and the inclusive curriculum. The physical environment and ethos of the classroom give vital clues as to its inclusive nature and, together with the way the curriculum is delivered, shows how provision can be made for children to achieve. While the way the physical environment is set up and how the curriculum is delivered are intertwined, for the purposes of this book they are separated out in order to make the intent of each obvious.

Chapter 12, The inclusive classroom, considers both the learning environment and the social environment of the classroom. Factors which affect learning, such as how seating is arranged, where resources are kept, the use of visual cues, labelling of classroom features and displays, are discussed. Additionally, this chapter raises some important issues about how pupils are grouped to support inclusion and how different groupings can be used for different tasks. The use of TAs is also considered in providing an inclusive learning environment.

In the final chapter, Chapter 13, The inclusive curriculum, attention is given to the teacher's responsibility to provide an engaging curriculum for all children. Rather than introducing different approaches, the chapter outlines how common teaching approaches can be used, but with more intensity, additional emphasis or with greater care. Making differentiated provision which moves away from the commonly used three-way differentiation is discussed and a model which values difference, meaningful experiences and tools for later life is offered. This chapter returns to the theme begun in Chapter 12 of how TAs are used to make the curriculum accessible and finally outlines a range of strategies which can be used to engage all children in their learning.

References

Department for Education (DfE) (2012) *Support and Aspiration: A New Approach to Special Educational Needs and Disability. Progress and Next Steps.* Cm 8027. London: The Stationery Office.

Department for Education (DfE) (2013) *Teachers' Standards.* Online: http://media.education.gov.uk/assets/files/pdf/t/teachers%20standards%20information.pdf (last accessed 31 Aug 2013).

Department for Education and Skills (DfES) (2004) *Every Child Matters.* Online: http://webarchive. nationalarchives.gov.uk/20130401151715/https://www.education.gov.uk/publications/ standard/publicationdetail/page1/cm5860 (last accessed 17 October 2013).

Moon, J. (2008) *Reflection in Learning and Professional Development: Theory and Practice.* London: Routledge Falmer.

Opie, C. (ed) (2004) *Doing Educational Research: A First Time Guide for Researchers.* London: Sage.Smyth, J. (1989) Developing and Sustaining Critical Reflection in Teacher Education. *Journal of Teacher Education,* 40(2): 1–9.

UK Government (2010) *The Equality Act 2010,* Chapter 15. London: The Stationery Office. Online: www.legislation.gov.uk/ukpga/2010/15/pdfs/ukpga_20100015_en.pdf (last accessed 30 Aug 2013).

Wellington, J., Bathmaker, A., Hunt, C., McCullogh, G. and Sikes, P. (2005) *Succeeding with Your Doctorate.* London: Sage.

List of acronyms

ADHD   Attention deficit hyperactivity disorder
AfL   Assessment for learning
ALS   Additional literacy support
ASD   Autistic spectrum disorder
ATL   Association of Teachers and Lecturers
BICS   Basic interpersonal communication skills
CAF   Common Assessment Framework
CALP   Cognitive academic language proficiency
CoP   Code of Practice
DCSF   Department for Children, Schools and Families
DDA   Disability Discrimination Act
DED   Disability Equality Duty
DfE   Department for Education
DfEE   Department for Education and Employment
DfES   Department for Education and Skills
DISS   Deployment and Impact of Support Staff
EAL   English as an additional language
ECM   Every Child Matters
EFA   Education for All
EHCP   Education, Health and Care Plan
EHRC   Equality and Human Rights Commission
ELS   Early literacy support
EP   Educational psychologist
EU   European Union
EYFS   Early Years Foundation Stage
FLS   Further literacy support
GCSE   General Certificate of Secondary Education
GED   Gender Equality Duty
GDP   Gross domestic product
HAPs   Higher ability pupils
HMSO   Her Majesty's Stationery Office
ICF   International Classification of Functioning, Disability and Health
ICT   Information Communication Technology
ID   Indices of deprivation
IDACI   Income Deprivation Affecting Children Indices
IEP   Individual Education Plan

IPU	Inter-Parliamentary Union
IQ	Intelligence quotient
IT	Information Technology
ITT	Initial teacher training
JRF	Joseph Rowntree Foundation
LA	Local Authority
LAC	Looked after children
LAPs	Lower ability pupils
LSS	Learning Support Service
MAPs	Middle Ability children
NALDIC	National Association for Language Development in the Curriculum
NC	National Curriculum
NCTL	National College for Teaching and Leadership
NHS	National Health Service
NLT	National Literacy Trust
NQT	Newly qualified teacher
OECD	Organisation for Economic Co-operation and Development
Ofsted	The Office for Standards in Education, Children's Services and Skills
ONS	Office for National Statistics
PE	Physical Education
PNS	Primary National Strategy
QTS	Qualified teacher status
RBA	Removing barriers to achievement
RQT	Recently qualified teacher
RTP	Registered Teacher Programme
SATs	Standardised Assessment Tests or Standardised Attainment Tests (both are used)
SEAL	Social and emotional aspects of learning
SEN	Special educational needs
SENCo	Special Educational Needs Co-ordinator
SENCoP	Special Educational Needs Code of Practice
SEND	Special Educational Needs and Disability
SENDA	Special Educational Needs and Disability Act
SS	Social services
SSP	Systematic synthetic phonics
TA	Teaching Assistant
TAC	Team around the child
TDA	Teaching and Development Agency
TS	Teachers' Standards
UK	United Kingdom
UN	United Nations
UNCRC	United Nations Convention on the Rights of the Child
UNESCO	United Nations Educational, Scientific and Cultural Organization
VAK	Visual, auditory and kinaesthetic (learning approaches)
WHO	World Health Organization

Part 1

Making reasonable adjustments

1 Understanding policy

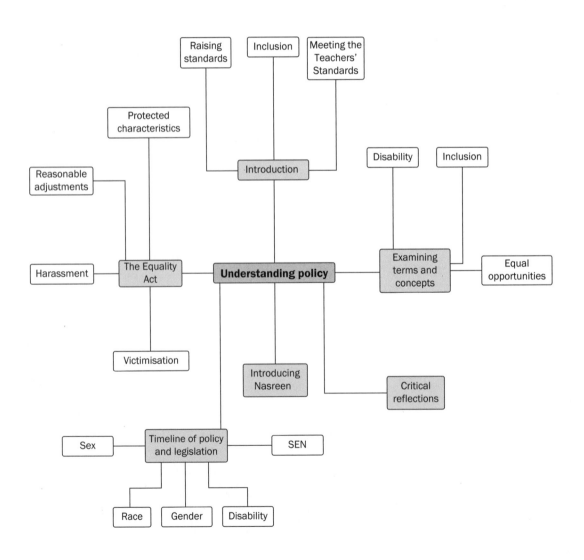

Introduction

The current emphasis in our schools is on standards and how well children achieve. This is driven largely through the framework set out by the Office for Standards in Education, Children's Services and Skills (Ofsted). This framework assesses a school against national standards and provides information for parents on how well the school is performing in order for them to make informed choices regarding schools for their children. The inspection process deliberately sets out to drive up standards of effectiveness and performance and to promote rigour in the way a school assesses and monitors its own performance and its capacity to improve. Assessment focuses on the achievement of pupils, the quality of the teaching, the behaviour and safety of the children, as well as the quality of the leadership and management of the school (Ofsted, 2013, p 5). Schools can no longer receive an Ofsted judgement of 'satisfactory'. Schools offering an 'acceptable' standard of education can be considered to be 'good', whereas schools which are not yet 'good' but not considered to be 'inadequate' are considered to 'require improvement'. Other categories which schools may be allocated are 'serious weaknesses' and 'special measures' (Ofsted, 2013, pp 5–6). Many teachers feel the pressure of impending inspections at one day's notice. If you have been into placement schools near or during the time of inspection you will be aware of the impact that this has on teachers.

Alongside the constant drive for achievement is the push towards the inclusion of all pupils. The 1997 Green Paper *Excellence for all Children: Meeting Special Educational Needs* was a commitment by the Labour government to improve the statutory framework for children with special educational needs (SEN). This was followed by other guidance and legislation such as:

*   the SEN Code of Practice (SENCoP) (DfES, 2001);

*   the Special Educational Needs and Disability Act 2001;

*   the Equality Act 2010 (UK Government, 2010);

*   most recently, the new coalition government's SEN Green Paper (DfE, 2011);

*   and its response *Support and Aspiration: A New Approach to SEN and Disability – Progress and Next Steps*. (DfE, 2012)

All of this policy and guidance presents the teacher with the dilemma of needing to provide inclusion for all children, while at the same time driving up standards for all.

Research by Farrell et al. (2007) suggests that there is neither a positive nor a negative relationship between the inclusion of children with SEN into mainstream schools and the achievement of other pupils, maintaining that many of the strategies that are good for children with SEN are also good for all children. However, Glazzard et al. (2010) consider that schools are reluctant to embrace an inclusive education agenda because of the increased emphasis on performance and school accountability (p 5).

Black-Hawkins et al. (2007) recognise that relationships are at the heart of understanding and developing inclusive practice in schools and that an individual's own values and beliefs, as well as those of the institution, play an important role in inclusive practices. They recognise that not all teachers feel confident about how to include all learners and that this can generate feelings of insecurity and lack of competence. They state

> If feelings such as fear, humiliation, failure, intolerance and anger are ignored then barriers to inclusion and achievement are strengthened. Similarly, these processes cannot be developed if pleasure, success, happiness, and confidence are not valued and if respect, responsibility, kindness and resilience are not encouraged. (p 31)

Their research considers that inclusive schools are continually looking to solve problems, to re-invent inclusion and to make dynamic links between policy and practice. Furthermore, Black-Hawkins et al. maintain that such schools are effective and able to compete well alongside other schools, not compromising standards for the sake of inclusive practice. Such schools use policies and practices which help to shape the values and beliefs held by those within and to promote a culture of high expectations and the valuing of all (2007, p 30). It can be seen, therefore, that for schools to work towards the achievement of all pupils alongside the inclusion of all, there needs to be a clear understanding of purpose. Successive governments have laid down their expectations through their policies, legislation and guidance. However, it is the responsibility of each school to determine how such policies are to be played out in its setting.

MEETING THE TEACHERS' STANDARDS

Links to Department for Education Teachers' Standards May 2012

Part 2.

Introducing Nasreen

All schools are required to have policies relating to equal opportunities for all children. This relates to any circumstance where children may be considered to be disadvantaged in relation to their peers. It can relate to physical access to a building such as via ramps and the size of doors, as well as access to all curriculum areas, including school trips. The following scenario considers the barriers to learning and participation which need to be removed for Nasreen to play a full part in her education experience.

SCENARIO

Nasreen is a 10-year-old Pakistani girl in Year 6. She has four brothers, two older and two younger than herself. Nasreen had a difficult birth. She has cerebral palsy. This means her speech is not always easy to understand and she has difficulty in walking unaided. She is a wheelchair user and needs help in toileting and dressing. Her hands are also affected by her cerebral palsy such that she is not able to hold a pencil, or a knife and fork. Nasreen's parents wanted her to attend the same school as her brothers, but due to her complex needs, she was unable to start school at the same time as her peers. She was eventually able to attend her local school after several modifications were made to the building and a part-time TA was appointed to support her both in her learning and health needs. As the TA was not full time and the school did not feel they could manage her needs without additional support, Nasreen initially only attended school in the mornings. She was often tired in the afternoon and would go home to rest. Now Nasreen is in Year 6, the TA support has increased and she is able to attend school full time. Her ability to learn is not impaired and she is able to read and understand at the same level as her peers. However, her access to the curriculum is a challenge. For example, the Information Technology (IT) suite is in a room accessed by stairs. There is no lift and so she is taught IT in a separate room away from her peers. Because of her difficulties in holding equipment and resources, Nasreen often just watches the other children as they engage in practical tasks, and the teacher is nervous about her engaging in science, food technology or PE where there could be considered to be health and safety risks. Nasreen needs regular physiotherapy, which is provided by the TA, but as the teacher does not want her missing out on class time, the physiotherapy is carried out at lunch time before Nasreen eats. This means that she does not eat with her peers and her opportunity to socialise at lunch time is reduced.

Nasreen's parents recently complained to the school as they felt she was being discriminated against with regard to access to a school visit. The class was being taken to a local theatre performance, but as the seats the children were allocated were upstairs and not wheelchair accessible, Nasreen was told that she had to sit with her TA downstairs or not take part in the visit. Nasreen's parents wanted the school to seat everyone downstairs so that Nasreen could be part of the social group, but the school felt that this would increase the cost of the visit and that some parents would not be able to afford the additional cost.

Critical questions

» *How do you think the school is making inclusive provision for Nasreen?*

» *What further inclusive practices could be carried out to improve Nasreen's educational experience?*

» *Consider Nasreen's experience of social inclusion. How could that be improved?*

» *How would you solve the dilemma of how to manage the theatre visit so that Nasreen can be part of her class?*

Having begun to consider how Nasreen is being included within a mainstream classroom, as well as some of the barriers to her learning and participation, consider the spidergram on page 6, which provides an overview of some of the issues raised in this scenario.

The spidergram provides an examination of inclusion as it relates to Nasreen, but it is also applicable to other similar incidents and situations. An examination of these issues will enable you to:

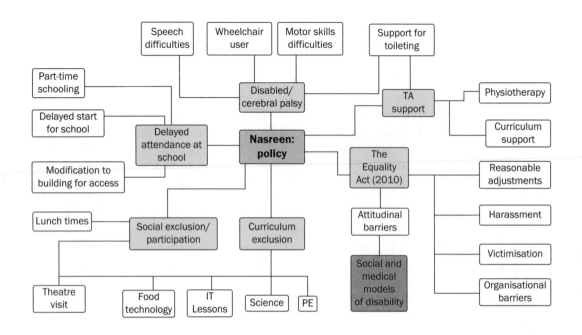

- be aware of legislation relating to disability discrimination in schools;

- understand how statutory guidance and policy documents influence and relate to practice in schools;

- identify specific examples of disability discrimination and how they can be overcome.

Additionally, this chapter examines relevant government policy and considers the implications of these for you as a beginner teacher within the context of placement. However, it is important to gain an understanding of some of the commonly used terms which are used when considering the needs of all learners. These are explored in the following section.

Examining terms and concepts

Over the years, various terms and labels have been used to identify children who are at an earlier stage of development or who are considered to have specific difficulties or barriers to learning. Many of the labels that were used to identify particular medical conditions or disabilities are now seen as terms of abuse, for example, spastic (now known as cerebral palsy), idiot, moron and cretin. Evans (2007) reminds us that it is important when talking about children with special needs that the child is seen first and not the disability. She therefore recommends that rather than using the term *the SEN child*, they should be referred to as *the child with SEN*. Similarly, rather than the *Tourette's child*, it should be the *child with Tourette's syndrome* (p 36). Language is constantly evolving, so it is worth taking a look at the language used in policy and guidance documents to gain a clearer understanding of the concepts and notions which are expected to be enacted in our schools and as part of your professional practice.

Disability

Professor Stephen Hawking, who has had motor neurone disease for most of his adult life, states that *disability need not be a barrier to success* (World Health Organization, 2011a, p 3), yet the World Report on Disability by the World Health Organization (WHO) states that more than 1 billion people worldwide, about 15 per cent of people, live with some form of disability. Around 200 million of these experience considerable difficulties in functioning and this figure is rising (WHO, 2011a, p 5). Despite Professor Hawking's assertion and own experience, it is known that people with disabilities have poorer health outcomes, lower educational achievements, less economic participation and higher rates of poverty than people without disabilities. This is considered to be because people with disabilities may not be able to access services such as health, education, employment and transport in the same way as other non-disabled people (WHO, 2011a, p 5). This can be seen in the scenario as Nasreen was not able to start school at the same time as her peers and was only able to attend part time in the first instance.

Barton considers that status is influenced by cultural images (2005, p 59), while the way people with disabilities are portrayed in the media is considered by Hodkinson and Vickerman (2012) to be detrimental to society's perception of disability. They consider how in fiction people with a disability can often be portrayed as objects of pity or as villains. Furthermore, they observe that newspapers often feature people with impairments in a sensational way, seeing them as different or other and therefore not part of mainstream life. The use of people with disabilities in advertising has often been centred on abnormality and a perceived helplessness or dependency. Such media portrayal promotes a negative conceptualisation of disability in society. This leads to the formation of attitudes, assumptions and expectations of disabled people based on stereotypes, and these can influence the classroom environment (pp 43–49). In a report by Mencap (2007), 82 per cent of children with a learning disability had been bullied, with 79 per cent afraid to go out because of the threat of being bullied. Additionally, 58 per cent of children had been physically hurt. This shows how children with a disability are at risk of social exclusion by their peers and how negative perceptions of disability threaten the inclusion of children with disabilities in our schools.

It is commonly believed that the Paralympics in London 2012 heightened the awareness and acceptance of people with disabilities. Indeed, a survey by Scope prior to the Paralympics suggested that 62 per cent of people with disabilities and their families believed that the games could change the way people think about them. Lord Coe stated that *we would never look at disability the same again*. A further survey carried out after the Paralympics showed that 72 per cent of people with a disability thought the games had made a positive impact on attitudes, 20 per cent of people with a disability considered the games had changed the way people talked to them, and a further 20 per cent of people surveyed considered that people were now more aware of their needs. However, discriminatory attitudes seemed to be hard to shift. Further questions in the survey revealed the following information.

* 54 per cent of people with disabilities experience discrimination on a regular basis.
* 84 per cent of people with a disability felt others patronised them.
* 63.5 per cent of people with a disability stated that people refused to make adjustments for them or to do things for them. (Scope, 2012)

It would therefore seem that while some people's perceptions of people with disability have changed, there are still entrenched views and attitudes which continue to provide disabling barriers for those with disabilities.

WHO has produced a framework for measuring health and disability known as the International Classification of Functioning, Disability and Health (ICF). This framework considers health and disability at both the individual and the population level and also includes a list of environmental factors. The ICF considers that disability can be experienced by anyone, through a decrease in health, an increase in age, or through accident or disease. It therefore becomes mainstream, with an emphasis not on cause, but on impact, thereby allowing all disability to be measured by the same yardstick. Additionally, the ICF considers the social aspects of disability, rather than seeing it as a medical or biological dysfunction (WHO, 2011b).

The medical and social models of disability

Booth and Ainscow (2002) state that within the medical model of disability, difficulties in learning are considered to arise because of deficiencies or impairments within the child. Impairments are seen as a long-term limitation of function, either physical, intellectual or sensory. According to the Office for Disability Issues, the Equality Act (2010) states that a person has a disability if he or she has a substantial or long-term adverse effect on their ability to carry out normal day-to-day activities (Great Britain, 2010, p 6). However, within the social model of disability, barriers to learning and participation arise because of the interaction between the child and their environment. The disabilities which arise may be because of *discriminatory attitudes, actions, cultures, policies and institutional practices* towards impairments or illness (p 6). While Booth and Ainscow acknowledge that there is little a school can do to overcome a child's impairment, they maintain there is a great deal to be done to reduce disabilities caused by discriminatory attitudes and actions as well as institutional barriers (p 7). It would seem that Nasreen's teacher is presented with some dilemmas with regard to how to include her fully in the educational and learning activities presented to the rest of the class, for example in IT, or in practical lessons such as science and PE. Yet teaching a child separately from her peers cannot be seen as full inclusion, and therefore attitudinal and organisational barriers need to be challenged. A further discussion of the medical and social models of disability in relation to children with special educational needs and disability (SEND) can be found in Chapter 7 (see page 113).

Critical questions

»   *Dr Stephen Hawking considers that disability need not be a barrier to success. Consider people with disabilities that you are aware of, either personally or in the public eye. How would you define success for them?*

»   *Examine the media portrayal of people with disabilities. How are they presented? Can you think of an advertising campaign which portrays disabled people in a positive way?*

»   *Consider how the media portrayal of people with a disability influences society's attitudes and behaviour. How are your attitudes and behaviours influenced by what you read or see on TV, the internet, in newspapers and in literature?*

» 	*If you had a child with disabilities such as Nasreen in your placement class, what barriers of attitude and action within yourself might you need to challenge?*

Inclusion

The new framework for the National Curriculum in England was published in February 2013. Within this document, the government's statement on inclusion is made plain. The previous National Curriculum Inclusion Statement had three principles:

* setting suitable learning challenges;

* responding to pupils' diverse learning needs;

* overcoming potential barriers to learning and assessment for individuals and groups of pupils. (DfEE, 1999, p 30)

These have now been reduced to two statements, but covering very similar ideals and values. They are:

* setting suitable challenges;

* responding to pupils' needs and overcoming potential barriers for individuals and groups of pupils. (DfE, 2013, p 9)

The new National Curriculum will be made mandatory in 2014. It has a strong emphasis on planning *stretching work* and *ambitious targets* and articulates the need for teachers to be aware of their duties under equal opportunities legislation. This includes the protected characteristics of disability, ethnicity, gender, sexual identity, gender identity, and religion or belief, and goes beyond making provision for children with SEN alone. Additionally, provision for children for whom English is not their first language is explicitly required (DfE, 2013, p 9).

The inclusion statements in the new National Curriculum outline clearly how the teacher should make provision for all learners, regardless of difference; however, Booth and Ainscow (2002) consider the concepts of inclusion that may underpin the teacher's actions and attitudes. They maintain that inclusion involves an unending process of learning and participation for all children. Participating means being able to learn alongside other pupils and being involved in shared learning experiences. It is about being *recognised, accepted and valued for one's self* (p 3). Armstrong also considers that inclusive education is concerned with the right for all to receive equal recognition, respect and treatment and that this centres on the acknowledgement of diversity. She states that this involves being an equal member of the community and neighbourhood schools (2008, p 11). Such a stance suggests that Nasreen is not in receipt of a fully inclusive experience, as the way the visit to the theatre is being managed suggests that she is being treated differently from her peers. Armstrong also points out that inclusion differs from integration in that integration is concerned with the perceived deficits of the child as creating barriers to participation, whereas inclusion considers the barriers to participation to be within the school or educational setting (Armstrong, 2008, p 11).

Barton maintains that inclusive education is *part of a human rights approach to social relations and conditions*, and that it is concerned with the well-being of all pupils and should be part of a whole-school, equal opportunities approach (2005, pp 59–60). Booth and Ainscow suggest that inclusion begins by recognition of difference between pupils and that inclusive approaches to teaching and learning build on such differences, but are concerned for the whole person and not just an impairment or barrier to learning (2002, p 4). Inclusive practice therefore involves a strong emphasis on the need for the teacher to plan lessons with the needs of all pupils in mind, where learning activities provide opportunity for all to participate (p 6).

Critical questions

» *What is your own definition of inclusion? How would you justify your view?*

» *What challenges do you think inclusion would present to you as a teacher?*

» *How could you ensure the participation of all children in your class?*

Equal opportunities

Inequality is a fact of life for some children. They may be born into circumstances which mean that they are disadvantaged and it is possible that they will carry this disadvantage with them into adulthood. Inequality can be seen in educational opportunity, aspiration, employment, housing and the expectations of others. According to WHO (2011a), children with disabilities often experience poorer health and greater risk of developing additional conditions. They are less likely to start school at the same time as other children and they are less likely to be employed. Due to people with disabilities being less likely to be employed, they are more likely to experience poverty, with insecurity about food, poor housing and exposure to poor sanitation. Additionally, because people with disabilities often need medication, those in low-income countries are 50 per cent more likely to experience severe health-related expenditure than non-disabled people.

Low income and deprivation are two factors in inequality. Poverty is defined as people living in households with an income of 60 per cent below the median for that year. During the 1980s, child poverty rose to 31 per cent and figures for 2010/11 stand at 27 per cent. This is 2.1 million children. Of the children in poverty, 61 per cent are in families with a working adult (Joseph Rowntree Foundation (JRF), 2012). Life expectancy has changed for men and women over recent years. Whereas women could expect to live at least as long as men, regardless of whether they lived in an area of deprivation or not, women in the most deprived areas now have a lower life expectancy than men in a less deprived area (JRF, 2012). The JRF also report that, over the last ten years, the proportion of income spent on housing has risen for the poorest 20 per cent from 26 per cent to 29 per cent. With regard to employment, figures show that 18 per cent of working-age households are workless, with only 2 per cent where no one ever worked. However, half of the adults in households where no one worked were under 25 years of age. This information shows that inequalities in life chances and expectations are very real for those in poverty and that over one-quarter of children in our schools are affected by factors related to deprivation. It is likely therefore that at some point during your teaching career you will encounter children for whom inequality is a fact of life. However, it is essential that you are aware of relevant national policy and familiar with how this is made practical in your school.

The Equality Act (2010)

The Equality Act (UK Government, 2010) consolidates existing law with regard to discrimination into a single legal framework and is designed to *reduce the inequalities of outcome resulting from socio-economic disadvantage* (p 3). Many of the concepts of discrimination remain the same as in previous legislation such as the Race Relations (Amendment) Act 2000 and the Sex Discrimination Act 1975, with nine protected characteristics being covered. These are:

- age;
- disability;
- gender reassignment, including transsexual;
- marriage and civil partnership;
- pregnancy and maternity;
- religion or belief;
- race;
- sex;
- sexual orientation. (p 4)

However, the characteristics of age and marriage and civil partnership are not covered within the section on schools.

Within the terms of the Equality Act (2010), schools are not allowed to discriminate with regard to who can be admitted, the way in which education is provided, the way in which pupils can access benefits or services, by not affording pupils access to benefits or services or by *subjecting the pupil to any other detriment* (p 55). Additionally, schools may not harass or victimise pupils in regard to admissions or the way in which education, benefits or services are provided, but rather are required to make *reasonable adjustments* (p 55).

Reasonable adjustments should be made where the provision, criteria or practice places a person with disabilities at a substantial disadvantage relative to a person who is not disabled. Similarly, where a *physical feature, or the lack of an auxiliary aid disadvantages a person with a disability, reasonable steps should be taken to avoid disadvantage* (p 10). According to the Equality Act (2010), disability discrimination occurs if a person is treated less favourably because of their disability. This is the same for the protected characteristics of sex or religion, and in the case of race, less favourable treatment includes being segregated from others (p 7).

When considering the scenario about Nasreen and the theatre visit, it would seem that reasonable adjustments should be made to avoid subjecting her to detriment and disadvantage. It is because of her disability and the lack of access to the upper floor of the theatre that the school is considering that she should sit separately from her peers and therefore be socially excluded. The physical feature disadvantaging Nasreen in this instance is the stairs. According to the Equality Act (2010), if substantial disadvantage occurs, then the physical feature should be removed, altered or reasonable means of avoiding it should be employed (p 11). Clearly, the decision in the scenario is concerned with how to avoid the stairs. The school's reasoning that having all children sit downstairs with Nasreen may make the visit too costly for other children should be countered by the school subsidising the visit so as to make it accessible for all. This would mean that reasonable adjustments were made and the requirement of the Equality Act regarding the affordability of benefits and services would be fulfilled.

However, equality is not about treating all children the same regardless of circumstance or situation. Some children do need different provisions from others in order to provide the same equality of opportunity. Consider the following scenario.

SCENARIO

A child with autism was made to wait in the queue at lunchtime as he was expected to behave the same as other children and not push in. This made the child extremely agitated, particularly as he could see the chocolate pudding he wanted being chosen by other children. As he drew near to the food counter, the child in front of him took the last piece of chocolate pudding. This was too much for the boy with autism, who threw his tray in the air and pushed the boy who had taken 'his' pudding. The boy with autism was pulled out of the queue and punished for his outburst, being made to sit alone.

In looking at this example, it could be considered that this boy was being treated unfavourably because of his disability. Because his perception of social situations was different from other children, he did not understand the concept of waiting, nor the idea of not being able to have the pudding he thought he was entitled to. It was an unrealistic expectation for him to be treated the same as the other children as his disability meant that such behaviour and understanding was beyond him at this point. While it might seem 'unfair' for him to be treated more favourably than others, to fail to do so would place him disadvantageously and mean the school was in danger of being discriminatory. In expecting the same behaviour from the boy with autism as other children, he was consequently denied the opportunity to sit with his peers to eat his dinner and therefore made to forfeit opportunities for social inclusion.

With regard to the protected characteristic of race, this includes colour, ethnic origin and nationality. Similarly, the protected characteristic of religion includes belief, lack of belief and lack of religion (UK Government, 2010, p 6). Clearly, it is possible that some children may have more than one protected characteristic, as in the case of Nasreen, who is of Pakistani origin as well as being disabled. The school would need to take into account both of these protected characteristics when making suitable educational provision for her. They would also need to be sure that they do not discriminate against any of her brothers or other family members because of Nasreen's disability, as this would be indirect discrimination under the terms of the Equality Act (2010, p 10). Indirect discrimination might involve abuse, teasing or bullying because of their sister. If the school were to discriminate against Nasreen's brothers because of race, then this would be direct discrimination as they are of the same racial origin.

If Nasreen's school considered that the best course of action with regard to the theatre visit was for her not to attend, and they put pressure on her to opt out, they could be guilty of harassment. The Equality Act (2010) states that harassment is where a person engages in unwanted conduct in relation to a protected characteristic and in doing so violates dignity or *creates an intimidating, hostile, degrading, humiliating or offensive environment* (pp 13–14). Victimisation is said to occur if a person is subject to detriment because they have carried out an action which is protected. For example, in a recent high-profile case, a member of the cabin crew of a well-known flight company was victimised for wearing a cross around her neck. As religion is a protected characteristic, her right to wear symbols of her religious beliefs was upheld. In schools, care must be taken not to victimise pupils who are taking part in the observance of religious festivals such as Ramadan and Eid.

Critical questions

Consider the practice you have observed while in school.

»   *What examples can you think of where schools have adhered to the requirements of the Equality Act 2010?*

»   *What examples can you think of where schools have made reasonable adjustments in order to fulfil the requirements of the Equality Act 2010?*

»   *Thinking about your own experiences as a pupil in school, were you aware of any children with disabilities in your class? How did the teacher seek to include them? What barriers to learning did the teacher seek to remove? Reflect on how this same child with a disability might be provided for today. What do you think the differences would be?*

The Equality Act 2010 is a significant piece of legislation with regard to discrimination and draws together much of the previous legislation regarding sex, race, disability and so on. However, it is important to gain a historical understanding of what legislation and policy was previously in place as it provides a context for this Act. This is now provided by means of the following timeline and goes beyond the Equality Act of 2010 to the shift in emphasis in policy and legislation as outlined by the coalition government from 2011. The timeline provides context rather than detailed discussion of each of the relevant policies and legislative documents, as most of the detail is covered in the relevant chapters within the book.

Timeline of most significant policy and legislation

Timeline of most significant inclusion policy and legislation from 1944, including provision for SEN, sex, gender and race.

1944   **Education Act in England and Wales:** Children were selected for specific types of secondary education based on psychometric testing at age 11.

1945   **The Handicapped Students and School Health Service Regulations:** A new framework of 11 categories of special education, including maladjusted, with educational provision only available in special schools.

1970   **Handicapped Children Education Act:** For the first time, children with severe cognitive disabilities were entitled to a school-based education.

1975   **Sex Discrimination Act:** This made it unlawful to discriminate against anyone because of their sex or whether they are married.

1976   **Race Relations Act:** A fresh provision with respect to discrimination on grounds of race.

1978   **Warnock Report:** The term special educational needs was introduced to replace the previous categorisation of handicap.

1981   **Education Act:** The Warnock Report was translated into legislation. Provision was made for all children to be educated in mainstream schools and parents should be consulted about their child's educational provision.

1985   **Swann Report: Education for All:** This is a commitment that all children, regardless of race, colour or ethnic origin, should have a good education.

1988   **Education Reform Act:** This Act paved the way for the National Curriculum with the introduction of statutory testing in primary and secondary schools. It also made provision for children to receive a *broad, balanced, relevant and differentiated curriculum*.

1994   **The Salamanca Agreement:** A commitment at the World Conference on Special Educational Needs where 92 governments pledged to work towards Education for All, especially those with SEN.

1994   **Special Educational Needs Code of Practice:** This Code of Practice introduced a 5-stage model.

1995   **Disability Discrimination Act (DDA 1995):** This Act made it unlawful to discriminate against a person in respect of any disability, with regard to employment, the provision of goods and services, education or transport.

1996   **Education Act:** The law states that children with learning difficulties are considered to have a need and that this need is special if special provision is required.

1997   **Green Paper: Excellence for All Children:** This paper introduced an inclusive approach.

1998   **The SEN Programme of Action:** This document recommended strategies to support inclusion, such as early intervention and staff training.

1999   **The MacPherson Report:** This document was produced as a result of the Stephen Lawrence Inquiry. Stephen Lawrence was a black boy murdered by white males and the police were accused of institutional racism in how they handled the case. This report recommended that the police should be subject to greater public control.

2000   **Race Relations (Amendment) Act:** This is an extension of the 1976 Act to include discrimination by the police and other public authorities.

2001   **Special Educational Needs and Disability Act (SENDA):** The law states that children with a statement of educational need must be educated in a mainstream school unless the child's parents do not wish this or the education of the other children is compromised.

2001   **Inclusive Schooling: Children with Special Educational Needs:** Guidance on the practical application of the statutory framework for inclusion.

2001   **Revised SEN Code of Practice:** This replaces the five stages of SEN with a graduated response from School Action through to School Action Plus and beyond to a statement of educational need.

2003   **The Every Child Matters Agenda:** This document is concerned with the right of children to enjoy and achieve and places a strong emphasis on effective multi-agency working.

2004   **The Children Act:** The principles of the Every Child Matters Agenda are made effective through this legislation.

2004   **Removing Barriers to Achievement:** Early intervention, removing barriers to learning and raising expectations and achievements are the key features of this document.

2004   **Ofsted Report: Special Educational Needs and Disability: Towards Inclusive Schools:** The main finding of this report was that children with social and behavioural difficulties provide the most challenge in terms of admission and retention.

2005   **The Disability Discrimination Act (DDA):** This Act provided a definition of disability whereby the effect of the disability on the person concerned is deemed to be substantial, adverse and long term.

2005   **White Paper: Higher Standards, Better Schools for All:** Stronger provision for children deemed to be Gifted and Talented is made in this paper, including personalised provision.

2007   **The Children's Plan: building brighter futures:** A 10-year plan for supporting families and involving parents in children's learning.

2007   **Guidance on the duty to promote community cohesion:** Responsibility is placed on schools to educate children and young people to live and work alongside others of diverse backgrounds, cultures, beliefs and faith.

2007   **Gender Equality Duty (GED):** Schools have a general duty to promote equality of opportunity between men and women and to publish a Gender Equality Scheme which shows how the school intends to fulfil its specific duties.

2007   **Disability Equality Duty (DED):** This is a requirement for all schools to show how they will respond to the legal requirements of the DDA (1995).

2009   **The Lamb Report:** An inquiry into SEN provision, parental confidence and how TAs are used in schools with the specific duty for Ofsted to report on the quality of the provision for disabled pupils and those with SEN.

2010   **The Equality Act:** All previous anti-discrimination legislation brought together in one document. Introduced nine protected characteristics.

2012   **Green Paper: SEN and Disability:** The coalition government set out their proposals for SEN. This includes condensing the two categories of SEN to one school-based category and replacing the statement of educational need with an Education, Health and Care Plan (EHCP).

2012   **Support and Aspiration: A New Approach to Special Educational Needs and Disability. Progress and next steps:** This document gives parents budgetary responsibility for children with SEN, provides details concerning early identification and assessment and the introduction of the EHCP from 0–25 years.

2013   **The Children and Families Bill:** The intention of this legislation is to improve services for vulnerable children such as those who are adopted, looked after children and those with SEN. It will make lawful the recommendations in the Green Paper 2012. (Wearmouth, 2009, pp 18–30; Glazzard et al., 2010, pp 1–3; Armstrong et al., 2011, pp 16–19)

Policy and politics

This chapter has provided a historical overview of policy and legislation which gives the context for current policy and practice with regard to equality in school. It is interesting to note that when the Labour government came to power in 1997, one of the first things it did was to introduce the Green Paper, *Excellence for All: Meeting Special Educational Needs* (DfEE), which outlined an inclusive approach, encouraging all children to be educated in mainstream schools where possible. Similarly, the new coalition considered that SEN should be one of the first things they turned their attention to in coming to power in May 2010. As well as simplifying the categories of SEN and introducing a single common assessment for the EHCP, one of the most significant commitments is that parents will be given the opportunity for control over the personal budgetary provision for a child who has an EHCP.

As a teacher, you need to be familiar with the main concepts and ideals contained in policy and legislation which must be adhered to. Schools are required to write policies which show how they will carry out the requirements of the law and it is imperative that you know how this will impact on your practice. When you are next in school, it would be helpful for you to be aware of the expectations of the policies the school has written and expects the staff to adhere to. This will provide you with an understanding of the ethos and practices of the school and will support you in working with children, parents, colleagues and other adults in the teaching and learning environment.

Critical reflections

»   *Consider a school where you have been engaged in teaching. How does this school continue to drive up standards while bringing about inclusion for all?*

» *Consider a child with SEN or disability that you have encountered while in school. What aspects of the Equality Act (2010) do you need to be aware of in order to make sure you make relevant and appropriate provision for this child?*

» *What discriminatory attitudes, actions, culture, policies or institutional practices that may create barriers to learning can you identify in any school you have been in, either as a pupil or a trainee teacher?*

» *The school where you are working as a trainee teacher is renewing its Disability Equality Scheme. What do you think are the most important elements to include in a new policy?*

Taking it further

Books and journals

Gerschel, L. (1998) Equal Opportunities and Special Educational Needs: Equity and Inclusion, in Tilstone, C., Florian, L. and Rose, R. (eds) *Promoting Inclusive Practice*. Oxon: Routledge.

While this chapter was written in 1998, which pre-dates the SENDA (2001), the DDA (2005) and the Equality Act (2010), it contains some important discussion regarding equal opportunities in relation to race and SEN. It also contains some useful advice about a rationale for a policy on equality which includes the role of parents, staff and governors.

Hodkinson, A. and Vickerman, P. (2012) *Key Issues in Special Educational Needs and Inclusion*, Chapter 7, Current Legislation Governing Special Educational Needs and Inclusion. London: Sage.

In this chapter, key policy relating to SEN is discussed, along with how changes in policy have been brought about because of shifts in principles. This chapter does consider the SENDA and examines how this impacts on current inclusive practice. The section on the identification of SEN and the stages of the CoP, however, are not consistent with the current government's policy which will bring about changes in 2014.

Marks, K. and Wood, M. (2008) Supporting Traveller Children, in Richards, G. and Armstrong, F. (2008) (eds) *Key Issues for Teaching Assistants: Working in Diverse and Inclusive Classrooms*. Oxon: Routledge.

This chapter is concerned with Traveller children, and while it does not directly mention the Equality Act (2010), it does outline how the Race Relations Act (2000) provides legal protection from discrimination for Traveller children. It also considers differences of culture, lifestyle and aspiration which may lead to prejudice. It is important to consider this group of learners within the context of the requirements of the Equality Act.

Richardson, R. (1999) Unequivocal Acceptance: Lessons for Education from the Stephen Lawrence Inquiry, in Nind, M., Rix, J., Sheehy, K. and Simmons, K. (2005) (eds) *Inclusive Education: Diverse Perspectives*. Maidstone: David Fulton.

This chapter provides a discussion of institutional racism as seen in the Stephen Lawrence Inquiry, but suggests how this also exists within education and the teaching profession. It considers teachers' attitudes towards black boys and non-Western traditions and heritages such as Islam. It includes charts and diagrams which consider racism in Britain, institutional racism in education and racial inequality in institutions.

Web-based materials

Tomlinson, S. (2012) The Irresistible Rise of the SEN Industry. *Oxford Review of Education*, 38(3): 267–286. Online: http://dx.doi.org/10.1080/03054985.2012.692055 (last accessed 4 October 2013).

> This article takes a historical perspective on SEN and how it has developed over time. It considers how SEN and behavioural issues were seen to be largely within those from the lower socio-economic classes but how middle-class parents are keen to claim their children have SEN if they are unable to achieve within a standards-driven education system.

References

Armstrong, F. (2008) Inclusive Education, in Richards, G. and Armstrong, F. (eds) *Key Issues for Teaching Assistants: Working in Diverse and Inclusive Classrooms*. Oxon: Routledge.

Armstrong, A.C., Armstrong, D. and Spandagou, I. (2011) *Inclusive Education: International Policy and Practice* London: Sage.

Barton, L. (2005) The Politics of Education for All, in Nind, M., Rix, J., Sheehy, K. and Simmons, K. (eds) *Inclusive Education: Diverse Perspectives*. Maidstone: David Fulton.

Black-Hawkins, K., Florian, L. and Rouse, M. (2007) *Achievement and Inclusion in Schools*. Oxon: Routledge.

Booth, T. and Ainscow, M. (2002) *Index for Inclusion: Developing Learning and Participation in Schools*. Bristol: Centre for Studies in Inclusive Education.

Department for Education and Employment (DfEE) (1997) *Excellence for All Children: Meeting Special Educational Needs*. London: The Stationery Office.

Department for Education and Employment (DfEE) (1999) *The National Curriculum Handbook for Primary Teachers in England*. Online: www.education.gov.uk/publications/eOrderingDownload/QCA-99-457.pdf (last accessed 15 February 2013).

Department for Education (DfE) (2011) *Support and Aspiration: A New Approach to Special Educational Needs and Disability: a Consultation* (Green Paper). London: HMSO.

Department for Education (DfE) (2012) *Support and Aspiration: A New Approach to Special Educational Needs and Disability. Progress and Next Steps*. Cm 8027 London: The Stationery Office.

Department for Education (DfE) (2013) *The National Curriculum in England Framework Document For Consultation*. Online: www.education.gov.uk/nationalcurriculum (last accessed 15 February 2013).

Department for Education and Skills (DfES) (2001) *Special Educational Needs Code of Practice*. London: The Stationery Office.

Evans, L. (2007) *Inclusion*. Oxon: Routledge.

Farrell, P., Dyson, A., Polat, F., Hutcheson, G. and Gallannaugh, F. (2007) Inclusion and Achievement in Mainstream Schools. *European Journal of Special Needs Education*, 22(2): 131–45.

Glazzard, J., Hughes, A., Netherwood, A., Neve, L. and Stokoe, J. (2010) *Achieving QTS Teaching Primary Special Educational Needs*. London: Sage.

Hodkinson, A. and Vickerman, P. (2012) *Key Issues in Special Educational Needs and Inclusion*. London. Sage.

Joseph Rowntree Foundation (JRF) (2012) *Monitoring Poverty and Social Exclusion*. Online: www.jrf.org.uk/sites/files/jrf/poverty-exclusion-government-policy-summary.pdf (last accessed 16 February 2013).

Mencap (2007) Press release. Online: www.mencap.org.uk/node/7000, (last accessed 13 February 2013).

Office for Disability Issues (2010) *Equality Act Guidance: Guidance on Matters to Be Taken into Account in Determining Questions Relating to the Definitions of Disability.* Online: http://odi.dwp.gov.uk/docs/wor/new/ea-guide.pdf (last accessed 12 October 2013).

Ofsted (2013) *The Framework for School Inspection.* Online: www.ofsted.gov.uk/resources/framework-for-school-inspection (last accessed 19 October 2013).

Scope (2012) Press release. Online: www.scope.org.uk/news/paralympics-poll (last accessed 17 October 2013).

UK Government (2010) *The Equality Act 2010*, Chapter 15. London: The Stationery Office. Online: www.legislation.gov.uk/ukpga/2010/15/pdfs/ukpga_20100015_en.pdf (last accessed 4 October 2013).

Wearmouth, J. (2009) *A Beginning Teacher's Guide to Special Educational Needs.* Maidenhead: Open University Press.

World Health Organization (WHO) (2011a) *World Report on Disability: Summary.* Online: www.who.int/disabilities/world_report/2011/en/index.html (last accessed 30 August 2013).

World Health Organization (WHO) (2011b) *International Classification of Functioning, Disability and Health (ICF).* Online: www.who.int/classifications/icf/en. (last accessed 14 February 2013).

2 Understanding identity and gender

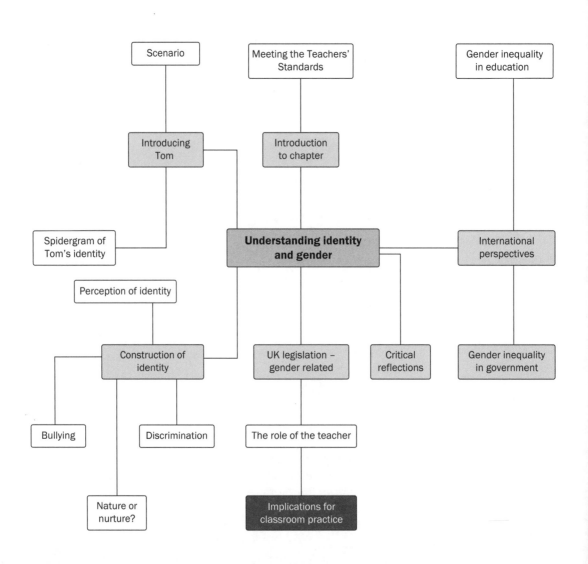

Scenario

Meeting the Teachers' Standards

Gender inequality in education

Introducing Tom

Introduction to chapter

Spidergram of Tom's identity

Understanding identity and gender

International perspectives

Perception of identity

Construction of identity

UK legislation – gender related

Critical reflections

Gender inequality in government

Bullying

Discrimination

The role of the teacher

Nature or nurture?

Implications for classroom practice

Introduction

In becoming an inclusive primary teacher it is vital to get to know and understand the children in your class. No class of primary children is the same as any other, and as a trainee teacher you will experience contrasting schools on your placements. All children have their unique characters and personalities, with specific and particular home backgrounds and life experiences which contribute to their sense of identity. Children in a class within an urban setting will have different expectations, opportunities and experiences from those in a rural setting. Similarly, white British children will have different cultural and religious values and traditions from children whose family embrace other culture, religions and language. While you, as a trainee primary teacher, will be concerned with delivering good-quality lessons to all pupils, you will also need to understand the identity of the children in your class and what makes them the people they are. Children who have difficult home lives may not be well placed to learn, whereas those who have supportive and nurturing home lives will more likely come to school able to successfully manage the social, emotional and learning challenges that are part of every classroom and playground. This chapter considers the various factors which contribute to a learner's identity and in particular those related to gender. It also examines your role as a trainee teacher in providing equality of opportunity within the classroom and in understanding how the identity of the child may affect their readiness to learn.

MEETING THE TEACHERS' STANDARDS

Links to Department for Education Teachers' Standards May 2012

TS 1; 7

Part 2

In working towards the DfE Teachers' Standards (2012a), you must provide a safe and stimulating environment for your pupils in which you show respect for pupils of *all backgrounds, abilities and dispositions* (p 7) and where you are a positive and constant role model in terms of values and attitudes. There is a strong requirement for you to manage classroom behaviour *using approaches which are appropriate to pupils' needs in order to involve and motivate them* (p 9), and in Part 2 of the Teachers' Standards, you are required to show tolerance of those who are from different faiths and beliefs and to respect the rights of others. This is supported by your need to understand the statutory frameworks within which you as a trainee, and later as a qualified teacher, will work and act. In fulfilling the Teachers' Standards, it is important that you not only know the requirements of the law such as the Equality Duty (2010) and of government guidance such as the *Code of Practice for Special Educational Needs* (DfES, 2001a), but that you know, understand and respect the individuals in your class and make provision for their learning. Knowing and understanding what makes children who they are and what contributes to their identity is an important first step in providing positive learning experiences for them.

Introducing Tom

Some of the issues concerned with identity can be seen through the following scenario. It is based on examples from classroom practice and shows many factors which contribute to Tom's identity. The scenario also provides a basis for thinking critically about how you as a trainee teacher could remove barriers to learning for Tom, while also providing positive learning experiences within an inclusive classroom environment.

SCENARIO

Tom is a 7-year-old boy. The teacher considers he has SEN. Tom is often late to school. His clothes are not always clean and he doesn't always have breakfast. His reading is well below his chronological age. He often has a TA to work with him. Tom often plays alone or with girls. The teacher has heard some children calling him 'gay'. Tom's mother is a single parent and is disabled. Tom has an older sister and together he and his sister are carers for their mother. They need to make sure she is out of bed and dressed every morning before they leave for school. Most of the domestic chores fall to Tom and his sister because of their mother's disability.

Now you have read the scenario, consider the critical questions below. These will help you to identify what school feels like for Tom, the family pressures and responsibilities that he carries, as well as explaining some of his attitudes and behaviours both within the classroom and in the playground. They will also stimulate you to think of what this means for you as a trainee teacher in terms of your own attitudes and values, as well as managing the responses and behaviours of other pupils and adults.

Critical questions

»   *Identify the different identities that Tom has in different environments, eg at home, in the classroom, in the playground.*

»   *Consider the effect that Tom's identity as a carer has on his ability to learn and socialise.*

»   *What important factors regarding Tom's identity do you as a trainee teacher need to take into account in providing positive learning experiences for Tom?*

»   *How would you encourage Tom's peers to build positive relationships with him?*

Having begun to consider Tom's identity and some of the factors which contribute to it, take a look at the spidergram on page 23.

This provides a more detailed overview of some of the issues raised by the scenario. An examination of these will enable you to:

•   recognise the complex nature of the construction of identity;

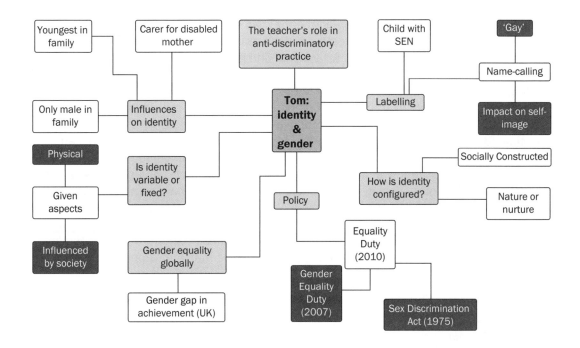

- identify and consider the impact of identity on children's achievement;

- recognise issues surrounding gender inequality at macro and micro level;

- identify opportunities for addressing the needs of boys and girls within the school environment;

- be aware of statutory guidance, research and data analysis which influences and underpins classroom practice.

These are now considered more fully in the following section.

The construction of identity

When you meet someone new, you introduce yourself. What you say provides some ideas about how you view yourself and what you consider your identity to be, but, more importantly, how you want others to view your identity. You might consider it important to describe your family background, your ethnicity or beliefs. You could talk about your job, your hobbies, your appearance or any possessions or pets. You may choose to offer some information about yourself and withhold other, or you could emphasise some parts of your identity, your skills or abilities, for example, and play down some aspect of your identity such as your age or status, depending on who you are introducing yourself to.

There are many factors which influence identity such as gender, family and position within the family, age, religion, the expectation of society, ethnicity, race, ability or disability. For Tom, he is the younger of two siblings. He is the only male in the household and has no obvious male role model. He is expected to take on some of the caring duties for his disabled mother and the fact that she is disabled means that she is not able to undertake many of the tasks traditionally expected of mothers, such as cooking and washing. Consequently, Tom is taking on some of these roles for himself, and given that he comes to school without breakfast and with dirty clothes he is not managing this too well. Further consequences of needing to support his disabled mother are that he does not have time to go and play with friends outside of school or to bring friends home to play. This contributes to his isolation in school. In addition, being constantly attentive to his mother at home means he does not have time to undertake any additional work to support his lack of progress, and because his mother is not mobile, there is no opportunity for her to attend school to discuss Tom's progress. In short, Tom's identity at home could be described as: male, younger of two siblings, carer for disabled mother, isolated from peers, belonging to female-dominated family, limited experience of childhood or opportunity to play, unable to undertake additional learning opportunities at home with limited home–school communication. It is clear to see that such factors have significant implications for how Tom views himself and how he places himself within the learning community at school. It is also obvious that Tom experiences many barriers to his learning.

The way Tom acts at home and the identity that he takes on in that environment is very different from the identity he takes on at school. This suggests that identity is not fixed, but rather shifts depending on a range of circumstances, such as peer group, environment, the expectations of society, the impact of stereotypes and the influence of prejudice. As a trainee teacher, when you go into school for your placements, you will portray yourself in a particular way. You will be keen to show yourself as a competent and effective teacher, a good team worker, ready to take advice, but also able to take initiative. You will act in a way that is in accordance with the expectations of a trainee teacher and for your time in school this will be your identity. Trainee teachers who do not take on the expected teacher identity or conform to expected behaviours are likely to find their school placements and relationships with their colleagues difficult. However, away from school and in social situations, you are likely to act very differently. You could be someone who is the life and soul of the party, or who spends their time online shopping, downloading music or using social networking sites. Maybe this is the first time you have been away from home and find the complexities of independent living difficult. In these circumstances, you will take on the identity of a student rather than a teacher. Therefore it can be seen that a person's identity is influenced by peer groups and the social expectations and constraints of the group as well as environmental factors. Thus identity can be considered to be socially constructed.

Critical questions

» *Construct a spidergram which details all the factors which make up your identity.*

» *Construct a second spidergram which considers the factors which you think show the identity of a teacher.*

» *Consider what aspects of the identity of a teacher you already show.*

» *Consider what aspects of the identity of a teacher you need to develop.*

» *Think about what aspects of your identity are not relevant to the identity of a trainee teacher and why.*

Perceptions of identity – gender related

For Tom, the aspects of his identity which are more prominent at home are those related to his role as a carer, with only female role models. However, within the school environment, he is faced with his peers, some of whom are boys who may have had strong male role models. Their home experiences are likely to be more about sport and other hobbies, possibly including competitive activities, rather than the cooking, washing and other household chores that are part of Tom's home experience. Tom may find he has little in common with his male peers, preferring instead the friendship of girls as he is used to a female-dominated environment.

Other children in the class may also have parents who place a high value on education and therefore from early childhood have provided an environment conducive to learning. Research by Horgan (2007) showed that children from disadvantaged backgrounds, such as Tom, are much less likely to participate in after-school activities due to the cost or practicalities of staying behind after school. Additionally, the research found that a significant number of boys from disadvantaged backgrounds complained about the length of the school day, the amount of work required and being shouted at by teachers; this led to them saying they hated school. By the age of nine or ten they were disengaged and there was a strong possibly of playing truant later on.

Bullying

Tom's playground experiences are related in part to his identity as a male. Alongside Tom's own perception of himself are issues concerned with others' perception of him and his identity. It would appear that some of the children have stereotypical views of how boys should play and who they should play with. Tom's behaviour does not conform to their assumptions and this leads to name-calling. In a DfES government research report, Oliver and Candappa (DfES, 2003) define bullying as involving *verbal abuse, physical aggression, or social ostracism repeatedly and over a period of time* (p 27). It carries with it the intent to be hurtful to another and as such is distinguishable from teasing or play. Most bullying in primary schools takes place in the playground and name-calling is one of the most common forms (p 18). Oliver and Candappa found that 51 per cent of children in Year 5 from six primary schools reported having been called names over the period of one term, and over a third of these pupils stated they had been hit on purpose. In addition, 34 per cent of pupils were subject to being ostracised, possibly due to gossip (2003, p 51). While it is often thought that girls are more prone to verbal bullying, the frequency of name-calling for boys and girls was found to be virtually the same, while gossip and spreading nasty rumours was also as frequent in boys as in girls (p 53–54). Further findings from this research suggest that incidents of bullying may be under-reported by parents, children and teachers and that bullying which is sexual or homophobic in nature is common (p 28). Slater (2004) considers that this type of bullying is largely unchecked (p 125). The impact of insults of a sexual nature, such as *gay, queer,* or *slag*, are shown in an autobiographical study by Vicars (2006). He also relates stories from students which show how such insults from childhood have had repercussions on the identities, future interactions and sexual behaviour of the children and young people concerned.

Friendships are important for the person experiencing bullying, in that friends could provide support, advice and a buffer against the bully (DfES, 2003, p 70). While primary school children are more likely to talk with their mothers first about the bullying, this may not be straightforward for Tom. The fact that he has few friends within school and possibly limited friendship skills makes him additionally vulnerable to bullying.

Discrimination

The way Tom behaves in the playground does not conform to other boys' perception of how boys should behave and therefore demonstrates assumptions about gender identity, which in turn leads to gender-based discrimination. This identification of difference from an assumed identity is an important factor in provoking name-calling. Children may exhibit difference from their peers for many reasons, and some of these will be concerned with conforming to cultural, religious or traditional expectations. Therefore identity is concerned not only with behaviour but with physical appearance. This may be a matter of dress, such as in head coverings for some girls, or the latest trainers or T-shirt. It may also relate to what is considered to be important to various subcultures, such as tanning, piercings, tattoos or hairstyles. Children who are physically disabled have physical characteristics that are different from other children. Similarly, children who are psychologically impaired, either through trauma (such as asylum seekers, the abused or neglected), or because of a medical condition, can be considered to be different from others. However, such differences contribute to the identity of the child and therefore need to be taken into account when providing social and academic opportunities. For Tom, the fact that he comes to school with unclean clothes contributes to an identity which other children perceive as unattractive. This again marks him out as different and makes him vulnerable to being discriminated against as well as socially isolated, as other children find it difficult to accept him within their social grouping.

There is considerable ongoing debate as to whether children express gender preferences because this is innate or genetic or whether it is due to social conditioning through gender-specific toys or gender-specific assumptions of behaviour, preferences and attitudes from parents and other adults. In other words, is being male or female nature or nurture?

Nature or nurture?

This debate considers what the essence of being male or female might be. It raises questions as to what constitutes maleness and femaleness and whether it goes beyond physical attributes. Bartlett and Burton use the term 'sex' to indicate our biological make-up and the term 'gender' to refer to what society expects maleness and femaleness to be like (2008, p 51). Kirkpatrick (2003) contends that *competent genital anatomy is neither sufficient nor necessary for gender identity* and that the most powerful influence on gender identity is the parents' belief that their child is a boy or a girl (p 562). She distinguishes between gender identity, which is the belief that a person is male or female, and gender role, which is the behaviours, attitudes and values that are considered to be masculine or feminine. For children in primary schools, these can be seen in the kinds of play that children engage in and the toys they choose. For Tom, while he might be undeniably male in terms of his biological make-up, his exposure to a female-dominated home life, along with domestic roles which are considered to be feminine, means that his play behaviour is also seen as feminine, especially by other boys who are likely to choose more masculine gender roles.

While it can be seen that nurture is considered to be a powerful factor in contributing to identity, more recent studies undertaken by Professor Timothy Bates suggest that key personality traits such as social skills and learning ability are influenced more strongly by genetic factors than was previously considered to be the case. His study of more than 800 sets of identical and non-identical twins shows that twins having the same genetic make-up are more likely to share the same personality traits than non-identical twins whose DNA is different. This study therefore provides evidence that nature is a more dominant factor than nurture (Collins, 2012). While this research does not take into account gender-related personality traits, it can be seen that Tom's identity will be influenced by both his genes and his environment.

International perspectives

Inequality between men and women exists in many countries throughout the world. In the UK, equality for women has made great strides since Victorian times when a woman's place was considered to be in the home embracing motherhood and domesticity. In 1870, the Married Women's Property Act meant that wages earned could be used for the wife's own purposes. Prior to this, any money earned by a wife was deemed to belong to the husband. In World War I many women took traditionally male jobs and roles while the male workforce was fighting. This helped to advance the feminist cause. Parity of voting rights has only been in place since 1928, after a long and determined fight by the Suffrage Movement, and in 1979 Margaret Thatcher became the first female prime minister in the UK. While there is equality with men at least in a legal sense, there are still some social and economic factors which mean full equality has not yet been attained. For example, men are more likely to own their own home, while women are more likely to rent from the social sector. Additionally, women's average earnings are less than those of men, with more men than women being employed in skilled trades or as managers or senior officials (Office for National Statistics, 2008).

While much of the above discussion concerns inequality for women, it is worth considering the matter of inequality for men. A mother automatically has parental rights for a child at birth; however, the father only has parental rights if he is married to the mother, they jointly register the birth, or there is agreement by the mother or through a court of law. When gaining parental rights through the court, the father needs to prove his degree of attachment and commitment to the child. This is not the case for the child's mother and this can therefore be considered to be discrimination against fathers (Directgov, 2012).

Similarly, although cases of domestic violence tend to see the woman as the victim, the charity Parity, which is concerned for equal rights for men and women, states that between one-third and one-half of victims of violence within intimate relationships are men (2012). Police records show a much lower proportion than this, but Parity suggests that this is due to fear of an unsympathetic response from the authorities. While there are over 400 publicly funded places of refuge for women who suffer violence, there are none for men. This means that many men choose to remain within their violent situations in order to protect their children. Further evidence of the unequal treatment of men is cited by Blackburn (2012). He observes that men are conscripted to wars more than women, that corporal punishment is used more for boys than girls and that it can be more severe. Furthermore, he comments that men are the recipients of violence more frequently than women, whether this is through casual crime, political unrest or genocide (Blackburn, 2012). From this it can be seen that gender equality is a complex matter. It is not simply a matter of rights for women or rights for men, but social justice for all.

Gender inequality in government

While there have been great strides towards equality for women in the UK, there is still a long way to go with regard to women in parliament. Data released by the Inter-Parliamentary Union (IPU) in June 2012 shows that only 22.5 per cent of government positions in the UK are held by women. This is on a par with countries such as Pakistan (22.5 per cent), but below other less-developed countries such as Senegal (22.7 per cent) and Latvia (23.0 per cent). Interestingly, only 16.9 per cent of the governing body in the United States are women, and in Kenya this figure is only 9.8 per cent. However, in other countries such as Kuwait and Saudi Arabia, there are no women in parliament at all. Surprisingly perhaps, the country with the largest percentage of women in parliament is Rwanda (56.3 per cent) with many European countries such as Sweden, Finland, Norway and Denmark showing figures between 44.7 and 39.1 per cent. (IPU, 2012). This shows that, worldwide, governance is predominantly male and that there is huge variation from country to country.

Gender inequality in education

UNESCO maintains that there is a strong human rights argument for equality in education. Educating girls brings improved livelihoods, a greater value of education and increased civic responsibility. In 2012, 56 per cent of the world's children of primary age were in countries where there was gender parity, in other words, equal participation in schools for boys and girls. However, at the secondary phase, the proportion dropped to 29 per cent for lower secondary and only 15 per cent for higher secondary. This means that, while there is gender parity at primary level for the majority of the world's children, gender equality (ie the right to benefit from education in terms of the social, economic and political development of society) at secondary level is much reduced for girls (UNESCO, 2012, p 24).

In 2010, 75 million children worldwide were excluded from education, 60 per cent of them girls living in Arab states and 66 per cent of them in south and west Asia (UNESCO, 2010). In many African countries such as Kenya, girls are expected to take on a significant share of the domestic chores and childcare. Daughters are often expected to marry early and therefore education may be viewed by parents as wasteful. Society may endorse the pressure for early marriage and there may be vulnerability to sexually transmitted disease such as HIV or AIDS. School systems and educational practices are not always conducive to the learning needs and preferences of girls, and even when girls achieve parity in educational access, their opportunities within the job market may be limited. Despite this, there has been significant progress in terms of gender parity at primary level.

According to UNESCO (2012, p 39) of 193 countries worldwide, 128 have achieved gender parity with regard to attendance at school. Of the remaining 65 countries, all but 8 favour boys. These include most of the African continent, Pakistan, India, Iraq, Saudi Arabia and Brazil. There is gender parity in education in most European countries, the United States of America, Canada and Australia, as well as in Iran, Russia and Japan. However, in China, Malawi, Bangladesh and Senegal, the gender balance in school favours girls. The fastest gain towards parity has been seen in sub-Saharan Africa and in the Arab states, where the proportion of countries achieving parity has quadrupled in the period between 1970 and 2009.

Bearing this in mind, UNESCO (2012) states that most countries need to address gender disparities, and in some situations this is concerned with educational outputs for boys rather than girls. While in developing countries boys may be advantaged in terms of access to education, once in school, girls are found to outperform boys (p 25).

Critical questions

» *Consider an incident or experience where you think you have been treated unfairly because of your gender.*

» *What are the underlying attitudes and beliefs which contribute to how you were treated?*

» *Consider how you feel about the way you were treated.*

» *Consider an incident when you may have used your gender to gain benefit. What were the circumstances which provoked this behaviour and how would you justify what you did?*

In the UK, the Equality Act (UK Government, 2010) is an attempt to provide a framework within which any form of discrimination is unlawful. The Equality Duty encompasses all other Equality Duties, including the Gender Equality Duty of 2007. All teachers are required to *promote equal opportunities and to provide reasonable adjustment ... as provided for in the Equality Act 2010* (DfE, 2012b, p 6). It is therefore crucial that as a trainee teacher you should be familiar with the requirements of such legislation in order to act appropriately within it.

UK Legislation – gender related

In 2007, the Gender Equality Duty was published. This meant that schools had a general duty to promote equality of opportunity between men and women, including boys and girls, and to publish a Gender Equality Scheme showing how the school intended to fulfil the implications of the Duty. The Equality and Human Rights Commission (EHRC) published the findings from detailed research into ways in which schools in England and Wales were carrying out their equality duties and to exemplify good practice (EHRC, 2011). The actions by schools that have resulted in positive pupil outcomes can be seen in the graph on page 30 taken from the report.

Critical questions

Using the information shown in this graph, consider the following questions concerning the action taken by schools to achieve equality of opportunity under the terms of the Gender Equality Duty (2010).

» *What percentage of schools did not take any action or know what action had been taken towards gender equality?*

» *What is the most frequent action taken?*

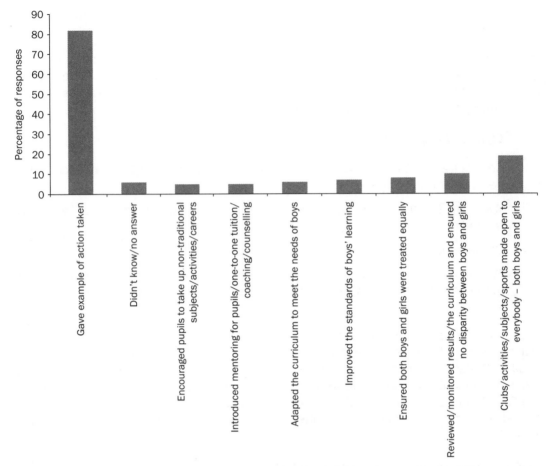

Figure 2.1 Gender Equality Duty-related action that has contributed to positive pupil outcomes
Source: *The Equality Duties and Schools: Report 70*. Equality and Human Rights Commission (2011).

»   *What two actions are aimed specifically at equality of opportunity for boys?*

»   *What do you think taking up non-traditional subjects/activities/careers might mean for boys and for girls?*

The EHRC (2011) research showed that only 20 per cent of schools considered there to be enough training on the Equality Duty and that they believed that new entrants to the teaching profession are *significantly more likely to need a lot of training* (p xii). Furthermore, while schools demonstrated that they were taking action to implement the Disability Equality Duty, this was more likely to be concerned with disability than with gender or race and therefore more sustained training and action is needed to address gender equality.

The Equality Act 2010 supports and develops the principles of the Sex Discrimination Act, the Race Relations Act and the Disability Discrimination Act. One of its nine protected characteristics is sex. This legislation states that schools cannot lawfully discriminate against pupils because of their sex or sexual orientation (DfE, 2012b, p 5). This applies to discrimination about a characteristic a person is thought to have, whether or not they have it, and is relevant to the incident of Tom in the playground where he is discriminated against by his peers as they are calling him *gay*. This could be considered to be harassment under the terms of the Equality Act. The DfE defines harassment as

> *unwanted conduct, related to a relevant protected characteristic, which has the purpose or effect of violating a person's dignity or creating an intimidating, hostile, degrading, humiliating or offensive environment for that person. (p 6)*

This is extended further to actions which cause offence, either intentionally or unintentionally, because of a protected characteristic. As a trainee teacher, you need to be aware of the implications of such legislation. While the Equality Duty does not cover the relationship between one pupil and another, if a teacher knows that children such as Tom are being bullied in the playground because of homophobic name-calling and does nothing about it, this could be seen as being complicit in the action and, as such, the school could be guilty of unlawful discrimination (DfE, 2013, p 4). The Equality Duty also makes provision for those who may be victimised because of a protected characteristic such as sex. This means that, as a trainee teacher, you must be careful not to treat a child such as Tom less favourably because he prefers to play with girls or exhibits what might be considered to be 'feminine' play behaviour. This would have implications for how you managed any situation where Tom might complain to you about how he is ostracised by the boys at playtime. Furthermore, it is important to know that should Tom's mother complain to the school about him being treated less favourably because of his supposed sexual orientation, it is unlawful for Tom to be victimised as a result of this complaint (p 6). Having outlined the requirements of the law for teachers with regard to gender issues, it is now important to consider the implications for classroom practice.

The role of the teacher

While it is reasonable for the class teacher to investigate whether or not Tom has special educational needs, it should not be assumed that this is the cause of his lack of progress. As Gerschel (2004) states, *it is difficult to say where 'underachievement' ends and 'special needs' begins* (p 53). Children who live in unsafe environments, who lack the basics of food, warmth and clothing, let alone access to educational tools such as computers and books, are considered to be less likely to succeed in their learning, particularly if their parents have a low income, as is likely to be the case for Tom. Mittler (2000) links social class and economic deprivation with underachievement, maintaining that *boys are more susceptible to social disadvantage in early childhood, girls more vulnerable at adolescence* (p 58). Additionally, Tom's difficulties with socialisation and the bullying that he receives in the playground are likely to have a deleterious effect on his self-esteem and therefore his willingness to grapple with work he finds difficult. All of these factors will impact on Tom's identity and therefore on his ability to learn.

One of the most important things any teacher must do is provide opportunities where children can develop a strong sense of positive self-esteem. This is particularly important for a child such as Tom, who is likely to have low self-esteem due to his reading difficulties, his peer relationships and his home circumstances. Schachter and Ventura (2008) consider that people such as teachers, parents, youth workers and mentors can be seen as identity agents, in that they are actively engaged with children in such a way as to support positive identity formation (p 454). This being the case, it is vital that when you are on placement, you provide positive learning experiences for all children. Some suggestions about how you might plan and deliver such learning opportunities are detailed in the next section.

Implications for classroom practice

Previous schools of thought have considered that delivering a more 'boy friendly' curriculum would engage boys' attention more fully and lead to an improvement in their achievement. However, there is little evidence from research to show that providing a gender bias in the curriculum enables boys to achieve more. Indeed, it has been found that such a gendered curriculum may lead to greater stereotyping where teachers ignore children's preferences and limit their choices (DCSF, 2009, p 6). This being the case, you need to think carefully about the choice of topic or theme you introduce to your class on placement and how you approach it. It is also important to be aware that not all slow readers are boys. Therefore, you need to make sure that you provide interest for all pupils and that you plan interactive, exciting and motivating lessons which engage all learners.

Providing reading partnerships with other more fluent readers or older children can be a very effective way of developing reading. In my own experience, I paired a Y6 pupil with dyslexia with a low-achieving Y3 pupil for 10 minutes' reading every morning. The reading of both pupils improved considerably and, although this pairing was initially meant to be for one term, it continued for a whole year, bringing huge benefits to the self-esteem of both pupils as well as greater acceptance with peers in the playground. Other reading-related activities could be reading clubs, where pupils recommend what is worth reading and which foster reading for enjoyment and not just to be able to accomplish academic work. Additionally, children can be sensitively paired in the class when doing work which involves reading in order to help them complete the task. It is important not to equate lack of reading ability with poor cognitive function. This is particularly so in children with dyslexia, who may be frustrated by work which is too demeaning for them, but which they cannot access due to their lack of reading ability.

The importance of male role models for reading is highlighted by the National Literacy Trust (NLT) (2012), who identify that girls tend to model themselves on their mothers and boys on their fathers with regard to reading behaviour. Therefore, if the mother is seen to read and not the father, boys are less likely to read for pleasure as it is not associated with their male role model (p 18). This is clearly a difficulty for Tom as he has no father figure. When I was a class teacher, I actively sought out male volunteers who could come into school to read with boys who were not motivated readers. One elderly retired gentleman came regularly each week to read with a particularly vulnerable boy in my class. This not only generated an enthusiasm for reading, but also provided a regular constant relationship which became very meaningful for both the supporter and the child. Another father I had contact with regularly read to all of his four boys; each of them fostered a love of books and reading by the time they were Y6 pupils, even though two of the boys had a reading age well below their chrono-logical age at age seven.

Having good resources available for reading is also important. This includes a good range of fiction and non-fiction and books for different interests and reading abilities. Similarly, the use of images and ICT can be very motivating and provide helpful clues to hesitant readers. The NLT found that one of the main reasons boys state they do not read is because they cannot find anything they are interested in (2012, p 24). Providing games which involve reading in order to play them is another way in which children can be motivated to read, perhaps without noticing. Such games can be played with any children, fluent readers or otherwise, and not just with a group of reluctant readers and the TA. They can be computer-based, board or card games. Furthermore, encouraging children to read material beyond their reading book is important. Children may prefer to read comics, 'how-to' manuals, instructions for activities or hobbies or labels from packets. The NLT found that the majority of reading undertaken by children outside of the classroom was digital, with only 7.7 per cent of boys and 8 per cent of girls reading books (2012, p 22). As a teacher, applaud every effort a child makes to read.

Although reading is key to literacy, it is important for children not to be hampered in their participation and achievement by their limited reading skills. Incorporating talk as a pre-task for writing is a useful strategy to employ. Also, the use of drama, speaking and listening, role play and hot seating to enable all children to be involved in thinking about what is being taught and expressing themselves as fully as any other member of the class. These strategies are endorsed in a four-year report undertaken by Cambridge University and focusing on the gender gap in achievement (Younger and Warrington, 2005, p 8). These strategies are good practice for all pupils, whether boys or girls, able readers or hesitant readers, and they are excellent pre-tasks for writing or other methods of recording. While this report does not reflect the current government policy, it nonetheless provides some useful ideas for classroom practice.

Many class teachers group their children by ability, often based on reading competence. This immediately draws distinctions between pupils, including the tasks they are given and the reading materials they have access to. While boys in the lower ability group tend to develop avoidance strategies for the work they find too difficult, girls tend not to mind being seen to read books which are too easy and therefore gain more practice and improve their reading. However, they may avoid books which they consider to be too hard and may therefore not develop their reading ability further. The avoidance of reading by boys means that they fall further behind their peers with the resultant loss of self-esteem (DCSF, 2009, p 6). While you may not have much choice about how you group children on placement, you need to be mindful of the effect of grouping on children's ability to achieve. Similarly, while many teachers see the use of a TA as vital to the progress of low-achieving children, such children can see this support as a stigma and resent the fact that this marks them out as different. TAs can be deployed with many children to develop their learning and it is very important that you as the teacher spend time with the children who are not achieving their potential.

Critical reflections

» *If you were to meet a child such as Tom on your placement, how would you make provision to develop his learning and social inclusion within the class and playground?*

» *How would you justify these to your class teacher?*

» *When you are on placement you receive a letter from a parent complaining that the literature you are using with the children portrays stereotypical gender identities and promotes traditional nuclear families. She wants you to offer literature which features families with children who have lesbian or gay parents. What are your feelings about this? How should you respond, bearing in mind the requirements of the Equality Duty 2010?*

Taking it further

Books and journals

Brewer, S. (2001) *A Child's World: a Unique Insight into How Children Think*. London: Headline (Hachette).

> This book provides a fascinating insight into what the world looks like through the eyes of a child. Chapter 5 'The engendered species' is about how boys and girls view themselves and each other and how and when they begin to take on the concept of gender.

Hayes, D. (2012) Establishing Your Own Teacher Identity, in Hansen, A. (ed) *Primary Professional Studies*, 2nd Edition. London: Sage.

> This chapter is concerned with what motivates you to teach and discusses the values that you may have as a teacher. It includes a section on the professional responsibilities of teachers and issues which might be faced on school placement.

Marsh, J (2000) 'But I Want to Fly Too!': Girls and Superhero Play in the Infant Classroom. *Gender and Education* 12(2): 209–220.

> This article details some research about the topic of superheroes, which is often thought to be a theme which will appeal to boys rather than girls. However, Dr Marsh challenges the stereotypical view of male superheroes and considers that teachers should provide opportunities for both girls and boys to explore this role.

Web-based materials

Equality – Discrimination against Men, MWM a film by Man Woman Myth. YouTube www.youtube.com/watch?v=3S7v4fuguHI (last accessed 4 October 2013).

> This is a short video which details the case of discrimination against men.

References

Bartlett, S. and Burton, D. (2008) The Influence of Gender on Achievement, in Richards, G. and Armstrong, F. (eds) *Key Issues for Teaching Assistants: Working in Diverse and Inclusive Classrooms*. Oxon: Routledge.

Blackburn, S. (2012) The Second Sexism: Discrimination Against Men and Boys, *Times Higher Education*, 5 July 2012. Online: www.timeshighereducation.co.uk/story.asp?storycode=420459 (last accessed 2 October 2013).

Collins, N. (2012) It's Nature, Not Nurture: Personality Lies in Genes, Twins Study Shows, *The Daily Telegraph*, 16 May 2012. Online: www.telegraph.co.uk/science/science-news/9267147/Its-nature-not-nurture-personality-lies-in-genes-twins-study-shows.html (last accessed 30 August 2012).

Department for Children, Schools and Families (DCSF) (2009) *Gender and Education – Myth Busters: Addressing Gender and Achievement: Myths and Realities*. Online: http://webarchive.nationalarchives.gov.uk/20130401151715/https://www.education.gov.uk/publications/eOrderingDownload/00599-2009BKT-EN.pdf (last accessed 17 October 2013).

Department for Education (DfE) (2012a) *Teachers' Standards.* Online: http://media.education.gov.uk/assets/files/pdf/t/teachers%20standards%20information.pdf (last accessed 7 October 2013).

Department for Education (DfE) (2013) *The Equality Act 2010,Departmental Advice* Online: www.education.gov.uk/aboutdfe/policiesandprocedures/equalityanddiversity/a0064570/the-equality-act-2010 (last accessed 17 October 2013).

Department for Education and Skills (DfES) (2001a) *Special Educational Needs Code of Practice.* London: The Stationery Office.

Department for Education and Skills (DfES) (2003) *Tackling Bullying: Listening to the Views of Children and Young People: Research Report 400.* Nottingham: DfES Publications.

Directgov (2012) *Parental Rights and Responsibilities.* Online: www.direct.gov.uk/en/parents/parentsrights/dg_4002954 (last accessed 2 October 2013).

Equality and Human Rights Commission (EHRC) (2011) *The Equality Duties and Schools: Report 70.* Online: www.equalityhumanrights.com/uploaded_files/research/rr70_equality_duties_and_schools.pdf (last accessed 2 October 2013).

Gerschel, L. (2004) Connecting the Disconnected, in Tilstone, C. and Rose, R. (eds) *Strategies to Promote Inclusive Practice.* Oxon: Routledge.

Horgan, G. (2007) *The Impact of Poverty on Young People's Experience of School.* Joseph Rowntree Foundation. Online: www.jrf.org.uk/sites/files/jrf/2098-poverty-children-school.pdf (last accessed 22 August 2012).

IPU (2012) Women in National Parliaments. Online: www.ipu.org/wmn-e/arc/classif300612.htm (last accessed 2 October 2013).

Kirkpatrick, M. (2003) The Nature and Nurture of Gender. *Psychoanalytic Inquiry: A Topical Journal for Mental Health Professionals*, 23(4): 558–71.

Mittler, P. (2000) *Working Towards Inclusive Education: Social Contexts.* London: David Fulton Publishers.

The National Literacy Trust (2012) *Boys' Reading Commission: A Review of Existing Research Conducted to Underpin the Commission.* Online: www.literacytrust.org.uk (last accessed 5 October 2013).

Office for National Statistics (ONS) (2008) *Focus on Gender.* Online: www.ons.gov.uk/ons/publications/re-reference-tables.html?edition=tcm%3A77-51144 (last accessed 2 October 2013).

Parity (2012) Male Victims of Domestic Abuse. Online: www.parity-uk.org/male_dom_abuse.php (last accessed 2 October 2013).

Schachter, E. and Ventura, J. (2008) Identity Agents: Parents as Active and Reflective Participants in their Children's Identity. *Journal of Research on Adolescence* 118 (3): 449–76.

Slater, C. (2004) Gay Students, Teachers and Research Action, in Armstrong, F. and Moore, M. (eds) *Action Research for Inclusive Education: Changing Places, Changing Practices, Changing Minds.* Oxon: Routledge.

UK Government (2010) *The Equality Act 2010*, Chapter 15. London: The Stationery Office. Online: www.legislation.gov.uk/ukpga/2010/15/pdfs/ukpga_20100015_en.pdf (last accessed 8 October 2013).

UNESCO (2010) *Inclusive Education.* Online: www.unesco.org/new/en/unesco/themes/gender-equality/themes (last accessed 2 October 2013).

UNESCO (2012) *World Atlas of Gender Equality in Education.* Online: www.uis.unesco.org/Education/Pages/unesco-gender-atlas-2012.aspx (last accessed 2 October 2013).

Vicars, M. (2006) Who Are You Calling Queer? Sticks and Stones Can Break My Bones But Names Will Always Hurt Me. *British Educational Research Journal* 32(3): 347–61.

Younger, M. and Warrington, M. et al. (2005) *Raising Boys' Achievement*. Report No. RR636. London: DfES. Online: http://webarchive.nationalarchives.gov.uk/20130401151715/https://www.education.gov.uk/publications/eOrderingDownload/RR636.pdf (last accessed 17 October 2013).

3 Understanding behaviour

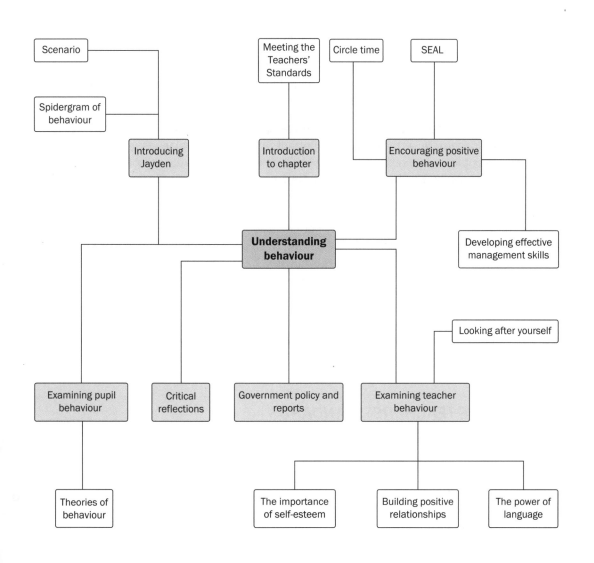

Introduction

During one of my teaching sessions recently, I asked a group of trainee teachers what they found most difficult about becoming a teacher. I anticipated many and varied responses from the group, including developing relevant subject knowledge, how to plan exciting and stimulating lessons, how to convey difficult concepts, manage the complexities of a busy classroom and make sure all children met their potential. However, the overwhelming response was their anxiety over managing difficult or challenging behaviour. On investigating this further, the trainees stated that they found this difficult because they felt the class could *get out of control* and that this was one of the biggest signs of failure and embarrassment. It was clear that the trainees felt a significant emotional burden and responsibility associated with managing the behaviour of the children in the class.

Experienced teachers also express concern about pupil behaviour. In 2010, the Association of Teachers and Lecturers (ATL) found that practising teachers considered pupil behaviour to have worsened over the past few years. Furthermore they found that:

- 51 per cent of staff reported that they had been verbally abused or threatened;

- 38.6 per cent of teachers had been intimidated or sworn at;

- 25.9 per cent of staff had experienced physical violence;

- 36.8 per cent of respondents had considered changing their career for reasons associated with behaviour. (ATL, 2010, p 4)

This might seem a pessimistic picture as there are also many classes of well-behaved children who are eager to learn. Nevertheless, it is important that you, as a trainee teacher, consider the factors which contribute to a positive learning environment as well as the reasons why some children present with challenging behaviour. Some children may have SENs affecting behaviour, while others may have a great deal of instability in their lives, perhaps living with violence, alcoholic family members, poverty or constant change. These children are more concerned about survival than learning. For other children, education may not be valued or other needs may take priority over developing a positive learning disposition. Whatever the reasons for children's challenging behaviour, it is important for you to provide a positive learning environment and to develop strategies that value and esteem children in order that they are well placed to choose to behave well.

As well as considering positive behaviour management, this chapter considers your own emotional development as a teacher and how fostering positive pupil–teacher relationships are important for good behaviour. It also considers government policy and relevant reports and guidance as well as providing some useful strategies to support good classroom management.

MEETING THE TEACHERS' STANDARDS

Links to Department for Education Teachers' Standards May 2012

TS 1; 2; 7

Part 2

Government policy and reports – England

Successive governments have been concerned about discipline in schools. The Elton Report (1989) and the Steer Report (DCSF, 2005) both highlight the need for teachers and those who train them to be aware of and put into practice the principles of good classroom management. Emphasis is placed on curriculum content and teaching methods to motivate children and reinforces the notion that poor behaviour can result because of the inability of the child to access their learning. The Elton Report (1989) urges initial teacher training (ITT) establishments to consider the personal qualities of prospective teachers in their interview and selection process, while the Steer Report (DCSF, 2005) recommends that trainee teachers should be given confidence and skills in how to manage behaviour. A section on 'What works in schools' is included with this in mind. These strategies include developing high levels of respect between parents, pupils and teachers with excellent levels of communication, effective behaviour and teaching and learning policies, a sense of professionalism and team working among teachers and a high level of pedagogical knowledge and practice (DCSF, 2005, p 72).

The recommendations of the Steer Report are developed further in the Behaviour and Discipline in Schools report (House of Commons Education Committee, 2011), where it is suggested that the 'What works in schools' approaches are incorporated into initial teacher training and in ongoing professional development for teachers (p 22).

However, although the Department for Education (DfE) endorses the expectation for the teacher to manage and improve children's behaviour within a climate of mutual respect, their recent guidance *Ensuring Good Behaviour in Schools* (DfE, 2012a) also includes a strong strand of discipline and punishment. There is a clear emphasis on *powers to discipline, disciplinary penalties, the power to search, reasonable force* and *exclusions*. Additionally, the requirement for the parent to make sure the child is well behaved at school is made explicit, with the possibility of a parenting contract or court-imposed parenting order if this does not occur (DfE, 2012a). This document places emphasis not just on the teacher to provide an effective learning environment and to manage behaviour accordingly, but also on parents to be responsible for their child's behaviour and education.

Alongside this government guidance, the Teaching Agency, now known as the National College for Teaching and Leadership (NCTL), published a description of the knowledge, skills and understanding that trainee teachers need to develop in order to manage pupil behaviour. This has implications for ITT (DfE, 2013). The requirements of the trainee include the ability to develop an effective personal style, self-management and reflection, as well as developing good relationships, understanding school systems and classroom management. These expectations are designed to complement the new Teachers' Standards.

All of the above documentation and guidance points to the need for the trainee to become equipped with appropriate behaviour-management skills and to develop the necessary personal and professional resources to provide a positive learning ethos. The following scenario allows you to consider some of these ideas further.

Introducing Jayden

This scenario introduces Jayden and Miss Parker and outlines an incident which could occur in a class with an inexperienced, ill-prepared or under-confident trainee. It is probably an example of the kind of experience a trainee dreads.

SCENARIO

A trainee teacher, Miss Parker, is working in a Y6 class. The children are doing written work. Jayden, who is known for challenging behaviour, is not getting on with his work. He is chatting to his neighbour, getting up and sharpening his pencil at the bin and fiddling with things on other pupils' tables while walking back to his place. He is not responding to Miss Parker's repeated requests to behave and get on with his work. Eventually, Jayden flicks his eraser across the room with his ruler and hits a girl in the face. She screams and cries while Jayden shrugs his shoulders and protests his innocence. The whole class are now interrupted in their work and watching to see what Miss Parker will do. She is angry and shouts at Jayden, demanding that he should apologise for his behaviour. He throws his pencil down and storms out of the class shouting and swearing. Some of the children are amused by this incident and smirk and snigger. Miss Parker does not know how to deal with the consequences of this situation nor how to regain control of her class.

Having read the scenario concerning Miss Parker and Jayden, consider the following critical questions. Through them you will begin to understand some of the complexities of managing behaviour and to think about the nature and quality of the classroom environment. They will also enable you to reflect on what Miss Parker might do differently another time and how relationships between the teacher and the pupils can impact on both specific and general classroom behaviour.

Critical questions

» *Why do you think Jayden is not doing his work?*

» *What could Miss Parker do instead of telling him to sit down and complete his work?*

» *What do you think the classroom environment is like during the incident above and what do you think the other children think about Miss Parker as a teacher?*

» *What emotions do you think Miss Parker feels during and after this incident and how does this affect her handling of the situation?*

» *What do you think Miss Parker's relationship with Jayden is like and how has this incident affected it?*

In considering Miss Parker and the way she manages Jayden's behaviour, a number of concerns and contributing factors can be identified. The following spidergram shows some of the issues raised by this scenario.

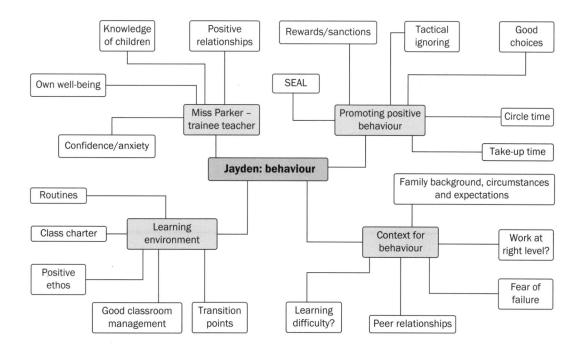

An examination of the issues raised by the scenario will enable you to:

- recognise how your own behaviour as a teacher impacts on pupil behaviour;

- understand the importance of building positive relationships in the classroom;

- be aware of the underlying causes of behaviour;

- understand the importance of social and emotional behaviours;

- know the importance of planning for positive classroom behaviour and how to implement it.

These are now considered in more detail in the following section.

Examining teacher behaviour

In any situation involving more than one person, there will always be different ways of looking at things. The ability to see beyond your own perspective is an important reflective quality to develop as a teacher. In the scenario above, Miss Parker had lost sight of the importance of fostering good relationships with all of the pupils in her class and had little confidence or strategies to deal with the situation as it escalated. All teachers, especially trainees, need to be self-aware, consider their body language and attitudes and accept that making a mistake is not failure, unless you are unable to learn from it.

Looking after yourself

The concept of Intelligence Quotient (IQ), traditionally related to the ability to manage linguistic and mathematical skills, is familiar to many. However, Howard Gardner (1993) developed the notion of multiple intelligences, and although logistic – mathematical and linguistic – intelligence is part of this, so are other intelligences, including musical, spatial, kinaesthetic, spiritual, moral, interpersonal and intrapersonal. Intrapersonal intelligence is concerned with knowing yourself and understanding your own feelings, fears and motivations, while interpersonal intelligence is concerned with the ability to understand the intentions and motivations of others. This is an important skill for building relationships.

Daniel Goleman considers the notion of different intelligences further, arguing that having a high IQ in itself does not prepare people well for successful careers and personal lives. He developed the idea of emotional intelligence (1996) which can be further subdivided into five domains:

- knowing one's own emotions – self-awareness;
- managing emotions – handling feelings;
- motivating oneself – becoming productive and effective;
- recognising emotions in others – building empathy;
- handling relationships – social competence. (Goleman, 1996, p 43)

Undertaking teaching practice can be a highly stressful as well as rewarding time. You will have lesson preparation, marking, innovative resources to make and the assessment of children's progress. In addition to this, you may have a long journey to and from your setting and will also have the necessities of life to attend to, such as sleeping and eating. There may also be tensions like those Miss Parker encountered with children you find difficult to manage or possibly like. Such children provide challenges enough, but if you are tired, anxious and lacking in confidence, then it is likely that you could become defensive, negative and lacking in self-esteem. Having an awareness of your own emotional state and then how to manage these emotions is important for all teachers, and failure to do so will leave you vulnerable in the classroom.

The importance of self-esteem

Jenny Mosley recognises the importance of building positive self-esteem for all teachers and provides a list of pointers to assess self-esteem. These include questions such as the following.

- Do you often lose your temper with the children?
- Do you worry about work when you are at home?
- Do you have personality clashes with certain children/colleagues?
- Do you feel that your efforts to make improvements are ineffective?
- Do you need to shout to gain pupils' attention
- Do you often give punishments for poor behaviour?
- Do you expect problems from children from certain backgrounds?
- Do you find it hard to praise children or colleagues? (2001, pp 18–19)

It would not be difficult for Miss Parker to answer yes to most of these questions. This would suggest that her self-esteem is low and that taking some measures to develop her own confidence would enable her to deal more effectively with Jayden's behaviour.

Jenny Mosley's (2001) *personal care plan* involves taking time out during the week to visit *wells*. These are spaces where you will find energy and restoration. They may involve reading books, watching films, having fun, developing friendships, enjoying hobbies or art, taking some exercise, eating, sleeping, meditating or enjoying nature (p 24–25). She cautions against the *box that pulsates guilt* – the box that teachers carry around with them which contains things they think they might do, but do not have time for – and encourages developing calming rituals such as breathing techniques, a long shower, enjoying a quiet cup of tea or taking fresh air. It is important for you to recognise that the most important resource in the class is yourself and neglecting your own well-being means you are less likely to have the capacity to develop positive relationships and give your children appropriate attention.

Building positive relationships

As teachers, you are role models for the pupils in your class. This is recognised in Part 2 of the Teachers' Standards, which requires you to treat *pupils with dignity, building relationships rooted in mutual respect* (DfE, 2012b). If you want pupils to treat you with respect, then you must model it within your classrooms.

All children need to know they can request your attention and that they will be listened to. This will enable them to feel valued and respected. Children who cannot get your attention through usual classroom interaction may well resort to gaining it through antisocial behaviour, even if this elicits negative attention (Mosley, 2001, p 14).

If, as a trainee teacher, you are feeling hassled and frustrated, this will show in your body language and children will recognise it. You will need to guard against the temptation to judge children because of their background, their reputation, the expectations you have of them or that other teachers impose on them. Your perceptions of children are betrayed in your behaviour and responses towards them, and those children who feel alienated from you or who have learned to distrust teachers will sense whether or not you accept them. Therefore you may need to work harder to offer a positive and valuing relationship to such children (Mosley, 2001, p 15). In the scenario, Jayden had a reputation for presenting with challenging behaviour. Along with Miss Parker's lack of confidence, this resulted in a situation which needed careful handling to avoid the kind of incident shown.

The power of language

Miss Parker repeatedly asked Jayden to 'behave'. However, Jayden's perception of what that might entail could be different from that of Miss Parker. In my own teaching experience, I found that asking children what 'behave' meant would provide me with a set of other non-specific statements like 'be good' or 'do what I am told'. Generalised statements should be replaced with specific instructions or questions such as 'What should you be doing?' Rather than repeated shouting across the classroom for Jayden to behave, Miss Parker should deny him the audience of the class and speak with him quietly. She should not tower over him in a show of power, but should be on a level with him and tell him specifically what he is to do. Rather than saying 'I would like you to sit down, please', she should simply and calmly say 'Jayden, sit on your chair, thank you'. Mentioning the child's name means it is clear who Miss Parker is addressing, and saying thank you relays an expectation that this should be done rather than a request. Miss Parker should then move away and allow Jayden the space to act appropriately.

As soon as Jayden does anything which relates to the expected behaviour, he should be praised. Other children who are behaving as expected should also be praised. I recently talked with some trainee teachers returning from their first placement in school. One of them remarked on how she seemed to be constantly nagging the children about their behaviour, until the class teacher suggested that she should praise expected behaviour instead. The trainee explained how this had completely changed the atmosphere in the classroom and turned restless, agitated children into well-motivated, respectful and enthusiastic pupils.

The trainees also commented on how they had learned about the importance of using their voices appropriately. They had begun to understand that noisy, shouting teachers often have noisy, shouting children and that keeping a quiet voice was effective in the classroom. Miss Parker had not yet made this discovery.

Miss Parker is clearly getting very frustrated at Jayden's behaviour and because she is afraid that the class is getting out of control, her own anxiety is building. She is likely to feel angry towards Jayden as he seems to be flouting her authority in the classroom and this is all taking place in a very public arena. Her reputation as a teacher is being challenged. Dealing with your own anger in the classroom is important, not least because such emotions will influence behaviour. It is therefore imperative that you consider what you will do when you get angry, rather than allow yourself to get angry and then wonder how to manage it. Anger in itself is not wrong, but how it is managed is vital. It is also beneficial to distinguish between annoyance, irritation, being fed up, frustration, anger and aggression (Rogers, 2006, p 184).

If on your placement it becomes necessary to speak with a child about something which has made you angry, then you should make sure that you can do this in a calm, non-threatening manner. Miss Parker made an unrealistic demand of Jayden by telling him to apologise. She could not enforce this apology and was setting up a confrontational situation which she was not going to win. In addressing the situation with Jayden, she should focus on the issue and not on the child. She might say something like 'I am annoyed because you flicked the eraser across the classroom'. Allowing cool-off time after such an incident helps both parties to calm down and reflect. After this, the teacher needs to work towards repairing and restoring the relationships within the classroom, whether or not the anger is justified. It is up to the adult to model expected behaviour (Rogers, 2006, p 186). It is also important to remember that all teachers will make mistakes. Admitting to them does not reduce your authority but enhances it, as it enables children to realise that mistakes can be made, but that acknowledgement and apology are the way to put things right (Mosley, 2001, p 17). Admitting to being human is a strength not a weakness.

Critical questions

» *Using Jenny Mosley's questions to assess self-esteem, how would you rate yours?*

» *What actions will you undertake while training to teach, but especially on placement, to develop a personal care plan?*

» *Imagine you are placed in Jayden's class for your placement. How would you establish and maintain positive behaviour in the class?*

» *Consider what your strategy will be for managing yourself in a situation in the classroom that makes you angry.*

Examining pupil behaviour

A re-reading of the scenario would suggest that Jayden is exhibiting a great deal of attention-seeking behaviour. He is chatting to his neighbour, drawing attention to himself by being out of his seat. His behaviour escalates when he flicks his eraser, and finally he storms out of the classroom, thereby gaining the attention of the whole class. While this behaviour might have been interrupted by the trainee teacher giving him appropriate attention earlier, there may also be other underlying reasons for his challenging behaviour. Children with low self-esteem may find they gain kudos with the class if they challenge the teacher. This may be particularly important to them if their social networks are limited. Other factors influencing Jayden's behaviour might be explained by some of the theories of behaviour outlined below.

Theories of behaviour

A child's home life and parenting are likely to have an impact on their behaviour. Work done by Bowlby (1953) on a child's attachment to their mother suggests that those who do not form firm attachments at an early stage are not likely to develop a secure emotional base for further development. Other children may have been subjected to trauma, have dysfunctional families or have a diagnosed SEN such as Attention Deficit Hyperactivity Disorder (ADHD), which means conforming to expected behaviours is more difficult.

Behaviourist theory suggests that it can be helpful to identify triggers that are sparked off by particular situations and use the ABC approach.

A antecedents – what happens before inappropriate behaviour occurs;

B the behaviour – the incident itself;

C the consequences – what happens as a result of the incident. (Cole, 1998, p 118)

The ABC approach involves looking for events or environmental circumstances that immediately precede unwanted behaviour. This could be something that has previously gone unnoticed, such as a child being provoked, ridiculed or teased and which may lead to the child lashing out physically or verbally or behaving inappropriately. It may also be related to a classroom environment which does not facilitate the child's learning well and thereby leads to a sense of frustration, thus sparking inappropriate behaviour. Identifying the antecedent helps the teacher to consider what can be done to prevent things from escalating further.

B refers to the behaviour itself. This is usually the incident to which teachers pay most attention as it is obvious. However, if teachers fail to look at the antecedent, children may feel unfairly blamed as, in their view, they were responding to something not seen or acknowledged. Teachers need to consider that there may be more to the story than meets the eye and understand that children who feel aggrieved are not well placed to learn.

High level

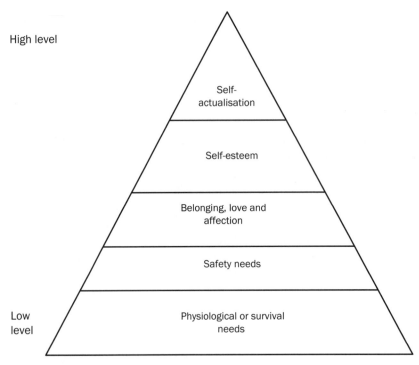

Self-actualisation

Self-esteem

Belonging, love and affection

Safety needs

Low
level

Physiological or survival needs

Figure 3.1 Maslow's hierarchy of needs

The consequences (C) are what result from the incident. These may be fractured relation-ships, a hurt child or a disruption in the classroom. Sometimes it is the consequences which will draw the teacher's attention to the fact that an incident has occurred. In the scenario, the ABC of behaviour would be:

A – antecedent – Jayden's low-level disruptive behaviour in class;

B – the incident – flicking the eraser across the classroom;

C – consequences – the trainee teacher shouting and the child storming out of the class.

If the trainee teacher had dealt with the antecedent – the low-level disruptive behaviour – more appropriately, it is possible that the incident with the eraser would not have occurred and there would have been no ill consequences as a result.

Many schools ascribe to the theory of Maslow's (1943) hierarchy of needs. This triangle of needs suggests that only when the needs at a lower level are met can a child's needs at the higher level be satisfied (see Figure 3.1).

It is not clear from the scenario whether Jayden's basic needs for food, sleep and safety are being met. However, it would seem that his constant craving for attention would call into question whether he feels he belongs and is accepted in the class. It is likely that his self-esteem is low and therefore his ability to reach his full potential is compromised.

Disruptive behaviour can be seen in children who face learning difficulties. In some of my own research in school, I found that teachers attributed children's inability to complete work to poor behaviour, whereas the children suggested that they lacked concentration because the work was too hard or uninteresting. Teachers continued to discipline the children for inattention, while the children continued with distracting behaviours as they felt unable to access their work. This kind of negative cycle builds hostility such as occurred between Jayden and Miss Parker and can only be broken by the teacher taking a different approach. While it is not stated that Jayden has SENs, it is possible that the work he has been set is not at the right level for him to achieve. It may be that this is at the heart of his disruptive behaviour. Therefore, it is imperative that Miss Parker considers the work required of Jayden and sets realistic and achievable expectations with support for him to succeed.

Critical questions

» *Consider the scenario from Jayden's perspective. Which of the behaviour theories identified above do you think are relevant to him?*

» *Given further insights into Jayden's behaviour, what advice would you give to Miss Parker to manage his behaviour?*

Having considered the scenario from both Miss Parker's and Jayden's perspectives, the next section considers some strategies and initiatives which can be implemented in the classroom to develop positive behaviour.

Encouraging positive behaviour

Developing a positive classroom ethos is both encouraging and motivating for pupils. Experiencing success provides further motivation for children. As a trainee teacher, you will be concerned about what you are teaching the children in your class. However, how you teach, your manner, your approach and the kind of learning environment you create will determine whether or not your children are encouraged, motivated and successful as learners. A much wider discussion of some of these issues takes place in Part 3; however, the following section considers two whole-school approaches designed to foster good self-esteem and supportive relationships. Both of these can be seen in many schools and you may well experience these approaches on placement.

Circle time

Jenny Mosley developed the concept of circle time to enable children to achieve their academic and social potential and thereby to provide a good foundation for adult life. The circle time model is based on respect for the whole person and is concerned with improving the well-being and morale of staff and pupils. It raises self-esteem and provides a safe and supportive learning environment which builds relationships and nurtures responsibility for others (Mosley, 2004, p 8). Circle time is where Golden Rules are created by the class, group or whole school. The Golden Rules are moral values such as honesty, co-operation, trust, listening and kindness, and they are created by the whole group sitting in a circle, sharing eye contact and providing openness of communication (Mosley, 2001, p 84).

Circle time gives the opportunity for children to learn self-discipline through a supportive framework. There is also a strong element of peer support, which encourages moral development. Through this means, children can be involved in a collaborative, solution-focused approach to issues which concern them. Circle time also provides an opportunity for children to develop empathy, to listen to someone else's point of view and see the consequences of their actions. It is not hard to imagine the difference that could be made to Jayden and his classmates if they each understood more fully the feelings and needs of the other and worked together to build welcoming friendships.

Social and emotional aspects of learning

The social and emotional aspects of learning (SEAL) approach has seven whole-school themes and is for children from Foundation Stage through to Key Stage 2. The five aspects of social and emotional learning, which are directly related to Goleman's notion of emotional intelligence, are taught and revisited each year through a spiral curriculum (DfES, 2005, p 8). The SEAL programme is designed to develop good personal and social skills and in doing so provide scope for children to be motivated and equipped to be effective learners, make and sustain friendships, manage conflict and strong feelings, work and play co-operatively and win and lose with dignity and respect for other competitors (DfES, 2005, p 7). Many of the activities are experiential, using visual and kinaesthetic approaches and involve the children in problem solving where they take responsibility for their own learning (p 27). The SEAL approach includes the use of circle time as an effective vehicle for the delivery of its curriculum, and, as such, the two approaches can be seen as complementary.

While the guidance for SEAL promotes a whole-school approach, it also recognises that some children benefit from additional work in groups, and others need an individual approach. Jayden could be seen as one such child. However, Miss Parker also needs to know how to manage inappropriate behaviour such as that described in the scenario. This final section considers such strategies.

Developing effective management skills

When teaching, it is important to understand the range of behaviour-management strategies which can be employed and how to prompt expected behaviour. It is best to shape and encourage required behaviour than to assume it will be given. It is also better to be proactive about expected behaviour than allow matters to escalate and require more significant interventions. The following strategies are taken from Dr Bill Rogers (2006), who ranked them from the least intrusive to the most intrusive. While his list is more extensive, the interventions listed below are of most relevance to the scenario.

*   *Tactical ignoring*: look for opportunities when a child is on-task and choose to ignore other unwanted behaviour.

*   *Tactical pausing*: while the teacher is giving instructions to the class she could briefly pause, showing she is expecting attention.

*   *Non-verbal cueing*: when a child is out of their seat or engaged in other inappropriate behaviour, the teacher could give 'The Look', or simply indicate with a hand gesture that the child should return to their seat.

*   *Descriptive cueing*: the teacher should describe reality. She could say something like 'This is time to be at your desk' if the child is out of their seat, or 'This is quiet reading time' if children are talking.

- *Take-up time*: this has been described earlier in the chapter. It involves giving an instruction or reminder and then moving away to allow the child to co-operate.

- *Behavioural direction:* this has also been explained earlier. It requires the teacher to direct a child specifically about expected behaviour, such as to sit on his chair.

- *Rule reminder*: the teacher will prompt the child by saying 'Remember our rule about respecting each other's things...' as she observes him fiddling with other children's possessions while out of seat.

- *Prefacing*: here the teacher would have focused on a positive issue prior to needing to discipline. She could have taken the opportunity to talk to the child about the work being attempted and then issue a reminder about expected behaviour.

- *Direct questions*: avoid the 'why' question. Children cannot always explain why and it tends to set up a confrontational situation. Children can be asked 'What should you be doing?', or told 'I need you to do your work in a way which does not annoy other children. How are you going to do that?'

- *Directed 'choices'*: this requires the teacher to give a sequence of 'when' followed by 'then', or 'after' followed by 'then'. For example, she could say 'When you are sitting down, I will come and help you with your work' or 'After you have done some work, you can take some time on the computer'.

- *'Choice'/deferred consequences*: in this instance, the teacher is dealing with continued disruption from a pupil and provides a consequential 'choice'. A child can be told 'If you choose not to respect other children's things, you will need to stay behind at playtime to discuss your behaviour'. This would be a reminder of a class rule followed by a consequence. If the child complained about having to stay behind at playtime, then he can be reminded that this is the choice he made by choosing to continue to fiddle with other pupils' belongings. When keeping a child behind at playtime, it is best to keep them for only a few minutes. Making a child with behavioural difficulties miss their opportunity to run around and expend energy at playtime is only creating a restless and possibly angry child for the next session.

- *Assertive comment/direction/command*: this requires the teacher to keep calm but be assertive. Commands should be short and delivered with eye contact. This intervention is described in the context of the scenario with Jayden earlier in the chapter.

- *Time out*: children who are constantly disrupting the class may need to take time out. This re-establishes an effective learning environment and defuses an escalating situation. Time out can be either within or beyond the classroom. If the child is to leave the classroom, they should be directed to a nominated place or teacher and remain there for the rest of the session. If the child refuses to leave the classroom, then a cue card, delivered by a responsible child to another class teacher will indicate that colleague-assisted time out is required. It is important that this intervention is prepared beforehand so that both you and your colleagues know what is expected and appropriate support can be offered.

Critical question

» *Consider each of the interventions in the list above, from least to most intrusive. What do you think the impact of each of these would be on Jayden and his class?*

As you can see from this chapter, positive behaviour management does not just happen. It needs a great deal of forethought, preparation and the building of valuing and esteeming relationships. I recently observed a trainee teacher who had no difficulties with behaviour in his class at all. The children were well behaved and compliant. However, his main method of control was his big booming voice which cut through all other conversation and dominated the classroom. He had little in the way of behaviour-management skills, relying on sheer force of volume. While this might have worked in this particular setting, he was not well equipped to provide an effective learning environment in another and more challenging setting. Not surprisingly, he was reluctant to go to another school to teach as he was afraid he might not be able to manage the children's behaviour. He was probably right. No teacher can *make* a pupil do anything against their will, and setting up confrontational situations only brings conflict and power struggles. It is better to consider ways in which change can be brought about. These include knowing and managing yourself, building positive relationships, knowing and understanding the children in your class, promoting positive behaviour and developing a range of behaviour-management skills. Becoming effective in these areas may not guarantee every child will become a perfect angel, but for the teacher to understand that the only behaviour they can control in the classroom is their own is an important step in providing a positive learning environment.

Critical reflections

»   *What government guidance and reports should you be aware of with regard to behaviour, and how will they enable you to fulfil the Teachers' Standards?*

»   *Think about your behaviour as a trainee teacher on placement. What steps will you take to ensure you are well placed to develop a positive learning environment?*

»   *Which behaviour-management skills do you think you do well? Which skills do you think you need to develop further?*

Taking it further

Books and journals

Mosley, J. (2004) *More Quality Circle Time: Evaluating Your Practice and Developing Creativity Within the Whole School Quality Circle Time Model.* Cambridge: LDA.

   This book provides a rationale for using circle time and is a valuable practice resource for developing circle time sessions in school.

Scruton, J. (2010) Challenging Students, Challenging Settings, in Richards, G. and Armstrong, F. (eds) *Teaching and Learning in Diverse and Inclusive Classrooms: Key Issues for New Teachers.* Oxon: Routledge.

   This chapter reflects on some of the reasons why children present with challenging behaviour. It considers some of the relevant government reports which provide a context for current government policy and guidance and suggests strategies for the newly qualified teacher to implement in the classroom.

Visser, J. (2005) Key Factors that Enable the Successful Management of Difficult Behaviour in Schools and Classrooms. *Education 3–13: International Journal of Primary, Elementary and Early Years Education,* 33(1): 26–31.

This article from John Visser, a well-known behaviour consultant, considers positive behaviour management to be an essential part of inclusive practice. It further reinforces the notion of good behaviour being built on positive relationships, advocates that behaviour can change and recommends a sense of humour as an important aspect of good classroom management.

Web-based materials

DfE (2011) *Getting the Simple Things Right: Charlie Taylor's Behaviour Checklists.* (last accessed 4 October 2013 at http://media.education.gov.uk/assets/files/pdf/c/charlie%20taylor%20 checklist.pdf.

Charlie Taylor is the government's expert advisor on behaviour management and was the Chief Executive of the Teaching Agency. He is the former head of a special school for children with social, emotional and behavioural difficulties. This document was produced as a result of a summit held with headteachers where they outlined the key principles for improving behaviour. It provides information and advice for headteachers in terms of developing a positive school ethos, but also a behaviour checklist for teachers for classroom practice.

References

Association of Teachers and Lecturers (ATL) (2010) Behaviour and Discipline in Schools: ATL's Submission to the Commons Select Committee. Online: www.atl.org.uk/Images/ATLBehaviourSubmissionConsultFinal1.pdf (last accessed 7 October 2013).

Bowlby, J. (1953) *Child Care and the Growth of Love.* Harmondsworth: Pelican.

Cole, T. (1998) Understanding Challenging Behaviour, in Tilstone, C. and Florian, L. (eds) *Promoting Inclusive Practice.* London: Routledge.

Department for Children, Families and Schools (DCSF) (2005) *Learning Behaviour: Lessons Learned. a Review of Behaviour, Standards and Practices in Our Schools (The Steer Report).* Online: www.education.gov.uk/publications/eOrderingDownload/DCSF-Learning-Behaviour.pdf (last accessed 4 October 2013).

Department for Education (DfE) (2012a) *Ensuring Good Behaviour in Schools: a Summary for Head Teachers, Governing Bodies, Teachers, Parents and Pupils.* Online: www.education.gov.uk/publications/eOrderingDownload/Ensuring%20Good%20Behaviour%20in%20Schools%20-%20A%20summary%20for%20heads%20governing%20bodies%20teachers%20parents%20and%20pupils.pdf (last accessed 4 October 2013).

Department for Education (DfE) (2012b) *Teachers' Standards.* Online: http://media.education.gov.uk/assets/files/pdf/t/teachers%20standards%20information.pdf (last accessed 31 August 2013).

Department for Education (DfE) (2013) *Improving Teacher Training for Behaviour.* Online: www.education.gov.uk/schools/careers/traininganddevelopment/initial/b00210912/improving-tt-beh (last accessed 4 October 2013).

Department for Education and Skills (DfES) (2005) *Excellence and Enjoyment: Social and Emotional Aspects of Learning Primary National Strategy.* Online: www.education.gov.uk/publications/eOrderingDownload/SEAL%20Guidance%202005.pdf (last accessed 4 October 2013).

Elton Report (1989) *Enquiry into Discipline in Schools.* London: HMSO. Online: www.educationengland.org.uk/documents/elton/index.html (last accessed 4 October 2013).

Gardner, H. (1993) *Frames of Mind: The Theory of Multiple Intelligences*, 2nd edn. New York: Fontana Press.

Goleman, D. (1996) *Emotional Intelligence: Why It Can Matter More Than IQ*. London: Bloomsbury.

House of Commons Education Committee (2011) *Behaviour and Discipline in Schools: Volume 1*. London: HMSO. Online: www.publications.parliament.uk/pa/cm201011/cmselect/cmeduc/516/51602.htm (last accessed 4 October 2013).

Maslow, A.H. (1943) A Theory of Human Motivation. *Psychological Review*, 50: 370–96.

Mosley, J. (2001) *Quality Circle Time in The Primary Classroom*, vol 1. Cambridge: LDA.

Mosley, J. (2004) *More Quality Circle Time: Evaluating Your Practice and Developing Creativity Within the Whole School Quality Circle Time Model*. Cambridge: LDA.

Rogers, B. (2006) *Classroom Behaviour: A Practical Guide to Effective Teaching, Behaviour Management and Colleague Support*. London: Paul Chapman.

4 Understanding race

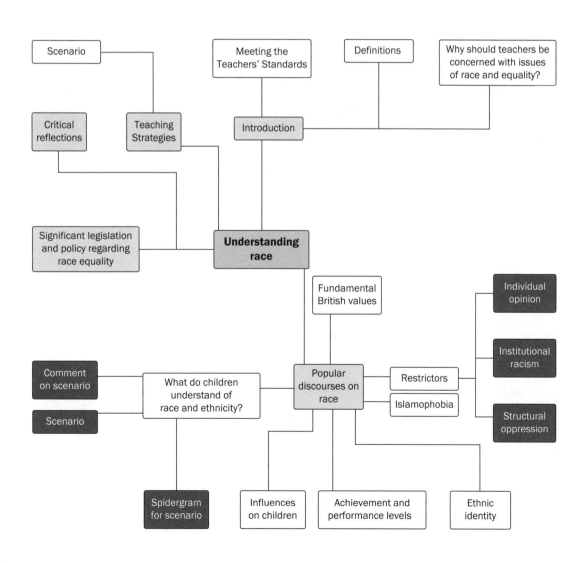

And if they all were English it would save a lot of fuss. And wouldn't it be nice for them if they were all like us.

1930s rhyme, in Brown, 1998, p 54

Introduction

This chapter asks you to examine your own beliefs about race and, in turn, your own prejudices. This will allow you to understand the values and beliefs of others and perhaps to discriminate between the fact and the fiction involved in race rhetoric.

MEETING THE TEACHERS' STANDARDS

Links to Department for Education Teachers' Standards May 2012

TS 1

Part 2

Meeting the Teachers' Standards requires you to set high expectations which inspire, motivate and challenge pupils. This is to take place within a safe and stimulating environment. Fundamental to the Teachers' Standards is the notion of mutual respect. This is to be demonstrated in tolerance and acknowledging the rights of others, including those with differing faiths and beliefs.

Critical questions

Pause for a moment and consider the following terms:

» *racism;*

» *culture;*

» *ethnicity.*

Now consider:

» *In what ways are the terms similar and in what ways are they different?*

» *Why do you think the terms sometimes get confused?*

» *How often do you think about your own race? In what situations?*

Write down a few notes on your own understanding of the term 'racism'.

» *Compare your notes with the following definitions. Do you agree or disagree?*

Definitions

Race

- Race is a social construct. It is a social relationship in which structural positions and social action are ordered, justified and explained by reference to the systems and symbols of belief which emphasise the social and cultural relevance of biologically rooted characteristics.

- Race is a social classification based on your physical features.

- Race is a changeable term and we have to understand the ways in which ideologies and structures construct certain groups in ways that presume they are naturally distinct. (Bhavnani, Mirza and Meeto, 2006, p 217)

Ethnicity

- Ethnicity is a sense of cultural and historical identity based on belonging by birth to a distinctive cultural group, for example, English, Indian, Irish or Afro-Caribbean. It is essentially a process of group identification. We can belong to at least one ethnic group but may also identify with several groups at the same time, for example, Ibo, Nigerian, African and Black Briton.

Culture

- Culture can be defined as the learned system of shared beliefs, systems of meaning, values, customs and behaviours which are transmitted from generation to generation. Culture exists in a constant state of change.

Why should teachers be concerned with issues of race and equality?

We live and work in a multicultural, multi-ethnic society within an interconnected world. Pupils bring into school different understandings and perspectives of what it means to live in a multi-ethnic society. The Guidance on the Duty to Promote Community Cohesion (DCSF, 2007) made a clear statement on the responsibility of teachers to prepare children for living in a diverse society.

The Early Years Foundation Stage (EYFS) (DfE, 2012a, p 2) seeks to provide *equality of opportunity and anti-discriminatory practice, ensuring that every child is included and supported.* The National Curriculum (DfE, 2013b) requests that *teachers should set high expectations for every pupil'* (p8). All children deserve an environment where they can be sure that they will be given the opportunity to excel and be treated fairly. Schools have a duty to:

- eliminate unlawful racial discrimination;

- promote equality of opportunity;

- promote good relations between people of different groups.

The curriculum alone cannot make a difference to race equality in the classroom – teachers and schools need a positive ethos and a commitment to engage.

Significant legislation and policy regarding race equality

You also need to be aware of the legislation and policy, past and present, that governs and controls behaviour towards each other in and out of school.

This race legislation has evolved over the last 50 years in response to the changing need to protect the vulnerable members of society. The significant legislation and policies regarding race equality are listed in the table below.

UK legislation regarding race equality

Legislation and policy	Date	Purpose	Outcomes
Race Relations Act	1976	Unlawful to discriminate on grounds of race, colour, nationality or ethnic or national origin	Discrimination laws applied to jobs, training, housing, education, provision of goods, facilities and services
Education for All – Swann Report into the education of children from minority ethnic groups	1985	Government committed to the principle that all children, irrespective of race, colour, ethnic origin, should have a good education which develops their abilities and aptitudes to the full and brings about a true sense of belonging to Britain The report comprehensively explored the issues which appeared to be preventing this from happening	*Many crucial recommendations were not implemented* *We believe that for schools to allow racist attitudes to persist unchecked in fact constitutes a fundamental mis-education for their pupils*
The National Curriculum	1999	Inclusion statement providing effective learning opportunities for all pupils, with three clear principles: 1. setting suitable learning challenges 2. responding to pupils' diverse learning needs 3. overcoming potential barriers to learning and assessment for individuals and groups of pupils	All schools had to provide an inclusive curriculum while maintaining an inclusive ethos in school
Macpherson Report Result of Stephen Lawrence Inquiry	1999	Requires that schools record all racist incidents; that all recorded incidents are reported to the pupils' parents/guardians, school governors and LEAs: – the numbers of racist incidents published annually – school's curriculum should value cultural diversity	Logging of racist incidents Recommendation for school curriculum to value cultural diversity
Race Relations Amendment Act	2000	Prohibited race discrimination in all public authority functions not already covered by the 1976 Act	Extended scope of 1976 Race Relations Act Extended protection against racial discrimination by public authorities
Every Child Matters (DfE)	2003	Promoted anti-racist practices, procedures and structures	To safeguard children

Legislation and policy	Date	Purpose	Outcomes
Children Act	2004	Safeguarding the welfare of children	A Children's Commissioner ensured children had a voice, to encourage working in partnership to protect children from harm
Removing Barriers to Achievement (DfE)	2004	Mainly for support of children with SEND, in addition to the SENCoP, but very inclusive of all children	Established that *All children have the right to a good education and opportunity to achieve their potential*
Guidance on the Duty to Promote Community Cohesion (DCSF)	2007	*Teaching, learning and curriculum* – helping children and young people to learn to understand others, to value diversity while also promoting shared values *Equity and excellence* – to ensure equal opportunities for all to succeed at the highest level possible, striving to remove barriers to access and participation *Engagement and extended services* – to provide reasonable means for children, young people, their friends and families to interact with people from different backgrounds and build positive relations	Promoted positive relations by engaging with local communities Recognition of diversity, equality of opportunity and inclusion within teaching
Equality Act	2010	Consolidates existing law into a single legal framework Many of concepts of discrimination remain the same as in previous equality legislation Some new areas, eg different types of discrimination (victimisation, harassment)	Simplified and strengthened laws on discrimination
Revised EYFS	2012	Guidance and principles for teaching Early Years *No child should be excluded or disadvantaged because of ethnicity, culture or religion, home language, family background, SEN, disability, gender or ability*	No child excluded or disadvantaged because of ethnicity, culture or religion, home language, family background, SEN, disability, gender or ability
National Curriculum 2013	2013	Guidance and principles for teaching KS1–KS3	Simplified inclusion statement by expectation by stating *teachers should set high expectations for every pupil* (p 8)

The cumulative effect of this legislation clearly established the principle that it is not possible to justify direct discrimination. It will always be unlawful to discriminate on the grounds of race. The other strong discourse coming through education policy is that ethnicity and culture should make no difference to expectations or to developing the potential of each child to the highest level.

Although legislation has made it unlawful to discriminate on the grounds of race, it is still insufficient in helping to integrate all members of society. Why, despite strong anti-discrimination laws, have we not managed a truly integrated society? What is preventing it?

Critical questions

» *Take a few moments to reflect upon why, in spite of ongoing legislation to protect against racial discrimination, it apparently continues. What do you think are the restrictors which work against full integration?*

» *Connelly (1998) suggested that the discourses on race define ways of interpreting the world. They underpin our knowledge of and the way we regard the social world. They influence and shape the way the social world is structured and organised and can shape individuals' subjective identities.*

Consider your position as a teacher in supporting children's understanding of race and identity. Make some notes and share your reflections.

Popular discourses on race

Restrictors

There are restrictors which act to prevent a fully integrated society. The main ones, examined in more detail in the next section, are:

- individual opinion – negative attitudes, prejudice and stereotyping;
- structural oppression;
- institutional racism (policies and practices).

Individual opinion

In Britain we have a certain freedom to be able to think and to act as we like, unless it infringes on other people's personal liberty or is unlawful. Bourdieu (1994) recognised that, although free to choose our thoughts and actions, we are also constrained by our *habitus*. This Bourdieu defines in terms of the way we develop and internalise our thinking, which in turn guides our future actions and behaviour. As we proceed through life, our habitus is reinforced and strengthened by our experiences. In this way, we habitualise the way we think and behave (Connolly, 1998). Our experiences begin to structure and define our view of the social world. As a result, we may come to believe in and support a very negative and rather stereotypical view of race. We develop prejudices. A major characteristic of prejudice is the rigidity with which the prejudice is maintained. New information does not alter our first understanding, instead it becomes twisted to fit the stereotypical preconceptions already held (the Swann Report, DfES, 1985).

Philips (2005) suggested *Integration is a learned competence ... it is not instinctive* (p 6). There are some media discourses that feed off people's negative anxieties – immigration being one of them. There has been a tolerance of diversity in Britain, which Philips (2005) suggests has resulted in a fragmentation of society. He maintains that UK society is becoming more divided by race and religion. *We are becoming more unequal by ethnicity* (p 7). Philips used the memorable phrase *UK is sleeping walking into segregation*. Burgess et al. (2004, p 14) suggested that schools *far from becoming sites of integration, are more segregated in the playgrounds than they are in their neighbourhoods.*

It appears we are preparing children to live in a diverse world but within a segregated community where there is little participation with other ethnic groups.

Critical questions

» *Consider what this might mean for you.*

» *What is your own experience of living in a multi-ethnic community?*

» *Do you have friends of a different ethnicity to yourself?*

» *How do we prepare children who live in an all-white community for living in a diverse society?*

Structural oppression

As described in critical race theory, structural oppression suggests that education policy is powerfully dominated by theories of white supremacy. Gillborn (2005) suggests that *despite rhetoric of standards for all, education policy in England is actively involved in the defence, legitimation and extension of white supremacy* (p 24).

He maintains that any improvement in race equity has arisen directly from resistance and protest from minority groups and gives examples of ways to adjust the inequities that currently exist in school by:

• securing testing;

• abandoning selective teaching and grouping;

• broadening the curriculum;

• diversifying the teaching force;

• genuinely acting on the results of ethnic monitoring.

In practice, however, high-stakes testing, school performance tables and selection by 'ability' are all increasingly being used – despite their *known* detrimental impact on many pupils, not just black students. Gillborn's examples seek to prove that race inequality and racism are continued features of the UK education system.

Institutional racism

Institutional racism, as identified and described by Swann (DfES, 1985), *is a way of describing the long established systems, practices and procedures, within education and the wider society, which were originally conceived and devised to meet the needs and aspirations of a relatively homogeneous society* (p 28). It is now recognised that these procedures have not only failed to take account of the multi-racial nature of Britain today but may also ignore or even actively work against, the interests of ethnic minority communities. These kinds of practices, while clearly and originally well intentioned and in no way racist in *intent*, can now be seen as racist in *effect*. They may deprive members of ethnic minority groups of equality of access to the full range of opportunities which the majority of the community can take for granted, or they may deny their right to have a say in the future of the society of which they are an integral part (Swann, DfES, 1985, p 28).

Institutionalised racism has also been described as *inaction in the face of need* (Jones, 2002). In schools, this could be inadequate access to books which reflect the cultural background of the children in school or certain assumptions being made about the progress levels of the ethnically diverse children.

This could be construed as unintentional racism, which was defined in the Rampton Report (1981):

> *A well-intentioned and apparently sympathetic person may, as a result of his education, experiences or environment, have negative, patronising or stereotyped views about ethnic minority groups which may subconsciously affect his attitude and behaviour towards members of those groups. (p 12)*

The Macpherson Report (1999, 6.45) first highlighted the institutionalised racism evident in the Metropolitan police force after the murder of Stephen Lawrence in 1993.

It is an indictment of the whole justice system that the murderers of Stephen Lawrence were only convicted in 2012, 19 years after his murder at a bus stop. Evidence suggests that racism continues to exist in the police force. Although black people are 30 times more likely than white to be stopped and searched by police in England and Wales, less than 0.5 per cent of searches have led to an arrest (Crown Ministry of Justice, 2010).

Racism violence in the UK continues. In 2011/12 UK police forces recorded 37,000 racially aggravated crimes, an average of 100 per day in England and Wales. These are recorded by the Office of National Statistics as taunts, harassment and assaults, and in some cases murder. For others, there is an underlying hostility and fear rather than acceptance towards certain cultures and faiths. These fears range from a fear of dilution of the mainstream culture to fear of complete annihilation.

Fundamental British values

There is some ambiguity surrounding the notion of fundamental British values. What are the nation's values? What does it mean to be British in a changing world? Is it 'fair play', individuality, tolerance, quirky humour, the National Health Service and a 'broadly Christian society'? Or do values and culture stem from a heritage of industrialisation, hard work, stiff upper lip and keeping calm under all difficulties.

Critical questions

»   *List what you think are the 'fundamental British values' referred to in the Teachers' Standards.*

» *What common British traditions would you expect to recognise in your everyday encounters?*

» *How do the nation's values and beliefs match up to your own?*

» *Suggest something that has been introduced by immigrants to Britain that is now totally assimilated into British culture.*

Islamophobia

There are some sharp dissonances stemming from recent violent acts involving people of extremist views. Since 9/11 there has been a rise in Islamophobia. Muslims in some spheres of the community are seen in a totally negative light. There is suspicion from some that any bearded male Asian is a fundamentalist Muslim extremist, likely to be venting destruction on capitalist imperialism. The truth is that the majority of Muslims abhor violence.

The media present quite a limited view. The following table shows how an open and unprejudiced perspective can interpret things quite differently.

Different views of Islam

Closed prejudiced view of Islam	Open unprejudiced view of Islam
Islam seen as?	Islam seen as?
The same everywhere, unbending unchanging	Varying in different places, with Muslims debating changes and different views
Having no ideas and values in common with other faiths and no links with them	Having some shared ideas and aims and valuing communication
Inferior, traditional faith, barbaric and sexist	Different, but not inferior and worthy of respect
Violent, aggressive, threatening	Peaceful and maybe partner in co-operating to solve shared problems
Not European	Long history in Europe with an influence on science and architecture
Not belonging in Britain	It is the faith of many British, French and German people
Always unfairly critical of 'the West'	Perhaps different perspective should be listened to
Too strict, especially on females and young people	Having strong moral standards
A faith which attracts extremists	Majority of Muslims are peaceful people who abhor violence
All Muslims are fundamentalist	Fundamentalists can be represented in all religions

Children may arrive in school with some very negative perceptions of certain groups in society, some of whom may be their peers. How, then, do you as a teacher manage this in a sensitive way?

Influences on children

The Teachers' Standards (DfE, 2012b) demand that you act as a role model and part of your role is to show that there is a bridge which connects home and school life.

Children bring into school their own experiences, ideas and perspectives of their place in society. Children's capacity to succeed in school is dependent on their social and cultural capital (Bourdieu and Wacquant, 1992). While children are attempting to make sense of this world they live in, they have to assimilate a range of conflicting information. As a teacher, you need to be aware of the influences that children obtain from home, because this affects their behaviour and acceptance of the school values and attitudes. If a child feels excluded from the culture of the school, for whatever reason, it may result in alienation and underachievement.

Ethnic identity

How do race and ethnicity impact on children's perceptions of themselves and of others? Schaffer (1996) found in research focused on ethnic identity that children from minority groups become highly self-conscious about their status. Observing the stages that children moved through in developing an ethnic identity, Schaffer found that young pre-school children categorised others by external appearances, for example, colour. Their acceptance of labels was limited to those such as 'I'm black'. Young school-age children begin to take account of more subtle differences, for example, food, customs, religion, birth place of parents. Nine-to-ten-year-olds realise the more important nature of ethnic identity – that the black person remains black despite putting on a wig or make-up.

Achievement and performance levels

While many young people from minority ethnic backgrounds achieve at the highest level, gaps for some groups remain unacceptably wide. For example, black Caribbean boys eligible for free school meals are among those making slowest progress. There is also an issue with the performance levels of children from mixed white/black Caribbean families. While school policy statements express commitment to tackling discrimination, racism and underachievement, these may only be in 'mono heritage' forms that often do not recognise mixed-heritage pupils. (Mai Simms, 2007) The highest performing group at 16 are Chinese girls, with those on free school meals outranking every other group except better-off Chinese and Indian girls. In contrast, after Gypsy, Roma and Traveller children, the lowest GCSE performance of any group defined by gender, free-school-meals status and ethnicity is that of white British boys eligible for free school meals.

The DfE (2013a) suggests that those schools successful in raising attainment of minority ethnic pupils focus on:

• high achievement;

• equal opportunities;

• the valuing of cultural diversity;

- the provision of a secure environment;

- the importance of challenging racism;

- partnership with parents and the wider community (school's stand on race equality made explicit);

- routinely monitoring how additional resources are used to ensure improved outcomes for targeted pupils;

- providing high-quality assessment, tracking and target-setting procedures, for individuals and groups to identify need and deploy resources effectively.

What do children understand of race and ethnicity?

SCENARIO

Milly and ethnicity

Children from a Reception class have been playing in the sand tray. A black child, Milly, leaves the activity crying. She won't tell you why. When you ask what happened, the children who are playing there say, 'She's just silly!'

Later on, you talk to Milly's mother and ask her to try to find out. The next day, her mother tells you another child had said, 'Take your dirty black hands off that toy, I'm playing with it!' You talk this over with the TA who works with you. She does not feel the incident is too serious. You disagree.

Critical questions

» What knowledge do you need to help you deal with situations such as this?

» How would you respond to the TA?

» What activities and discussion would you introduce that would help children to see that racism is not acceptable?

» How would you involve parents and keep them informed about the work that you are doing?

Comment on the scenario

This spidergram on page 64 provides a more detailed overview of some of the issues raised by the scenario. An examination of these will enable you to recognise the issues surrounding race inequality at the macro and micro levels. You need to:

- recognise the complex nature of the role of the teacher and what might be your next steps in dealing with the situation;

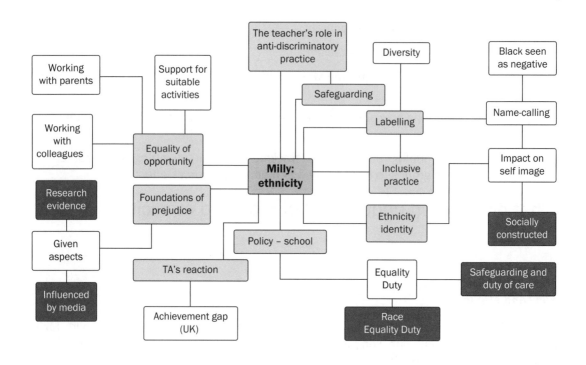

- identify and consider the impact of race and ethnicity on children's emotional development and academic achievement;

- identify opportunities for addressing the needs of ethnic minorities within the school environment;

- be aware of statutory guidance, research and data analysis which influences and underpins classroom practice.

There is a micro and a macro way of dealing with incidents of this type; ignoring it is not appropriate. The TA may think that it is an innocent remark, but there is a suggestion that the child is developing negative attitudes towards peers of a different ethnicity and race. If this behaviour is ignored there is a chance that it will be repeated. The victim, Milly, may then feel that the teacher is indifferent to racism. So consideration needs to be given to the impact on Milly and the wider implications for her future emotional and academic development. There is also the involvement of the other children and how they may have been affected by the incident.

The TA is deliberately side-stepping the issue by suggesting that the children are too young to be aware or too young to know any better. However, research by Milner (1983, in Brown, 1998, p 13) and further supported by Siraj-Blatchford (1994) confirmed that children between the ages of 3 and 5 learn to attach value to skin colour; there is an acknowledged hierarchy with white at the top and black at the bottom. If this evaluation remains unchallenged in the child's thinking then there is a risk that he or she will continue to believe that black people are inferior and grow up with very racist stereotypical beliefs.

There may be a 'so what' kind of attitudinal response to the idea of challenging racist actions. Some teachers have been accused of being too politically correct, too concerned to appease in the name of equality. But the teacher's role in this scenario is one of safeguarding. There is a need to convey that it is not acceptable to denigrate any child. Teachers have a moral and legal duty to make sure that there are no injustices in the classroom. There are also the wider implications for the school policy on inclusion which you may like to consider.

Critical questions

Consider the scenario again.

» *Will a rebuke be sufficient? It will show that the behaviour is unacceptable, but will it be sufficient to aid the perpetrator's understanding of why racist remarks are wrong?*

» *In what ways can additional teaching strengthen the message?*

» *How can a situation whereby the perpetrator feels that their own habitus is under attack be avoided?*

» *How can a more holistic school approach be instigated? What might the school need to do?*

» *How can the teacher help the children to understand their own behaviour?*

» *How could future partnership with the TA be resolved?*

Teachers are advised to be proactive in educating pupils about cultural and ethnic diversity across the curriculum.

Teaching strategies

There are different ways of educating pupils about cultural and ethnic diversity. It might be through an inclusion policy, a multicultural curriculum, positive anti-discriminatory practice – or a variety of strategies. There may be challenges to encompassing diversity. Factors inhibiting the valuing of diversity include:

• the absence or low numbers of minority ethnic groups in some schools – *There just isn't the diversity here* (Head teacher);

• diversity not being identified as a school priority;

• a lack of teacher knowledge about ethnic diversity and confidence in addressing such issues. (Maylor and Read, 2007; see also Cline et al., 2002; DfES, 2005)

It might be felt that racist attitudes and behaviour are less common in schools with few or no ethnic minority pupils. This is regrettably far from the case. The pervasive influence of racism through ignorance and ill-informed stereotyping can have a quite marked effect on the attitudes of youngsters in these mono-cultural areas. Brown (1998) suggests that anti-discriminatory practice and a culturally appropriate curriculum equips educators and children to actively challenge inequality and injustice (p 42).

The difficulty lies in implementing an appropriate cultural curriculum without it being perceived as tokenistic.

SCENARIO

Focus on Chinese New Year

A trainee teacher planned to arrange a day of festivities around Chinese New Year. She designed a variety of activities, making Chinese fans and lanterns in art, a dragon dance, eating noodles with chopsticks and attempting writing with fine brushes. She brought in some Chinese artefacts and thought about incorporating stories of Genghis Khan. Her class teacher was less than enthusiastic, suggesting that the whole idea was tokenistic and the children's view of China and Chinese people would remain very stereotypical.

Critical questions

» *What are the positive and the negative perceptions of China that the children could gain from these activities?*

» *Are there aspects of this scenario which might aid a child's understanding of the world?*

» *What other ways are there of introducing China and Chinese culture to young children?*

Consider the following strategies and decide (a) which are appropriate multicultural strategies and which are anti-discriminatory and (b) which strategies could be used singly or together to support a school's approach to racial equality?

» *Formulate equality policy in consultation with parents and relevant members of the community.*

» *Arrange an 'International Day' when parents are asked to bring food and cultural items associated with their country.*

» *Ensure school procedure and practices are accessible to all parents.*

» *Arrange a fashion show where children are asked to come dressed in a traditional national costume.*

» *Implement culturally appropriate curricula that include the past and present experiences and contributions to the human progress of women, black, working-class or disabled people.*

» *Children celebrate Diwali, Chinese New Year and Eid even if there are no children from these groups in the school.*

» *Racist and sexist remarks are challenged in a non-threatening and supportive way.*

Any teacher will find it difficult to change attitudes single-handedly. Inclusion has to be a whole-school policy and one that is strongly led. This is determined by the effectiveness of the strategies and actions that will eliminate discrimination, promote equality of opportunity and good relations between different racial groups (CRE, 2002).

There remains a justification that a teacher's role is to maintain an ethos of fairness and justice in the classroom. Each child should feel a sense of value and belonging in school and this should also be reflected in society for all ethnic groups.

Martin Luther King's words are still an aspiration:

> I have a dream that my four little children will one day live in a nation where they will not be judged by the color of their skin, but by the content of their character.
>
> Martin Luther King, 1963

Critical reflections

» *Return to your definition of racism. What are your thoughts now?*

» *If you had to prepare a section in a school's inclusion policy on race equality what do you think should be included in the aims and principles for the school?*

» *What examples of partnership with the community would you expect a school to maintain?*

» *What elements do you consider important in a curriculum that values diversity?*

Taking it further

Books and journals

Connolly, P. (1998) Racism, Culture and Identity: Towards a Theory of Practice, in Connolly, P. (1998) *Racism, Gender Identities and Young Children: Social Relations in A Multi-Ethnic, Inner-City Primary School*. London: Routledge

This chapter uses a theoretical framework of Bourdieu's theories of habitus, field and capital which helps to define racism as not just about ideas and structures but also about the way that racism influences children's subjective identities. Connolly sees racism as something children and adults come to internalise, which in turn shapes their actions, behaviour and collective identities.

Richards, R. (2010) Not In My Image – Ethnic Diversity in the Classroom, in Richards, G. and Armstrong, F. (eds) *Teaching and Learning in Inclusive Classrooms-Key Issues for New Teachers*. London: Routledge.

In this chapter Richards discusses the lack of black minority ethnic teachers and staff in schools. He indicates current figures show there are 27% of black minority ethnic children in primary schools and 23% in secondary schools; yet only 6.3% of teachers are from a BME background (2011 school census). There is not just a lack of BME teachers but also a noticeably curtailed career path. Richards points out that there are significantly fewer BME staff as heads and senior teachers compared to figures for white teachers. It is unlikely that the level of BME adults in the classroom is likely to match the current future ethnic school population. This means a certain challenge for teachers in being sensitive to the needs of the minority ethnic groups within the school and classroom.

Web-based material

One of the most remarkable pieces of classroom research focused on discrimination was attempted by Jane Elliot in 1968 in Iowa, USA, two days after the assassination of Dr Martin Luther King.

The project, known as The Class Divided or Blue Eyes /Brown Eyes, is available for viewing on YouTube: www.youtube.com/watch?v=VeK759FF84s (last accessed 4 October 2013).

Over a period of days, first, the blue-eyed children were told they were better than the brown-eyed, and then the roles were reversed. The result was that the children rose to those expectations of being better, feeling power over those who were in the role of the inferior. Some dastardly behaviour was observed of the children to each other. After the project, the children were able to speak about their feelings. One of the outcomes of the project was the noticeable change in the attitude towards learning of the children when placed in the different groups. Fourteen years later, Jane Elliot brought the group together again as adults. They described what a powerful experience it was for them and how it had positively affected their attitudes to discrimination throughout the rest of their lives.

SRtRC (2011) Show Racism the Red Card: Guidance for Initial Teacher Trainers: Preparing Student Teachers to Tackle Racism and Promote Equality in the Classroom. Online: www.srtrc.org/uploaded/ITT%20ED%20PACK.pdf (last accessed 4 October 2013).

This is a campaign that uses top footballers to educate against racism. The booklet is aimed at supporting trainees in tackling racism in class. There are useful audit pages and practical activities. The project is supported by the NUT and NASUWT and funded by the Department of Communities and Local Government.

References

Bhavnani, R., Mirza, H.S. and Meeto, V. (2006) *Tackling the Roots of Racism: Lessons for Success*. Bristol: The Policy Press.

Bourdieu, P. (1994) Rethinking the State: Genesis and Structure of the Bureaucratic Field. *Sociological Theory*, 12(1): 1–18.

Bourdieu, P. and Wacquant, L.J.D. (1992) *An Invitation to Reflexive Sociology*. Oxford: Blackwell.

Brown, B. (1998) *Unlearning Discrimination in the Early Years*. Stoke on Trent: Trentham Books.

Burgess, S. Wilson, D. and Lupton, R. (2004) *Parallel Lives? Ethnic Segregation in the Playground and the Neighbourhood*. Centre for Market and Public Organisation, (CMPO) Working Paper Series No. 04/094. CMPO and Dept. of Economics, the University of Bristol.

Cline, T., De Abreu, G., Fihosy, C., Gray, H., Lambert, H. and Neale, J. (2002) *Minority Ethnic Pupils in Mainly White Schools*, Research Report 365. London: DfES.

Commission for Racial Equality (2002) *Towards Racial Equality: An Evaluation of the Public Duty to Promote Race Equality and Good Race Relations in England and Wales* London: CRE. Online: www.equalityhumanrights.com/uploaded_files/EqualityAct/PSED/research_doc_towards_racial_equality.pdf (last accessed 22 October 2013).

Connolly, P. (1998) *Racism, Gender Identities and Young Children: Social Relations in A Multi-Ethnic, Inner-City Primary School*. London: Routledge.

Crown Ministry of Justice (2010) *Race and the Criminal Justice System*. Online: www.gov.uk/government/publications/race-and-the-criminal-justice-system--3 (last accessed 4 October 2013).

Department for Children, Schools and Families (DSCF) (2007) *Guidance on the Duty to Promote Community Cohesion*. Nottingham, DSCF Publications.

Department for Education (DfE) (2012a) *Statutory Framework for Early Years Foundation Stage: Setting the Standards for Learning Development and Care for Children from Birth to Five*. Online:

http://webarchive.nationalarchives.gov.uk/20130401151715/https://www.education.gov.uk/publications/eOrderingDownload/EYFS%20Statutory%20Framework.pdf (last accessed 4 October 2013).

Department for Education (DfE) (2012b) *Teachers' Standards*. Online: http://media.education.gov.uk/assets/files/pdf/t/teachers%20standards%20information.pdf (last accessed 4 October 2103).

Department for Education (DfE) (2013a) *Ethnic Minority Achievement*. Online: www.education.gov.uk/schools/pupilsupport/inclusionandlearnersupport/mea/a0013246/ethnic-minority-achievement (last accessed 4 October 2013).

Department for Education (DfE) (2013b) *The National Curriculum in England: Framework Document for Consultation*. Online: www.education.gov.uk/consultations/index.cfm?action=conResults&consultationId=1881&external=no&menu=3 (last accessed 4 October 2013).

Department for Education and Skills (DfES) (1985) *Education for All (The Swann Report)*. London: HMSO.

Department for Education and Skills (DfES) (2005) *Developing the Global Dimension in the School Curriculum*. No. 1409-2005DOC-EN. London: DfES with DFID.

Department for Education and Skills (DfES) (2007) *Diversity and Citizenship in the Curriculum*, Research Report 819. Nottingham: DfES Publications.

Gillborn, D. (1990) *'Race', Ethnicity and Education*. London: Unwin Hyman.

Gillborn, D. (2005) *Education Policy as an Act of White Supremacy: Whiteness, Critical Race Theory and Education Reform*. London: Educational Foundations & Policy Studies, Institute of Education, University of London.

Jones, C.P. (2002) Confronting Institutionalized Racism. *Phylon* (1960) 50(1/2): 7–22.

Macpherson, W. (1999) *The Stephen Lawrence Inquiry*. London: The Stationery Office.

Mai Sims, J. (2007) Thai-British Families: Towards a Deeper Understanding of 'Mixedness', in Mai Sims, J. (ed) *Mixed Heritage: Identity, Policy and Practice*. London: Runnymede Trust Publications. Online: www.intermix.org.uk/academic/Jessica%20Mai%20Simms.asp (last accessed 4 October 2013).

Maylor, U., and Read, B. with H. Mendick, A. Ross and N. Rollock (2007). *Diversity and Citizenship in the Curriculum: Research Review*. Research report 819. London: DfES.

Milner, D. (1983) *Children and Race: Ten Years on*. London: Ward Lock Educational.

Office for National Statistics (2013) Online: www.statistics.gov.uk/hub/crime-justice/police/police-activity (last accessed 2 September 2013).

Philips, T. (2005) *After 7/7: Sleepwalking to Segregation*. Online: www.humanities.manchester.ac.uk/socialchange/research/social-change/summer-workshops/documents/sleepwalking.pdf (last accessed 4 October 2013).

The Rampton Report (1981) *West Indian Children in our Schools*, Interim report of the Committee of Inquiry into the Education of Children from Ethnic Minority Groups. London: HMSO.

Schaffer, H.R. (1996) *Social Development*. Oxford: Blackwell.

Siraj-Blatchford, I. (1994) *The Early Years: Laying the Foundations for Racial Equality*. Stoke on Trent: Trentham Books.

Siraj-Blatchford, I. and Clarke, P. (2000) *Supporting Identity Diversity and Language in the Early Years*. Oxford: Oxford University Press.

5 Understanding learners in poverty

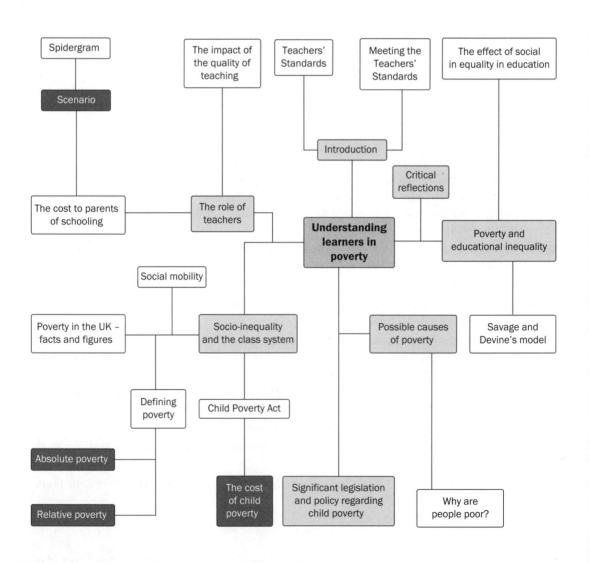

I no longer believe that the poverty endured by all too many children can simply be measured by their parents' lack of income. Something more fundamental than the scarcity of money is adversely dominating the lives of these children.

Field, 2010, p 14

Introduction

This chapter explores the impact of child poverty on educational attainment, investigating and highlighting some of the fundamental effects of living in poverty. It provides the opportunity to reflect on and consider the causes of poverty, the government strategies designed to combat the most damaging effects and the expectations upon teachers regarding children's achievement.

Questions are raised about the continued inequalities in British society and how poverty in particular affects a child's attainment in education. There have always been class divisions in the UK, recognisable in socio-economic stratification, but there appears to be an ever growing disadvantaged section of British society that does not have access to the same opportunities as other societal groups. This inequality continues despite successive UK governments' efforts to equalise the life chances of the population. The welfare state was initiated by Beveridge in 1942 and was designed to protect the poor from the very worst risks of poverty, but both the National Health Service and the benefit system are now creaking under the demand for their services. The fact remains that poverty still has not been eradicated, in spite of the many political promises to the contrary.

Teacher's standards

The DfE (2012) Teachers' Standards that are important in this chapter are the specific ones that deal with pupil expectations and aspirations. There is a need to provide equality of opportunity for all children, to enable them to learn in an environment that is supportive to their needs. Some children start with a disadvantage that is difficult to bridge. It has been shown statistically that the attainment gap at five years old increases in the primary school years so that the highest achievers from low-income households are eventually overtaken by the lower-achieving children from the more affluent backgrounds (Field, 2010). For teachers, it is essential to provide an education that enables all children to succeed and to fulfil their aspirations.

MEETING THE TEACHERS' STANDARDS

Links to Department for Education Teachers' Standards May 2012

TS 1

Part 2

Socio-inequality and the class system

> *The rich man in his castle*
> *The poor man at his gate*
> *He made them high and lowly*
> *And ordered their estate*
> *All things bright and beautiful.*
>
> Cecil Frances Alexander (1848)

This verse from the hymn *All Things Bright and Beautiful* exemplifies the traditional, almost feudal, class system in Britain in the nineteenth century. It reflects a time when class distinction was very clearly demarcated. The ruling class came from the rich land-owning aristocracy, the merchants formed the middle class, and at the lowest end was the poorly educated and economically poor working class. It was seen as God's will and therefore one was expected to accept one's inevitable status in life. But there have been social and economic changes since then. Changes in the education system have allowed and supported upward mobility, but politicians have admitted that there has not been much progress in alleviating the inequality associated with economic poverty which impacts upon social mobility and educational achievement.

Political parties may have differing perspectives, but over the last 20 years, each party has pledged to achieve *equality of opportunity* for all.

Poverty in the UK continues to exist alongside high economic prosperity. The Organisation for Economic Co-operation and Development (OECD) highlights particular international issues and facts about poverty. It suggests there is a long-term trend towards greater inequality and that the gap between rich and poor in OECD countries has reached its highest level for over 30 years (OECD, 2011). The advice is for governments to act quickly to tackle economic inequality.

Statistics for the UK indicate:

*   1 per cent of the population controls 23 per cent of the national wealth;

*   the bottom 50 per cent of the population controls 6 per cent of the national wealth.
    (OECD, 2010)

These statistics are supported by a report from the National Equality Panel (2010) which suggest that there are *deep seated and systemic differences between social groups* with income and wealth related to people's circumstances and characteristics.

Social mobility

Education has been seen as the passport to social mobility. But not everybody is able to assimilate the values and aspirations of education as a pathway to success. The concept of social mobility indicates a successful and progressive society. It reflects well on the educational system and has positive repercussions on the economy. But too often parental disadvantage translates into childhood disadvantage, and not all sections of the population achieve either educational or economic success. There are some who have been stuck at the bottom of the social order for generations. Education has not been successful in alleviating their plight. This has been acknowledged as a particular weakness of the English educational system: *right from the early years, there is a strong association between low family income and poor educational outcomes ... It is often called our 'long tail of underperformance'* (Ofsted, 2013, p 5).

Poverty in the UK – facts and figures

Poverty, as indicated by eligibility for free school meals, is strongly associated with low attainment, and more so for white British students than for other ethnic groups.

Figures from Oxfam's poverty facts (Oxfam, 2013) indicate that:

- one in five people (13 million people) in the UK are living in poverty;
- the UK has a higher proportion of its population living in relative poverty than most other EU countries: of the 27 EU countries, only six have a higher rate than the UK;
- 3.8 million children live in poverty;
- 2.2 million pensioners live in poverty;
- women are the majority in the poorest groups.

Defining poverty

Seebohm Rowntree devised a process for defining poverty in the 1900s which is still used today. He was specifically concerned with determining what sum of money would allow families to achieve a minimum standard of living. Families below this level of income were deemed to be poor; above it they were not. In calculating the number of poor families, Rowntree made a distinction between those households that simply did not have enough money to meet his minimum living standard and so ward off poverty and those families whose income could achieve this standard but who decided to spend part of their income in other ways.

Poverty has been defined by Townsend (1979, p 88) as

Individuals, families and groups in the population can be said to be in poverty when they lack resources to obtain the type of diet, participate in the activities and have living conditions and amenities which are customary or at least widely encouraged and approved, in the societies in which they belong.

From this definition we can say that poverty is affected by

- material conditions – needing goods and services, or low standard of living;
- economic position – low income, limited resources, inequality or low social class;
- social position – lack of social capital through lack of entitlement, dependency or social exclusion.

Absolute poverty

The term *absolute poverty* describes the extreme end of poverty based on the minimum standard required to live. It follows the research carried out by Rowntree and is a way of measuring the level of spending required to purchase a bundle of essential goods which consisted of food, safe drinking water, sanitation facilities, health, shelter, clothing, education and information. It is the minimum standard required to live but involves the severe deprivation of human need. It can be used to compare poverty globally.

Relative poverty

Relative poverty is the term more frequently used in comparison with the average and median incomes of an individual country. In the UK, it refers to a household that is living on below 60 per cent of the median income.

Child Poverty Act 2010

The Child Poverty Act (2010) defined four areas of child poverty and set targets that require the government to produce child poverty strategies that run through to 2020 and are refreshed every three years. These four challenging UK-wide targets are based on the proportion of children living in:

1. relative low income (whether the incomes of the poorest families are keeping pace with the growth of incomes in the economy as a whole) – target is less than 10 per cent;

2. combined low income and material deprivation (a wider measure of people's living standards) – target is less than 5 per cent;

3. absolute low income (whether the poorest families are seeing their income rise in real terms) – target is less than 5 per cent;

4. persistent poverty (length of time in poverty) – target is to be set in regulations by 2015.

The Act establishes an accountability framework to make sure progress is continuously made and the 2020 goal is met.

The cost of child poverty

The targets are necessary not only because of the socio-economic impact of poverty but because of the rising cost to the public purse. In 2008, the Joseph Rowntree Foundation estimated that child poverty cost the country £25 billion a year. In 2013, with the addition of the pupil premium and the early entitlement for two-year-olds spending, and with other expenses of benefits and post-tax earnings factored in, the cost of child poverty had risen to £29 billion. It is likely that costs could rise to £35 billion by 2020, which is equivalent to 3 per cent of the gross domestic product (GDP) (Hirsh, 2013).

The possible causes of poverty

Why are people poor?

There are a variety of theories which attempt to rationalise why we continue to have a high proportion of the population living in poverty.

Pathological explanations lay the blame on the individual, attributing poverty to the characteristics or behaviour of poor people. These behavioural characteristics do not take account of other factors which can affect the lives of those in poverty.

- **Individualistic explanations**: poor people are assumed to be inadequate, have made bad choices and chosen their lifestyle.

- **Familial:** poverty is believed to run in families, termed generational poverty.

- **Sub-cultural views**: the 'culture of poverty', which holds that poor people 'adapt' to poverty.

Structural explanations explain poverty in terms of the society where it occurs.

- **Class-based explanations**: poverty is the result of people's economic marginality limiting their life chances.

- **'Agency' views**: poverty is attributed to the failures of public services.

- **Inequality:** poverty is attributed to inequalities in the structure of society, leading to denial of opportunity and perpetuation of disadvantage, eg inequalities of income, wealth, race and gender.

Poverty and educational inequality

Child poverty and unequal opportunities are inextricably linked. If parents themselves have been disadvantaged and are without qualifications, for whatever reason, they are likely to be in no-income or low-income sections of society. Such families are likely to be living in areas of low cost, sometimes inadequate, housing in disadvantaged neighbourhoods. As a consequence, the children are less likely to gain good qualifications at school, and so the perpetuation of disadvantage continues.

The effect of social inequality in education

We should be careful, however, about creating a deficit model for what has been termed a 'culture of poverty'. Poverty does not make people poor parents, but it does greatly amplify and concentrate the other risk factors. There is a danger of creating a discourse of blame around the children and their families when really the problems lie within the structure of society. Within such a negative discourse, those individuals who do not succeed through education or the workplace are deemed to be failures and in part held responsible for their own failure. Poverty therefore needs recontextualising as primarily a cultural problem. Reay (2001, 2002) has argued that working-class pupils are constructed by the education system in terms of what they 'lack', the deficit model, which can lead to them feeling worthless and

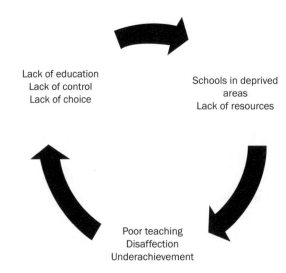

Figure 5.1 The cycle of educational poverty

educationally inadequate. Children and young people who are statistically more likely to 'fail' can quickly become demotivated and may subsequently come to see themselves as having no value or use in society (Archer and Francis, 2007).

A young person living in poverty at 16 has an increased risk of still living in poverty in their 30s and older (Field, 2010).

Social groupings or class may dictate one's values, attitudes and beliefs and therefore one's aspirations. Differences in income may not be the only determining factors in a child's aspirational levels. The theories of Bourdieu (1993) once again come to the fore here, where class is seen as a combination of cultural capital, economic wealth and social capital. In the recent Great British Class survey undertaken by Savage et al. (2013) a person's social capital was seen to be as important as their wealth.

Critical questions

» *Which class are you and why? Do you think that training as a teacher will have any effect on your social mobility?*

» *How are you now perceived by your family?*

» *Where do teachers fit in the stratified rankings of society?*

» *What are the expectations that society has of teachers as a professional group?*

» *Is an unequal society necessarily a class-ridden society?*

Savage and Devine's model

In Savage and Devine's latest model (2013) the three dimensions of a person's 'capital' were defined as follows.

- *Economic capital* concerns wealth, a person's occupation, monetary assets and savings.

- *Cultural capital* concerns social connections, the people known to that person, whether they were engaged in organised groups like political parties, sports teams or social groups. This includes those known in face-to-face social interaction, not those known as friends on social networking sites.

- *Social capital* concerns interests – education, participation in cultural activities and how people spend their spare time.

Summary of Savage and Devine's social structure

Class category	Definition
Elite	Very high economic capital (especially savings) high social capital, very high highbrow cultural capital
Established middle class	High economic capital, high status of mean contacts, high highbrow and emerging cultural capital
Technical middle class	High economic capital, very high mean social contacts but relatively few contacts reported, moderate cultural capital
New affluent workers	Moderately good economic capital, moderately poor mean score of social contacts, though high range, moderate highbrow but good emerging cultural capital
Traditional working class	Moderately poor economic capital though with reasonable house price, few social contacts, low highbrow and emerging cultural capital
Emergent service workers	Moderately poor economic capital, though with reasonable household income, moderate social contacts, high emerging (but lowbrow) cultural capital
Precariat	Poor economic capital, and the lowest scores on every other criterion

Critical questions

» *In what ways do class judgements tend to focus around social protocols and etiquette and markers of culture rather than wealth?*

» *Does social inequality arise because of poverty and not class? Explain your answer.*

Savage and Devine described the precariat as *the most deprived of the classes … on all measures* (p 243), and yet they constitute 15 per cent of the population, thus forming a relatively large social class. It is the children from this group who are at most risk.

In his report focusing on preventing poor children becoming poor adults, Field (2010, p 39) found overwhelming evidence that children's life chances are most heavily predicated on their development in the first five years of life. Details quoted suggest that by the age of three, a baby's brain is 80 per cent formed, and his or her experiences before then shape the way the brain has grown and developed.

Ability profiles at that age are highly predictive of profiles at school entry. By school age, there are very wide variations in children's abilities and the evidence indicates that children from poorer backgrounds do worse cognitively and behaviourally than those from more affluent homes.

Field's report (2010) suggested that schools do not effectively close the attainment gap that is recognisable on school entry. It was found that children who arrive in the bottom range of ability tend to stay there. The report concluded that although *later interventions to help poorly performing children can be effective in general, the most effective and cost-effective way to help and support young families is in the earliest years of a child's life* (Field, 2010, p 5). Field recommended that high-quality integrated services aimed at supporting parents should be provided, with a caveat that even if the money were available to lift all children out of income poverty in the short term, this move might not in itself close the achievement gap.

Significant legislation and policy regarding child poverty

Successive governments have introduced legislation or invested in research in order to alleviate and address the inequalities in society. The following table is a list of the most significant government interventions through legislation since the Beveridge Report in 1942.

Legislation regarding child poverty

Legislation, policy and reports	Date	Purpose	Outcomes
Beveridge Report	1942	Laid the foundations of the welfare state	Established welfare state and expectations about what the government would provide
Convention on Rights of the Child	1989	Universally adopted resolution from United Nations The right to a **childhood** (including protection from harm) The right to be **educated** (including all girls and boys completing primary school) The right to be **healthy** (including having clean water, nutritious food and medical care) The right to be treated **fairly** (including changing laws and practices that are unfair on children) The right to be **heard** (including considering children's views)	Principles ratified in the Children Act
Children Act	1989	Emphasised parental responsibilities and social services to protect and promote children's welfare	Children have greater protection within the law

Legislation, policy and reports	Date	Purpose	Outcomes
The National Curriculum	1999	Inclusion statement providing effective learning opportunities for all pupils with three clear principles: 1. setting suitable learning challenges 2. responding to pupils' diverse learning needs 3. overcoming potential barriers to learning and assessment for individuals and groups of pupils	All schools had to provide an inclusive curriculum while maintaining an inclusive ethos in school
UN General Assembly-World Fit for Children	2002	New agenda for world's children	180 countries adopted 21 specific goals and targets for next decade
Labour Government introduced targets to reduce child poverty	2002	Target to reduce child poverty by 25% by 2004/05 To halve child poverty by 2010 and eradicate by 2020	Targets not met
Every Child Matters (DfE)	2003	Economic well-being: not being prevented by economic disadvantage from achieving their full potential in life	Framework for safeguarding of children
The Child and Working Tax Credits	2003	Reform of the tax and benefit system	Guaranteeing family income Attempts to tackle child poverty
Children Act	2004	Safeguarding the welfare of children	A Children's Commissioner ensured children had a voice. Aimed to encourage working in partnership to protect children from harm
Child Poverty Act	2010	4 targets to eradicate child poverty by 2020	Placed a duty on the government to eradicate child poverty by 2020
Equality Act	2010	Consolidates existing law into a single legal framework Many concepts of discrimination remain the same as in previous equality legislation Some new areas, eg different types of discrimination (victimisation, harassment)	Simplified and strengthened laws on discrimination

Legislation, policy and reports	Date	Purpose	Outcomes
Coalition government commissioned *The Foundation Years: Preventing Poor Children Becoming Poor Adults*. The report of the Independent Review on Poverty and Life Chances (Field 2010)	2010	Report to investigate the problems that living in poverty causes and how it affects life chances of children	Emphasised the risks of living in poverty and the effect on child's individual attainments Recommendations to change the definition of child poverty
Government published *A New Approach to Child Poverty: Tackling the Causes of Disadvantage and Transforming Families Lives*	2011	Coalition's strategy on tackling poverty for 2011–2014 - Strengthening families- Encouraging responsibility - Promoting work - Guaranteeing fairness - Providing support	New government's strategies made clear
Government Strategy for improving social mobility *Opening Door, Breaking Barriers*' Cabinet Office		Strategies for breaking the transmission of disadvantage from one generation to the next	Brought together a range of policy initiatives affecting children and young people
Revised EYFS	2012	Guidance and principles for teaching Early Years: *No child should be excluded or disadvantaged because of ethnicity, culture or religion, home language, family background, SEN, disability, gender or ability*	Ensure continuity of approach in Early Years settings
National Curriculum 2013	2013	Guidance and principles for teaching KS1–KS3	Inclusion requirements simplified, teachers required to set *high expectations for every pupil* (p 8)
Unseen Children Access and Achievement: 20 Years On www.ofsted.gov.uk/accessandachievement	2013	A review of the current pattern of disadvantage and educational success across England. Focus on economic disadvantaged- those eligible for free school meals	New proposals for EY support. New study proposals for 16–19-year-olds New strategies for training of teachers

The role of teachers

Education has a unique ability to correct the inequalities of class or background.
(Blair, 2006, cited in Reay, 2008, p 464)

Schools and Early Years settings do have a part to play in encouraging and supporting children and young people's academic success, teaching vital personal and social skills and encouraging positive attitudes. There is strong evidence that schools have made some difference to children's life chances. School influence on attainment can be as significant as social background, and the impact of schools is up to three times greater for the disadvantaged. But money, parenting, relationships, culture and community also influence children's aspirations. Bright children can easily lose their competitive advantage if they are struggling with poverty and chaotic home lives in poor neighbourhoods. Other children can develop ability and confidence if they have aspirant, supportive parents, good schools, cultural capital and additional private tuition. The findings that the brightest five-year-olds from poorer homes are overtaken by the progress of their less gifted but richer peers by the time they are ten are a reminder of this.

The impact of the quality of teaching

Wilshaw, using Ofsted reports of 2011/12 as evidence, suggests that the quality of teaching makes a crucial difference to pupils' learning and achievement, particularly in disadvantaged schools (Ofsted, 2013, p 74). He suggests the characteristics of outstanding teaching include:

- excellent leadership of behaviour;

- excellent attitudes to learning;

- lessons that challenge pupils according to their needs and abilities;

- encouraging pupils to be actively involved in decision-making;

- specific strategies for high achievers.

High-quality teaching is seen to be a most effective element in the redistribution of equality. The effects of high-quality teaching are especially significant for pupils from disadvantaged backgrounds: over a school year these pupils gain 1.5 years' worth of learning with very effective teachers, compared with 0.5 years with poorly performing teachers. In other words, for poor pupils, the difference between a good teacher and a bad teacher is a whole year's learning (Sutton Trust, 2011).

Strategies for recruitment and retention of teachers who can provide good-quality teaching in areas of disadvantage are already in place. Several government initiatives, such as the Registered Teacher Programme (RTP) and Teach First, have been devised to achieve this goal.

Recent research on the state of the teacher labour market identifies a range of issues affecting teacher supply and retention for all schools, but with the potential to impact hardest on socio-economically disadvantaged schools. The impact of school can also be put at risk by factors such as high staff turn-over, and this is particularly significant in schools in disadvantaged areas where there are problems recruiting and retaining high-quality teachers.

Ofsted (2013) stresses the need for strong and multiple incentives to attract the best teachers to the schools and areas of the country that need them most.

Since 2011, government policy has focused on giving targeted pupil premium funding to individual schools to support the work they do with disadvantaged pupils. It has been suggested that the increased pupil premium should be used to attract and retain good-quality teachers in disadvantaged schools. There has also been some discussion about payment by results, but this has yet to be finalised with teachers' unions approval.

Other schemes designed to attract and retain trainees to disadvantaged schools are linked to extra pay over and above the current starting salaries. This is a very similar proposal to the old system of educational priority areas, where teachers received extra payments for teaching in more challenging schools. Rather than incentivising teachers through pay, there have also been suggestions from the teaching profession to focus more on reducing the amount of assessment currently carried out in schools.

It has also been argued that the preoccupation with educational standards through setting, streaming and league tables has increased social segregation within the education system both nationally and internationally (OECD, 2010; Reay, 2008, p 26). The relentless pursuit of targets is considered to be undermining creative teaching and there has been a call for schools to focus more on inclusion with an emphasis on justice, fairness and respect.

The GCSE performance tables have charted a year-on-year improvement in the proportion of pupils attaining five or more higher grades. But inequalities of attainment between certain social class and ethnic groups are growing. There is an argument that suggests that league tables emphasise the differences in performance between social classes and ethnic groups and they are therefore seen to be driving up inequality.

Critical questions

»   *In your opinion, what are the benefits and drawbacks of publishing school results as league tables?*

»   *Consider the justification of bringing in payment by results to the teaching profession.*

»   *Part of the teacher's role is seen to be a 'social engineer'. In what ways can teachers redress the imbalance of society?*

Cost to parents of schooling

Although a state school education is 'free', there are a number of costs to parents/carers associated with a child's schooling that can have a significant impact on family budgets. Examples include school uniforms, sports kit and school trips, lunches, books, donations to charities and after-school clubs. A DfES survey (2003) found that the total spending per year averaged £799 for primary school children and £968 for secondary school children. Annual spending on girls (£876) was found to be higher than spending on boys (£855). These figures are from 2003 so many of the costs will have risen and, given the current austerity climate, there will be more families who find the extra costs demanded difficult to pay. Thus more children run the risk of being stigmatised and possibly bullied. The school trip is usually associated with academic learning but there is always the expectation of a 'donation' from the family. In 2007, the School Admissions Code made clear reference to the importance of limiting the costs of school uniform and trips. Schools often do have contingency funds, but this is not consistent in all schools and some adults find it difficult to ask for this help from the school. For families with more than one child in school, the difficulties are compounded.

For parents living in poverty there is not a great deal of choice about which school their child attends. There is no other option than to choose the school that the child can walk to.

For the school trying to engage with a depressed community there are difficulties, too. But there are markers of deprivation such as the Indices of Deprivation (ID 2000, ID 2004, ID 2007 and ID 2010), which have been used very widely for a range of purposes, including by central government as criteria for allocating resources efficiently for programmes such as Community First and Troubled Families, and under the previous administration: the Neighbourhood Renewal Fund and Working Neighbourhoods Fund.

Income Deprivation Affecting Children Indices (IDACI) allow schools and other educational settings to claim extra funding on a sliding scale of need, using the child's post code.

SCENARIO

Billy's story

Billy is in a Year 1 class and has been stealing food from the other children and eating it in the toilet. He often falls asleep by late morning. He soils himself and the other children call him Smelly and Stinky.

Critical questions

Consider the scenario.

»   *Why might Billy be behaving like this?*

»   *As Billy's teacher, what are the actions you feel you could take?*

Comment on scenario

If you encounter a child such as Billy in your class, it is important for you to be aware of what you can do and who you can talk with to share your concerns. The first consideration is to make sure that the welfare of this child is known to the named safeguarding Protection Officer in school. The issues that can arise through poverty may also require monitoring through the protection of safeguarding structures in school and through the social services at-risk register.

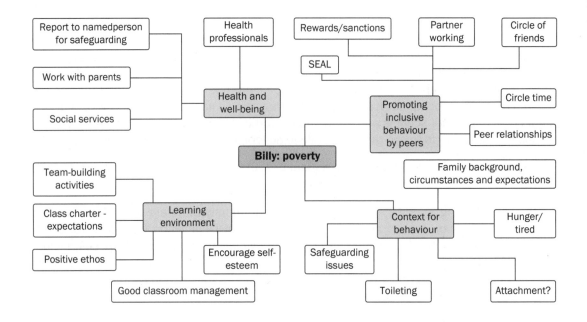

An examination of the spidergram above indicates ways in which this scenario can be tackled. There are complex and sensitive issues contained which require careful handling.

There are two main issues, both of which impact on Billy's learning ability.

1. Billy's welfare.

2. the way the other children are treating him.

With regard to Billy's welfare, an interview with his parents is essential to understand why Billy might be behaving like this. You will need to judge whether the parents also require some support in dealing with the problems. You may need to involve the SENCo and also the named safeguarding officer. This is essential because links may need to be made with social services.

You need to be aware of the guidance for safeguarding children and monitor Billy closely.

You may require help from parents in supplying changes of clothing for Billy. If this is not possible then you will need to make sure that there are some spare clothes available for him. Decisions about who will assist him to change also have to be made.

It is important to also consider the involvement of outside agencies. Once you have the parents'/carers' permission, you can involve medical professionals, for example, the school nurse or doctor in the first instance. Billy may have an eating disorder or a medical complaint that is the reason for his hunger and bowel disorder. You may need to assist in making appointments.

The second issue is with the class and the way they are treating him. You need the class to re-bond with Billy. He is currently ostracised by his peers because he smells very unpleasant.

It is not surprising that he is friendless, but you need to instigate all the inclusive class-management strategies to support and encourage inclusive behaviour towards Billy to ensure that he does not become isolated.

Critical reflections

» *In your view, what are the major effects of poverty on a child's education?*

» *What can teachers and schools do to remove the barriers to achievement?*

» *In what ways can schools avoid the high cost of 'free education'?*

» *How can schools and parents/carers work together to avoid making too many demands on scarce resources?*

Taking it further

Books and journals

Ridge, T. (2013) 'We Are All in This Together'? The Hidden Costs of Poverty, Recession and Austerity Policies on Britain's Poorest Children. *Children & Society*, 27(5): 406–417.

Article first published online: 9 Aug 2013 at. DOI: 10.1111/chso.12055.

Ridge claims that the drive towards eradicating childhood poverty in the UK has faltered. She suggests that the political landscape has shifted from structural explanations of poverty and disadvantage towards a more deficit model rooted in perceived individual failings and immoral behaviour. The article claims that the current government policies promote a discourse of difference and deficit which has had profound repercussions for disadvantaged families. The author claims there is no meaningful and effective engagement with children's expressed concerns when the government has a legislative requirement to consult with children and young people. Ridge proposes that children are fearful about debt and financial insecurity, with some children experiencing bullying at school. Severe cuts to local authorities have also affected provision for low-income families. Ridge suggests that poverty is a very localised experience and, unlike more affluent children with access to transport and commodified leisure opportunities, low-income children are effectively contained and constrained within their local neighbourhoods, thus exacerbating the feeling of isolation and exclusion from mainstream society.

Web-based material

Ofsted *Access and Achievement*, background papers. www.ofsted.gov.uk/resources/access-and-achievement-background-papers (last accessed 4 October 2013)

Ofsted *Unseen Children: Access and Achievement 20 Years On.* Ref: 130155. www.ofsted.gov.uk/resources/unseen-children-access-and-achievement-20-years (last accessed 4 October 2013).

These reviews of recent research evidence examine what works in closing the gap in educational achievement for children and young people living in poverty. There are several papers that were presented as evidence to the Unseen Children Access and Achievement (2013) panel. It contains some good examples of strategies that have worked in improving outcomes for children and young people. For example:

- engaging parents and raising parental aspirations;

- developing social and emotional competencies;

- supporting school transitions;

- providing strong and visionary leadership.

OECD (2011) *Divided We Stand* video http://youtu.be/ZaoGscbtPWU (last accessed 4 October 2013).

> The gap between rich and poor in the OECD countries has reached its highest level for over 30 years, and governments must act quickly to tackle inequality, according to a new OECD report, *Divided We Stand*. The UK remains one of the most unequal countries in the developed world. This is an accessible short video that explains visually what this means for the UK and its international partners:

BBC *The Class Divide* www.bbc.co.uk/comedy/collections/p00gs4vy#p00hhrwl (last accessed 4 October 2013).

> The categories of upper, middle and working class have long existed as a simple way of defining the stratification of society. This is a famous television sketch (1966) 'I know my place' by John Cleese, Ronnie Barker and Ronnie Corbett, which is successful in visually illustrating the way society has been demarcated into three distinct but socially separate groups, the working-class man, definitely knowing his place as the one with the lowest-ranking status of the three.

Oxfam – Poverty in the UK www.oxfam.org.uk/what-we-do/issues-we-work-on/poverty-in-the-uk?intcmp=hp_216_hych3_uk-food-banks_2013-08-01&ol=kMUYyxuW2Nw (last accessed 4 October 2013).

> The UK is the seventh-richest country in the world and yet over half a million people are now reliant on emergency food aid. It has been noticed in supermarkets that children who shoplift are not taking treats from the sweet counters but substantial food that they need to eat. Church Action on Poverty, Oxfam and the Trussell Trust believe that everyone in the UK should have enough to eat. This short film gives an insight into the help and support being given.

References

Archer, L. (2007) Social Justice in Schools: Engaging with Equality, in Dillon, J. and Maguire, M. (eds) *Becoming a Teacher: Issues in Secondary Teaching*. Berkshire: Open University Press.

Archer, L. and Francis, B. (2007) *Understanding Minority Ethnic Achievement*. London: Routledge.

Bourdieu, P. (1993) *Sociology in Question*. London: Sage.

Brunwin, T. (2003) *The Cost of Schooling*. London: DfES. Online: http://dera.ioe.ac.uk/id/eprint/5220 (last accessed 4 October 2013).

Child Poverty Act (2010) Online: www.education.gov.uk/childrenandyoungpeople/families/childpoverty/a0066302/the-child-poverty-act (last accessed 4 October 2013).

Department for Education (DfE) (2012) *Teachers' Standards*. Online: http://media.education.gov.uk/assets/files/pdf/t/teachers%20standards%20information.pdf (last accessed 4 October 2013.

Field, F. (2010) *The Foundation Years: Preventing Poor Children Becoming Poor Adults. The Report of the Independent Review on Poverty and Life Chances*. London: Cabinet Office.

Hirsch, D. (2013) *An Estimate of the Cost of Child Poverty in 2013*. Centre for Research in Social Policy, Loughborough University.

Hirst, D. (2007) *Chicken and Egg: Child Poverty and Educational Inequalities*. London: Child Poverty Action Group.

National Equality Panel (2010) *An Anatomy of Economic Inequality in the UK – Summary*. Online: http://sticerd.lse.ac.uk/dps/case/cr/CASEreport60_summary.pdf (last accessed 4 October 2013).

Ofsted (2013) *Unseen Children: Access and Achievement 20 Years On*. Report Ref: 130155. Online: www. ofsted.gov.uk/resources/unseen-children-access-and-achievement-20-years (last accessed 22 October 2013).

The Organisation for Economic Co-operation and Development (OECD) (2010) *Annual Report 2010*. Public Affairs Division, Public Affairs and Communications Directorate. OECD.

Organisation for Economic Co-operation and Development (OECD) (2011) *Divided We Stand: Why Inequality Keeps Rising*. An Overview of Growing Income, Inequalities in OECD Countries. OECD. Online: www.oecd.org/els/soc/49499779.pdf (last accessed 4 October 2013).

Oxfam (2013) *Poverty in the UK*. Online: www.oxfam.org.uk/what-we-do/issues-we-work-on/poverty-in-the-uk (last accessed 4 October 2013).

Savage, M., Devine, F., Cunningham, N., Taylor, M., Li, Y., Hjelbrekke, J. et al. (2013) A New Model of Social Class? Findings from the BBC's Great British Class Survey Experiment. *Sociology*, 47 (2): 219–50.

Sutton Trust (2011) *Improving the Impact of Teachers on Pupil Achievement in the UK – Interim Findings*. Online: www.suttontrust.com/public/documents/1teachers-impact-report-final.pdf (last accessed 4 October 2013).

Reay, D. (2001) Finding or Losing Yourself? Working-Class Relationships to Education. *Journal of Education Policy*, 16(4): 333–46.

Reay, D. (2002) Shaun's Story: Troubling Discourses of White Working Class Masculinities. *Gender and Education*, 14: 221–33.

Reay, D. (2008) Tony Blair, the promotion of the 'active' educational citizen, and middle-class hegemony. *Oxford Review of Education*, 34(6): 639–50. Online: DOI:10.1080/03054980802518821 (last accessed 4 October 2013).

Townsend, P. (1979) *Poverty in the United Kingdom*. London: Allen Lane.

6 Understanding learners with English as an additional language

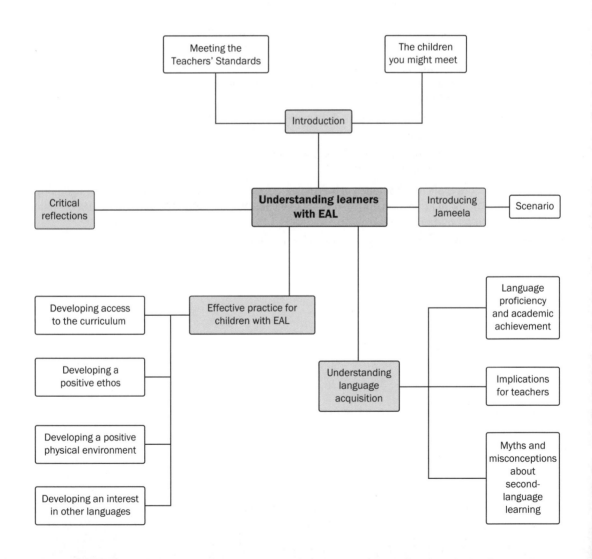

Introduction

This chapter considers the various groups of children you could meet who have EAL, and looks at their cultural backgrounds and previous experiences. It provides some theory about the way children with EAL acquire language and how this affects their learning, leading to an examination of how this will influence the way you teach and provide learning experiences for such children.

MEETING THE TEACHERS' STANDARDS

Links to Department for Education Teachers' Standards May 2012

TS 1; 2; 5

Part 2

Britain is a multicultural country and this is reflected in the populations of its schools. While some schools have only white British pupils, others have a wide range of pupils from many different countries speaking a range of languages. According to the DfE (2012), in some schools in Birmingham, Bradford and the Borough of Westminster, over 90 per cent of the pupils speak English as an additional language (EAL). There are at least two schools in Blackburn where more than 97 per cent of the pupils do not speak English as their first language. The local authority areas which have the highest number of pupils with EAL are Tower Hamlets (74 per cent) and Newham (71 per cent), and those with the lowest number of pupils with EAL are Halton (0.8 per cent), Redcar and Cleveland (0.8 per cent) and Derbyshire (1.1 per cent) (National Association for Language Development in the Curriculum (NALDIC), 2012a).

There are 577,555 primary school children who do not speak English as their first language; this is one child out of every six. Taking into account children in secondary schools who have EAL, there are over one million children aged between 5 and 18 who speak over 360 languages between them. The most spoken languages are Punjabi (1.7 per cent), Urdu (1.6 per cent), Bengali (1.3 per cent) and Polish (0.8 per cent). Other languages include Arabic (0.6 per cent), Somali (0.6 per cent), Chinese (0.3 per cent) and Albanian (0.2 per cent) (NALDIC, 2012b). It is most probable that as you go through your training to be a teacher, you will be given a range of different experiences in contrasting placements. As TS 5 relates specifically to teaching children with EAL, you are likely to be given experience in a school where there are a number of children who do not have English as their first language.

The children you might meet

People from other countries have been arriving and settling in the UK for many years. The most common reason in the past has been in order to secure employment. After World War II, Britain had a significant labour crisis. As a result, workers from Poland and Italy, who had been allies during the war, were welcomed. Additionally, workers from the West Indies were encouraged to move to Britain to take up jobs.

Over the last 50 years, Britain has seen a rise of people entering the country who are seeking asylum. These include people from war-torn countries or where they fear persecution. Aspinall and Watters for the Equality and Human Rights Commission (EHRC) (2012) report that in the 1970s, 28,000 African Asians with British passports were admitted because they had been expelled from Uganda by the dictator Idi Amin, and that between 1979 and 1982, 12,500 Vietnamese people arrived (p 2). Clearly children in our schools from these families are likely to have a good grasp of the English language as they will have been born and brought up in the UK. However, some of them will also speak their native language in their homes and English may not be their first language.

Confusion can arise over the differences between asylum seekers and refugees. While both groups are similar in that they have been are forced to leave their country for their own safety, Aspinall and Watters (2010) defines asylum seekers as those who have applied for asylum and are waiting for a response or who have had their application refused. Refugees, however, are those who have applied for asylum and are recognised with refugee status. This will grant them *humanitarian protection* including *exceptional leave to remain* or *indefinite leave to remain* (p 2). The numbers of people entering Britain for asylum peaked in 2002 at over 85,000. In 2008, 19,395 asylum seekers came to Britain. Of these, 3,505 (13 per cent) came from Afghanistan, 3,165 (12 per cent) from Zimbabwe, 2,270 (9 per cent) from Iran, 2,255 (9 per cent) from Eritrea, and 1,850 (7 per cent) from Iraq (Aspinall and Watters, 2010, p 3). Other countries from which people sought asylum include Sri Lanka, China, Somalia, Pakistan and Nigeria. Of all applications for asylum in 2008, 30 per cent were given refugee status or leave to remain, while the remaining 70 per cent were refused permission.

Asylum seekers may be unaccompanied children, single men or women, families with young children, single parents with children or older people who have left family behind. Many of them will by the very nature of being forced to leave their country have experienced trauma. As a teacher you may well need to consider what children with EAL may bring to school with them in terms of past experiences and understanding, and how this impacts on their readiness to learn. It may also be necessary for you to consider children's physiological needs, for example, whether or not they have enough to eat, opportunity for decent sleep and so on. Evans (2007, p 13) comments on children newly arrived in Britain who have been known to steal food from the bird table at school in order to take it home to other family members. Clearly knowledge of the child's and family's experiences will enable any teacher to deal with this kind of incident with understanding and sensitivity.

Critical questions

Consider the information you have just read.

» *What information did you find the most surprising and why?*

» *How do these statistics compare with the way asylum seekers and refugees are portrayed in the media?*

» *What alternative languages to English have you encountered (a) as a pupil in school and (b) as a trainee teacher?*

» *What other languages do you speak and how easy do you find learning another language?*

Introducing Jameela

Some of the issues related to teaching children with EAL can be seen in the following scenario. It is based on examples from classroom practice and outlines how a child with EAL could be perceived and managed in school. It considers curriculum concerns as well as the social aspects of school life and raises questions as to how a child such as Jameela can be given appropriate access to learning.

SCENARIO

Jameela has managed to escape from Syria where the civil war has been raging for some time. She is nine years old. Jameela's older brother was killed in some of the fighting which Jameela witnessed. Naturally, she is traumatised by this event. Her parents have stayed in Syria, they are trying to continue to work; but Jameela has escaped with her younger sister, Fatima, and her grandmother. None of the family who fled to England speaks English; their native language is Arabic. Both Jameela and Fatima attend local schools, but Jameela attends the junior school and Fatima the infant school, which is on a separate campus, and therefore they do not see each other at school. The school has mainly white British children, but there are a few children from other countries such as Poland, China, India, Sri Lanka and Iraq. Some of the children have come to Britain as their parents have come to study in the local university or for jobs in the local hospitals. Most of the children already have some basic English and the school assumes such children are capable of picking up further English just by interacting with other English-speaking children. Little specific provision is made for them. However, it is recognised that Jameela has specific needs due to her recent arrival and complete lack of English; therefore a dedicated teacher is employed to come to school to work with her. The teacher comes twice a week for half an hour and withdraws Jameela from the class for one-to-one support. Jameela is very timid and withdrawn and rarely speaks, particularly in the classroom. She watches what other children do and copies their actions. The class teacher has placed her in the same group as children with SEN as she considers she will get more support through increased TA time.

The critical questions ask you to consider Jameela's experience of school and in particular how she makes sense of the day when she has little English language. Think about the provision the teacher has made for Jameela and how this might support her language acquisition and development.

Critical questions

» *How can the class teacher enable Jameela to feel accepted within the class?*

» *How can the class teacher communicate effectively with Jameela?*

» *What provision can the class teacher make in order to communicate and build relationships with Jameela's grandmother?*

» *Do you think the provision of a specialist teacher is a good way of developing Jameela's language? Explain why.*

```
┌──────────────┐        ┌──────────┐        ┌──────────────┐                    ┌────────────────┐
│   Identity   │        │ Valuing  │        │Social aspects│                    │  Valuing and   │
└──────────────┘        │ culture  │        │  of school   │                    │ understanding  │
                        └──────────┘        └──────────────┘                    │   children's   │
┌──────────────┐                                                                │  knowledge     │
│  Belonging   │                            ┌──────────────┐  ┌──────────────┐  │  of language   │
└──────────────┘        ┌──────────┐        │  Jameela:    │  │Understanding │  └────────────────┘
                        │ Good EAL │        │ Learner with │  │  language    │
                        │ practice │        │     EAL      │  │ acquisition  │  ┌──────────────┐
┌──────────────┐        └──────────┘        └──────────────┘  │     and      │  │  Cummins'    │
│Relationships │                                              │ development  │  │  quadrants   │
└──────────────┘                                              └──────────────┘  └──────────────┘
                        ┌──────────┐        ┌──────────────┐  ┌──────────┐
┌──────────────┐        │  Labels  │        │  Learning    │  │ Seating  │      ┌──────────────┐
│    Ethos     │        └──────────┘        │ environment  │  └──────────┘      │  Myths and   │
└──────────────┘                            └──────────────┘                    │misconceptions│
                                                                                └──────────────┘
```

» *How can the class teacher encourage friendships between Jameela and other class members?*

» *Consider how Jameela is seated in the classroom. What are the benefits and limitations of this grouping with regard to Jameela's learning?*

Having considered some of the concerns around Jameela and her language development, the spidergram above identifies specific issues faced by children such as Jameela with EAL and how the class teacher can make provision for their needs to be met.

Understanding language acquisition

Language is a prime means of communication. It requires the ability to listen, to be able to make sounds and to employ some level of cognition which involves understanding. The ability to hear or accept language with understanding is known as receptive language, while the ability to offer language to another is known as expressive language. This could mean verbal communication, but it could also mean signing or gesturing.

Frederickson and Cline (2009, p 240) outline the knowledge and skills they consider to be involved in becoming competent in language use and communication. These are:

- knowing the forms of language used, how the words sound and go together;

- using these forms to convey meaning and understanding what other people mean when they use them;

- understanding the social conventions that determine how people use language to each other so as to appreciate another person's intentions as well as communicate their own;

- varying the style of communication and language to suit the different needs of listeners within a conversation;

- understanding how the use of language and its conventions vary within the social and cultural context.

This shows that the acquisition of language is a complex and multifaceted process which needs more attention than simply immersing the child with EAL in a new language and expecting them to pick it up. As a teacher of children with EAL it is important for you to have an understanding of the knowledge and skills a child requires in order to gain competency so that you can set appropriate expectations and make suitable provision. Clearly children in the early stages of acquiring a second language will be at different levels of competence in these areas and therefore the provision you make will need to take this into account.

Communication is an important social tool. It provides the means whereby relationships can be established and nurtured. Children whose main means of communication is in a different language from their peers will be socially disadvantaged as well as poorly placed to develop cognitively, as their ability to use both receptive and expressive language will be limited. Glazzard et al. (2010, p 61) comment on the work of Vygotsky, who asserts that language development is about the interaction between the environment and the pupil's cognitive skills. Such development takes place in a sociocultural context, is influenced by the cognitive skills of the pupil and develops over time at different rates. This indicates that supporting children with EAL to develop effective social relationships and to be valued as members of the class is vital in terms of additional language acquisition.

Language proficiency and academic achievement

The work of Jim Cummins considers the idea of basic interpersonal communicative skills (BICS) and cognitive academic language proficiency (CALP) in relation to learning an additional language. He defines BICS as being fluent in a language for conversational purposes, while CALP is the ability to understand and express in written and oral form the concepts and ideas which are necessary for academic success in school (Cummins, 2008, p 71). While both BICS and CALP develop from birth through social encounters, Cummins maintains that CALP becomes distinguished from BICS through schooling, as this involves the language that children require in order to succeed in their learning. For children with EAL, the significance of this is that while children may display conversational and peer-appropriate fluency (BICS), the language that supports academic progress (CALP) takes longer to develop. It is considered that becoming proficient in BICS usually takes about two years, while becoming proficient in CALP can take between five and seven years. This means that a seven-year-old child may be proficient in BICS by the time they are nine years old, but may not be proficient in CALP until they are between twelve and fourteen years of age. This will have particular implications for any teacher preparing children for Key Stage 2 National Curriculum tests (SATs) prior to transition to secondary school.

Teachers who do not understand the difference between BICS and CALP and the implications for children with EAL are in danger of misidentifying children as having SEN. They may place unrealistic expectations on the children and assume that because their conversational fluency is age appropriate, their ability to use CALP, or language which supports academic progress, will be similar. Roessingh (2006, p 92) likens BICS and CALP to an iceberg, suggesting that BICS is the *above-surface language*, which may account for possibly only 10 per cent of the overall proficiency of an academically successful learner. CALP is the *below-the-surface* language proficiency which underpins cognitive processes. It is concerned with the language of the classroom, less with non-verbal cues and more with abstract concepts. For children to reach their full academic potential they need to become proficient in CALP.

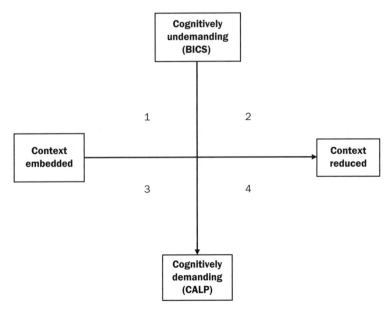

Figure 6.1 Cummins' quadrants

Cummins developed a framework which shows how context can support children's language development (see Figure 6.1).

The framework has a horizontal continuum from context embedded to context reduced, while the vertical continuum is about the task or activity, which may be placed on the line between cognitively undemanding and cognitively demanding. This gives four quadrants.

1. Context-embedded tasks requiring cognitively undemanding language or BICS (quadrant 1) use simple grammar forms and high-frequency vocabulary related to everyday conversation and concrete objects.

2. Context-reduced BICS (quadrant 2) is concerned with initial reading skills and writing for personal needs such as lists and notes. Common vocabulary such as that used within sport, hobbies and celebration is used at this stage and there are the beginnings of integrating grammar and vocabulary.

3. Context-embedded tasks requiring cognitively demanding language (CALP) (quadrant 3) require an increased amount of vocabulary, including some academic language. Visual representations may be used instead of concrete objects and there is a shift from learning to read to reading to learn. At this stage, the learner with EAL may have high-frequency words, some academic language and some common vocabulary, leading to about 8,000 words in all.

4. Context-reduced, cognitively demanding CALP (quadrant 4) is concerned with more abstract language and concepts, metaphors and imagery. It uses specialised vocabulary and more complex language structure. It is at this stage that the learner with EAL will be able to manage extensive use of reading and writing in essays and debate (Roessingh, 2006, p 93).

In devising learning activities for children with EAL, you will need to be aware of the demands you are making of the children in terms of CALP, and consider how you will provide appropriate levels of context to both support and challenge the EAL learners in your class.

Critical questions

» *Consider the following activities which a child with EAL may face in school. Place each activity within the appropriate quadrant on the Cummins framework and give reasons for your choice, taking into account the degree to which context is provided and whether the tasks demand BICS or CALP.*

» *Writing a poem;*

» *choosing food at lunchtime;*

» *writing a recipe;*

» *carrying out a science experiment;*

» *writing up the science experiment;*

» *reading a book for information for a project;*

» *talking with friends;*

» *understanding basic maths calculations;*

» *role play;*

» *asking to go to the toilet;*

» *worksheets with visual clues;*

» *relaying a message from home;*

» *using the computer;*

» *watching the teacher model good writing;*

» *undertaking a revision SATs paper;*

» *getting changed for PE.*

» *What does engaging in these activities tell you about the kind of expectation you might have of a child who has been learning English as an additional language for (a) one year, (b) three years, (c) five years?*

» *How would your approach to each task change depending on your knowledge and understanding of the children's level of language proficiency?*

Myths and misconceptions about second-language learning

McLaughlin (1992) outlines several popularly held misconceptions about how a second language is acquired and considers the implications for classroom practice.

• *Children learn second languages quickly and easily.* McLaughlin (1992) maintains that the language proficiency required of a child is less than that required of an ad in order to be considered competent. Children's vocabulary is smaller and therefore can be mastered more quickly. While it is assumed that children are less inhibited about making a mistake than adults, children can often be more embarrassed with their peers than adults.

- *The younger the child, the more skilled in acquiring an additional language.* McLaughlin refers to research (Stern, Burstall and Harley, 1975; Gorosch and Axelsson, 1964; Buehler, 1972; Florander and Jansen, 1968; Genesse, 1981, 1987) which shows that children who have begun to learn an additional language at an older age outperform those who have begun to learn an additional language earlier. However, where children are taught an additional language at an early age, their pronunciation is likely to be better.

- *The more time students spend in a second-language context, the quicker they learn the language.* This 'structured immersion' is where children receive all of their instruction in English and have additional support of specialist classes often out of the classroom. This is the approach taken by the school in the scenario previously outlined. However, children who have exposure to their home language as well as English are found to acquire additional language skills just as well as those in English only environments.

- *Children have acquired a second language once they can speak it.* This myth has already been discussed at length through the work of Cummins and BICS and CALP outlined above.

- *All children learn a second language the same way.* Different cultures use language in different ways. For example, in many Western countries, language is used in an analytical way, to convey information and to solve problems using clear and logical thinking. However, children from other cultures may use language differently and find this logical, reasoning approach frustrating and alien. Furthermore, McLaughlin (1992) maintains that middle-class, urbanised parents teach their children through language; however, children from other societies may learn through being alongside others, observing and through supervised participation. In some cultures, children will learn from their peers, having been taught to be quiet when adults are present and to have little interaction with them. This highlights again the importance of peer relationships for children with EAL.

Implications for teachers

All of the factors discussed above need to be taken into account when teaching children with EAL and you may need to challenge your own attitudes, unlearning what you previously believed. When interacting with children with EAL you will need to be aware that children find additional language learning as difficult as adults and therefore you should avoid expecting them to speak publicly in English if they are not ready to do so. You will need to have realistic expectations of learners with EAL, accepting that while learning a language at a younger age may mean better pronunciation, it does not mean greater proficiency in the longer term. It is vital to realise the importance of the home language in developing EAL. It provides strong bonds between home and school and can enable the child to participate more fully in school life while their English is developing. Children are likely to be more responsive to a teacher who values and is sensitive to their cultural background (McLaughlin, 1992).

You will also need to be aware of the cultural differences in how language is used and how children learn. The norm of the school environment is to pay attention and to persevere in achieving tasks; however, children from other cultures may appear to be inattentive and to move on from tasks. Having an awareness of different cultural expectations will enable you to manage these differences more effectively. Similarly, providing a range of different learning activities such as peer tutoring, co-operative learning and small-group work, as well as individualised instruction, will enable children with EAL to interact and learn from their peers, thereby providing them with an approach that will enable them to engage with their learning (McLaughlin, 1992).

Critical questions

The school where you are teaching has just received a number of families who have come from Iran. Nasreen has been placed in your class. She is five years old. She speaks Farsi. Considering the myths and misconceptions above:

» *What expectations would you have of her on her first day in school?*

» *What approach would you take to enable her to settle into your class and be well placed for learning?*

» *What do you know about the culture of Iran, its oral and written language, traditions and religion? How will this help you to support Nasreen and what more do you need to find out in order to support her better?*

After Nasreen has been in your class for a few weeks, she arrives at school one morning and hands you a note written in Arabic. She is crying. You cannot read the note. What action will you take on receiving this note?

Effective practice for children with EAL

Having considered some of the theory and research relating to learning English as an additional language, it is important to consider how this has a bearing on good classroom practice. Your attitude towards children from different cultures and with different languages will be quickly sensed by all the children in your class, no matter what their background and culture. Having EAL should be promoted and celebrated, not seen as a problem or an imposition. The Primary National Strategy (PNS) (DCSF, 2007, p 4) has as a key principle that bilingualism is an asset and recognises that *the first language has a continuing and significant role in identity, learning and the acquisition of additional languages*. While the current government has archived many of the materials produced by the PNS, many of the principles and approaches put forward in this documentation remain valid for teachers of children learning EAL.

The children in your class will notice how you welcome children with EAL, how you introduce them to other pupils, where you seat them, how you address them and how you support their learning in the class. Your own attitudes and behaviour will set the tone and expectations for how the other children respond to children with EAL. The PNS (DCSF, 2006a, p 11) claims that *school teaches in three ways: by what it teaches, how it teaches and by the kind of place it is*. Your role as teacher is fundamental in this.

All children should expect to come to school without anxiety, well motivated, confident and ready to learn. The PNS (DCSF, 2006a, p 7) outlines three interrelated prerequisites which apply to all learners for effective learning.

- Children need to feel safe, settled, valued and secure – a sense of belonging.

- Children need to be able to relate new learning to previous experience.

- No child should be expected to be cut off from their own language and culture within the school environment.

It is your responsibility as the teacher to ensure that the environment is conducive for learning for all children, including those with EAL.

Developing a positive ethos

Creating an ethos of acceptance for all children depends, in part, on the extent to which policies are adhered to. For example, all policies on bullying and racist incidents must be carried out so that all children understand the importance of treating everyone fairly (DCSF, 2006a, p 11). Schools convey an inclusive ethos not only by how they treat their pupils, but by how welcoming they are to parents and carers, how they communicate with them, how they consider their preferences and background and also by the extent to which they are willing and able to employ staff from a range of different cultural backgrounds, including the different languages spoken. Creating a positive ethos then depends on the relationships which are formed between pupils and the teacher as well as the family of the pupil and the teacher, alongside the physical environment of the school.

All children have their own distinct identity. Each of us belongs to a range of different cultures and communities, leading to unique and dynamic identities and loyalties (DCSF, 2006b, p 2). Within the mix of different elements that make up the identity of a child with EAL will be their culture, religion, nationality, ethnic origin, family expectations, particularly gender-specific expectations, aspirations, roles and interests. Teachers who work with children from different cultural backgrounds need to ensure they value the identity of such children, taking an interest in their celebrations, festivals and customs. This will increase motivation and enthusiasm and provide an environment where children feel safe and accepted and are willing to take risks with regard to language learning. The PNS (DCSF, 2006a, p 13) states that teachers tend to spend more time with pupils who are from the same background as themselves and less with children whose backgrounds they know little about.

Teachers should avoid giving the impression that their own culture, with its attendant values and beliefs, is the only one which matters, and should actively cultivate an interest in the lives and experiences of the children in their class. Children with EAL should be supported in gaining skills in becoming collaborative and active learners. This includes providing an atmosphere where all children's contributions are valued, ideas will not be dismissed, children's first language can be used as well as English and where adults and children work together to create meaning (DCSF, 2006a, p 17).

It is also important for children whose first language is English to be encouraged to accept children whose first language is something different. Along with this should be an understanding that different people do things in different ways, have different customs, traditions and expectations, but they have many similarities also. All children should be encouraged to develop a sense of empathy towards others, which will build a sense of class identity in which all class members belong. This sense of belonging will transcend the differences between individuals and provide an effective learning environment for all pupils (DCSF, 2006a, p 19).

Developing a positive physical environment

Children with EAL will feel more comfortable in the school environment if it reflects objects, decorations and surroundings with which they have some familiarity. The PNS (DCSF, 2006a, p 20) recommends that it is better for the child with EAL to experience an environment where diversity is celebrated and all children are included rather than a 'Eurocentric' environment. It is suggested that unless teachers consciously work at providing a diverse environment, then it will default to the Eurocentric mode where white children and teachers are those who really belong and other children are more likely to be marginalised. The PNS recommends that in order to promote diversity, visual displays should include positive images of minority ethnic groups; people from diverse cultural and religious backgrounds should be represented in *non-tokenistic and non-stereotypical* ways and the work of a range of children, including those learning EAL, should be placed on display. The colours and decorations used on wall displays should be carefully chosen so as to reflect other cultures and not just those familiar to those from white European urban culture. Other members of staff who may be better acquainted with patterns, designs and fabric which is more representative of the cultural background of the range of children in the school will be a rich source of advice and support.

In displaying children's work it is important to use a wide range of linguistic script. Reading material in reading areas and role-play areas should reflect the range of languages spoken in the class, and material from relevant community groups can be included to provide something familiar to the children. Letters for parents should be available in the home language of the parents to enable them to understand what is being communicated. Where this is difficult and your school does not have experience of working with children with EAL, then it is important to make links with leaders from other communities so that bridges can be built and children and families welcomed within the school environment (DCSF, 2006a, p 21).

Developing an interest in other languages

Teachers of children who are learning EAL need to be well informed about the different languages represented in their class and school. For example, families who are from Pakistan may read and write in Urdu as it is the official language for administration and education. However, most families in Britain with a Pakistani heritage will speak Punjabi, while Gujarati is the first language of most Indian-heritage families in Britain. Gujarati does have a written form, but speakers of this language may not have developed literacy skills within this language. A teacher may assume that because children are from the same cultural heritage they speak the same language; however, as explained above, children may have a different first language from other children and they may not be able to understand each other. This illustrates the complexity of understanding different languages and how they may be used for communication. It is therefore vital for the school to gather information about the first language of the EAL learner and to engage with the community in order to understand the linguistic needs of their children, thereby making the best provision for their learning (DCSF, 2006a, p 23).

As a class teacher you should not make assumptions about how at ease children with EAL may be about speaking their own language in school. Some children may be embarrassed and uncertain about whether their language will be valued. The PNS (DCSF, 2006a, p 27) suggests the following ways in which bilingualism or multilingualism can be celebrated.

- making a list of children who speak different languages;

- showing places in the world where this is the first language;

- giving a few facts about each language;

- including the same sentence written in a variety of different scripts and community languages to allow comparison to be made.

Critical questions

You have just gained your first teaching post and will be working in a school where over 60 per cent of children have EAL. You have a Y3 class.

» *How will you prepare the physical environment of your classroom to be welcoming to all children? Consider the seating arrangements, wall displays, the reading area, physical arrangement of furniture and so on.*

You have been invited to an Introductory Day to meet your new class prior to beginning at the school.

» *How will you introduce yourself to the children, what expectations will you set within the class and what will you do to get to know the children?*

Developing access to the curriculum

Building on prior knowledge is important for all children in providing a hook to develop their learning further. Bilingual strategies build on the child's first language, and where there are members of staff who speak the same language as the children learning English, this provides an opportunity for common experiences and knowledge to be shared, as well as connections, appropriate stimuli, examples and analogies (DCSF, 2006c, p 12). Providing artefacts and allowing collaborative time can also provide opportunities for the child with EAL to build on previous knowledge and experience. Similarly, creating a shared experience, such as a visit, a visitor, a practical activity, video or performance, will enable all learners to bring their unique experience to the task, and through collaboration each child can participate and benefit (p 13).

The PNS suggests that, where possible, children with EAL could be introduced to new ideas prior to the session in their own language and that these could be reinforced afterwards, also in their first language. Clearly, this depends on there being someone in the school who shares their language and who can support this task. However, it is believed that pre-teaching a lesson enables the child to access the lesson content more readily while it is being taught to the rest of the class. During the lesson, class discussion can support understanding, particularly if this includes using the child's first language. Figurative language and culturally specific references can be explained, as well as grammatical terms. During discussion, children can compare language and use cultural knowledge to make connections. This way both children with EAL and children with English as their first language can gain a wider understanding of each other's culture and heritage and deeper social relationships can be fostered (p 13).

When teaching classes which include EAL learners, the learning intention and success criteria can be offered in the predominant first languages to be found in the class. Children can be partnered with other children who share their language during discussion time in order to clarify expected learning and to consolidate new knowledge. Children sharing the same language can question each other and engage in dialogue to develop understanding further (DCSF, 2006c, p 16).

Care needs to be taken over the provision of resources. The PNS (DCSF, 2006a, p 36) maintains that where the cultural context goes beyond the familiar, this can cause a barrier to learning. For example, if talking about places of worship, pictures of mosques and temples should be shown as well as churches. Similarly, the way families are depicted spending their leisure time will be different depending on cultural expectations. A white British family may be shown going to a pub for a meal for a pleasant activity, whereas for some children from other cultures drinking alcohol is associated with behaviour which is disallowed. Where some children in the class may associate pictures of an airport with going on holiday and happy memories, other children, who may be newly arrived in the country, may associate airports with sadness, separation, loss and painful memories. It is also important to be aware that social mixing between sexes is discouraged in some cultures. With this in mind, images of social gatherings should be selected with care.

Children's popular culture can be a useful vehicle to support learning and to engage all learners. It provides much opportunity for conversation and the sharing of interests. This may be a television programme, film, book, current music, game, fictional character, play, show, celebrity or sports personality. All of these ideas are best supported by experiential learning and are likely to engage and motivate (DCSF, 2006c, p 38).

Teaching approaches for children with EAL need to be carefully selected in order to maximise learning opportunities. Some of these, such as sharing the learning intention in other languages, giving scope for the child to talk in their first language, providing appropriate pictorial representation, pre-teaching information and working collaboratively, have already been discussed. The PNS (DCSF, 2006c, p 19) also recommends modelling as a way of supporting new learning. Modelling should show children what to do, how to do it and what to say or write in order to do it. This is particularly important when developing subject-specific language. The PNS (p 20) also advocates recasting and remodelling as a way of dealing with errors when children are developing new language. For example *When I came to England I flied in an aeroplane* can be recast and remodelled into *When you came to England you flew. Was it a big aeroplane?*

Clearly, the spoken word, listening, reading, comprehension and writing are all important in language learning. The PNS (DCSF, 2006c) advocates that word recognition and comprehension should be taught within a rich language environment of songs, poems, rhymes, storytelling and book sharing. Structured phonics sessions, as well as multi-sensory activities including the use of ICT are recommended. Children with EAL should also be supported in reading for meaning; this includes the understanding of vocabulary, cultural context, reading which involves double meanings and inference (p 35). Texts chosen should be culturally appropriate, with familiar contexts and of interest to the child. Fictional characters should be appropriate for the culture to which the child belongs and positive images of ethnicity and gender should be portrayed.

In gaining confidence in writing, children with EAL may need to be shown where to start on the page and may need help with the orientation and flow of their writing when attempting English, as Arabic, for example, is written right to left. Children may also need to be shown how to form their letters and be taught the letters of the alphabet because their own language may have a completely different alphabet and script (DCSF, 2006c, p 48). A graphic area can be created in the classroom and children can be encouraged to contribute to this by writing in their own script. All children can be given the opportunity to look at different writing forms, comparing them, noticing differences and similarities.

Critical questions

You are planning your first week's lesson in the school where you have secured your first teaching position. 60 per cent of your Y3 class has EAL. Some of the children have only been in this country for a few months. Others have been here since birth.

» *How would you plan a literacy lesson on poetry?*

» *What teaching approaches would you use?*

» *What resources would you use and why?*

» *How would you group the children in your class and why?*

» *How would you build on children's previous knowledge and experience?*

» *How would you expect the children to record their ideas or poem?*

As you can see from this chapter, there are many children in our schools who are learning English as an additional language. These children are from diverse cultural backgrounds and heritages, some of whom have experienced trauma, loss and separation. It is important for the well-being of all of these children that their traditions, religion and language are valued and respected. They should be accepted within the communities of our schools and supported to belong. Their families and communities should also be embraced.

As a teacher in school and encountering children with EAL, you will need to consider your own values regarding such children and how you would include them in the classroom. You will also need to be aware of how learning theory such as Cummins BICS and CALP will affect your practice. Many of the strategies suggested for children with EAL are also useful for all learners; however, you will need to get to know the children with EAL in your class, to understand their heritage, language and traditions, in order to make specific and sensitive provision to develop them as competent learners.

Critical reflections

» *In thinking about the information given in this chapter and your own experiences, how competent do you think you would be to teach children with EAL effectively?*

» *What do you think your strengths are?*

» *What do you think your limitations are?*

» *What steps do you need to take to develop your practice further?*

» *Would you consider a job in a school where 97 per cent of the children had EAL? Why/ why not?*

Taking it further

Books and journals

Mistry, M. and Sood, K. (2010) English as an Additional Language: Assumptions and Challenges. *Management in Education*, 24(3): 111–114.

> This research paper considers some of the assumptions that are made about children who have EAL. It provides a review of some of the key issues associated with EAL provision and reports data which on analysis suggests strategies for further good practice.

Soan, S. (2004) Bilingual Learners, in Soan, S. (ed) *Additional Educational Needs: Inclusive Approaches to Teaching*. London: David Fulton Publishers.

> This chapter considers issues relating to teaching in a bilingual classroom. It provides discussion on a whole-school approach, classroom management and assessment. It is an easy-to-read chapter and provides both background understanding and strategies for teaching.

Web-based material

Refugee Council: www.refugeecouncil.org.uk/ (last accessed 4 October 2013).

> This website gives background information to many of the situations worldwide where people are having to flee their country. It gives stories of people who have sought asylum and also those who have helped asylum seekers and refugees. As well as providing this important information, it provides updates on current areas of human disaster and how people can get involved, from signing relevant petitions to volunteer work.

National Strategies for Supporting Children: www.teachfind.com/national-strategies/supporting-children-learning-eal (last accessed 4 October 2013).

> This web page provides invaluable suggestions for how to include children with EAL. It gives a list of models of collaboration which can be employed in the classroom, as well as very comprehensive guidance for teachers who may have little access to expert support.

References

Aspinall, P. and Watters, C. (2010) *Refugees and Asylum Seekers: A Review from an Equality and Human Rights Perspective*, Equality and Human Rights Commission Research Report 52. Online: www.equalityhumanrights.com/uploaded_files/research/refugees_and_asylum_seekers_research_report.pdf (last accessed 4 October 2013).

Cummins, J. (2008) BICS and CALP: Empirical and Theoretical Status of Distinction, in Street, B. and Hornberger, N.H. (eds) *Encyclopedia of Language and Education*, 2nd edn, vol 2: Literacy (pp 71–83). New York: Springer Science + Business Media LLC. Online: http://daphne.palomar. edu/lchen/CumminsBICSCALPSpringer2007.pdf (last accessed 4 October 2013).

Department for Children, Schools and Families (DCSF) (2006a) *Primary National Strategy Excellence and Enjoyment: Learning and Teaching for Bilingual Pupils in the Primary Years. Unit 3: Creating an Inclusive Culture.* Online: http://webarchive.nationalarchives.gov.uk/20110809101133/ nsonline.org.uk/node/85322 (last accessed 4 October 2013).

Department for Children, Schools and Families (DCSF) (2006b) *Primary National Strategy Excellence and Enjoyment: Learning and Teaching for Bilingual Pupils in the Primary Years. Culture and Identity: Ethos Environment and Curriculum.* Online: www.naldic.org.uk/Resources/NALDIC/ Teaching%20and%20Learning/pri_pubs_bichd_214206_011.pdf (last accessed 4 October 2013).

Department for Children, Schools and Families (DCSF) (2006c) *Primary National Strategy Excellence and Enjoyment: Learning and Teaching for Bilingual Pupils in the Primary Years. Unit 2: Creating the Learning Culture: Making It Work in the Classroom.* Online: http://webarchive. nationalarchives.gov.uk/20110809101133/nsonline.org.uk/node/85322 (last accessed 4 October 2013).

Department for Children, Schools and Families (DCSF) (2007) *Primary National Strategy Supporting Children Learning English as an Additional Language: Guidance for Practitioners in the Early Years Foundation Stag.* Online: http://webarchive.nationalarchives.gov.uk/20110208164652/ http://nationalstrategies.standards.dcsf.gov.uk/node/84861 (last accessed 4 October 2013).

Department for Education (DfE) (2012) *EAL Pupils by School.* Online: www.naldic.org.uk/Resources/ NALDIC/Research%20and%20Information/Documents/ealschool1.xls (last accessed 4 October 2013).

Evans, L. (2007) *Inclusion.* London: Routledge.

Frederickson, N. and Cline, T. (2009) *Special Educational Needs, Inclusion and Diversity*, 2nd edn. Maidenhead: Open University Press.

Glazzard, J., Hughes, A., Netherwood, A., Neve, L. and Stokoe, J. (2010) *Achieving QTS Teaching Primary Special Educational Needs.* London: Sage.

McLaughlin, B. (1992) *Myths and Misconceptions About Second Language Learning: What Every Teacher Needs to Unlearn*, Education Practice Report 5. Online: www.ocmboces.org/tfiles/ folder835/46%20NATIONAL%20CENTER%20FOR%20RESEARCH%20ON%20CULTURAL%20 DIVERSITY%20AND%20SECOND%20LANGUAGE%20LEARNING.pdf (last accessed 4 October 2013).

NALDIC (2012a) *EAL Pupils in Schools.* Online: www.naldic.org.uk/research-and-information/eal-statistics/eal-pupils (last accessed 4 October 2013).

NALDIC (2012b) *Languages in Schools.* Online: www.naldic.org.uk/Resources/NALDIC/Research%20 and%20Information/Documents/School%20census%20January%202011%20language%20 data.xls (last accessed 4 October 2013).

Roessingh, H. (2006) BICS-CALP: An Introduction for Some, a Review for Others. *TESL Canada Journal/ Revue TESL du Canada*, 23(2): 91–96. Online: www.teslcanadajournal.ca/index.php/tesl/ article/viewFile/57/57 (last accessed 4 October 2013).

7 Understanding learners with special educational needs and disabilities

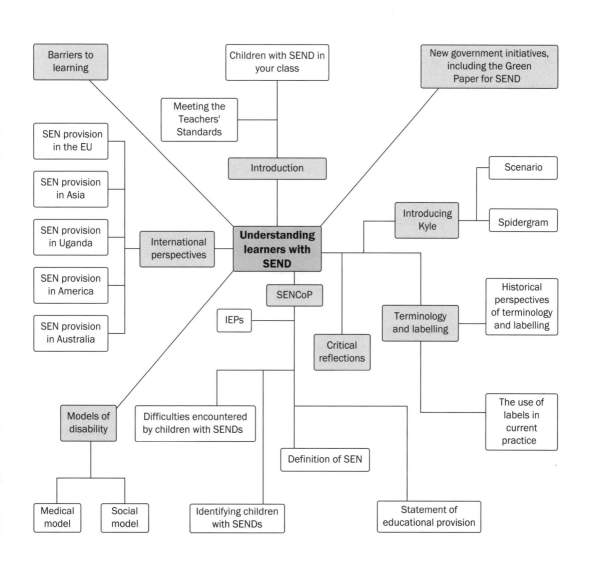

Introduction

When you go into schools as a trainee teacher you are likely to encounter in your class a number of children who are considered to have special educational needs and disabilities (SENDs). These are children for whom special provision needs to be made in order for them to learn and develop. The SEN Code of Practice (DfES, 2001) states that *all teachers are teachers of children with special educational needs* (p 47), therefore you will need to become acquainted with the requirements of children with barriers to learning and how such barriers can be removed or minimised. Such children could be those with medical conditions such as hearing or visual impairments; speech and communication difficulties, including children with autism; behavioural difficulties, including children with ADHD and specific learning difficulties, such as those with dyslexia.

Some children may not have recognised labels but find that certain aspects of the school environment and culture inhibit their learning. As a trainee teacher, you will need to be aware of how you teach and organise your classroom such that all children have the maximum opportunity to learn and fulfil their potential.

Children with SEND in your class

There are more children in our schools with SENDs than there were 50 years ago, and there are a number of reasons for this. Children with learning difficulties, even those as significant as profound and multiple learning difficulties, can now be educated in a mainstream school if the parents request it and the needs of the child can be met within it. This includes giving the child access to a broad, balanced and relevant education, including a relevant curriculum (DfES, 2001, p 7). My first introduction to this as a practising teacher was with a seven-year-old child who came into my mainstream class with no speech. She had seizures as a baby and they still racked her body at times in the classroom. She was unable to sit without support and came to school in a buggy. She was doubly incontinent, drooled all the time, making noises which I did not understand. She had a developmental age of 18 months. She provided me with some of the greatest challenges as well as the greatest joys of my teaching career and was accepted without question within our school community. Having her in my class radically changed the way I viewed children with learning difficulties and how I carried out my professional practice.

Children who are born prematurely may be developmentally delayed. The survival rate of babies born at 22–25 weeks has increased from 40 per cent in 1995 to 53 per cent in 2006, according to a study funded by the Medical Research Council. However, the study carried out by Field et al. (2008) also found that although survival rates had increased, there was no difference in the level of ongoing illnesses or complications from premature birth, such as respiratory problems, brain damage or cerebral palsy. Therefore, although more children survive, they often have remaining health complications. As a teacher it will become your responsibility to provide a supportive and positive learning environment for all children.

This chapter looks at how you as a teacher can best meet the needs of children with SENDs in your class. It also considers the systems and procedures you will need to be aware of when making provision for such children. Although, as a trainee teacher on placement you would not be expected to take a lead in progressing children through the processes of the SEN

Code of Practice (SENCoP), having an understanding of the code, the relevant terminology and its implications will enable you to engage in effective practice.

MEETING THE TEACHERS' STANDARDS

Links to Department for Education Teachers' Standards May 2012

TS 1; 2; 5

Part 2

Introducing Kyle

As a trainee teacher you will need to make provision for all learners in your class. For some children this might be a question of carefully crafted differentiation, while for other children you may need to make specific and personalised provision. The following scenario is an example from practice. It outlines the specific behaviours of a child with learning difficulties in a Y2 class and considers the role of the teacher in meeting his needs. It also gives the opportunity to examine guidance given in the SENCoP (DfES, 2001) and the implications for the class teacher in carrying it out.

SCENARIO

Kyle's class teacher is concerned about his behaviour and willingness to engage in learning in the classroom. He appears to understand the lessons, but he does not offer any verbal contribution or much written work. He is taken out of class each morning to work on writing skills with a TA, but he seems uncomfortable working in the corridor, as other children frequently walk past. His hair is long and his nails are uncut and dirty. In the classroom he only has one friend he is willing to talk to or work with and he seems to retreat into his own world at times. He can sometimes be found hugging or licking the metal support pillars in this modern school building.

Kyle's mother, Mrs Robinson, visits school regularly to express her concerns about his lack of progress in school, in particular his writing. She is aware that his reading is below the expectation for his age. Kyle's mother has commented that he does not like to be touched or hugged and that when she takes him to the hairdresser he screams and refuses to get into the chair. She can only cut his toe and finger nails while he is asleep at night. Kyle never seems to want to bring friends home for tea and when his mother has invited friends on his behalf he ignores them, leaving Mrs Robinson to entertain them herself.

Kyle's mother makes him do handwriting practice every night at home and wants the school to do more to engage him in his learning. Kyle's SENs are recognised by the school and he is being supported by the school with individualised provision. However, the class teacher wants his learning and behaviour to be assessed by outside agencies. Both the class teacher and the SENCo suspect that Kyle may be on the autistic spectrum and think an assessment will help identify his difficulties. Kyle's mother is resistant to this suggestion, considering that further assessment will result in him being given a label and stigmatised. She thinks that his behaviour can be modified and that his main difficulty is his reluctance to write.

The critical questions below will help you to consider the perspectives of the different people involved in this scenario as well as what action might be undertaken to advance Kyle's learning and behaviour. In considering these activities you will become more aware of your own values and beliefs with regard to children with SEND and how you might provide for them in your class. You will also examine your own knowledge and understanding of the systems and processes which the CoP requires.

Critical questions

» *What can the class teacher do to engage Kyle in his learning?*

» *How can the class teacher encourage Kyle to make more friends or to work co-operatively with more children?*

» *What advice as class teacher would you give to Kyle's mother in response to her resistance to Kyle being assessed further?*

» *What would the benefits be for Kyle if he was assessed by outside agencies?*

Having begun to consider some of the issues surrounding Kyle and the management of his SENs, the following spidergram will enable you to identify a broader picture with implications for teachers, parents and, not least, the child.

This spidergram on page 110 provides an overview of some of the issues which are evident in the scenario. In looking at these in more detail you will be able to:

* consider your own values and principles;

* be aware of the roles and responsibilities of the SENCoP;

* be aware of the initiatives of the new government, including the proposals of the Green Paper on SEND;

* consider how to support children with specific barriers to learning.

These are now outlined in more detail below.

Terminology and labelling

In considering the concept of special education needs and the implications for the teacher, it is useful to gain some understanding of the context for current practice. Much of this has centred on what has been seen as a need to identify and label children and educate them accordingly.

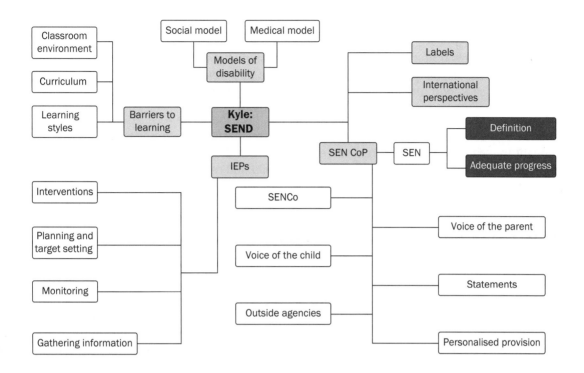

Historical perspectives of terminology and labelling

In 1870, the Elementary Education Act made attendance at school compulsory for all children. Previously, education had been only for the privileged, but the 1870 Act gave entitlement for other children to receive schooling. However, in order to make provision for children who did not make progress as quickly as others, a dual system was introduced. This meant that children not considered appropriate for mainstream education were sent to special schools (Wearmouth, 2001, p ix). Such a system required the categorisation of children and gave rise to groups of children labelled as imbeciles, feeble-minded and idiots and with medical conditions such as Mongolism (now known as Down Syndrome). Many of these terms are now seen as terms of abuse. While those considered to be 'feeble-minded' were able to receive an education, the 'imbeciles' were consigned to an asylum and the 'idiots' were considered to be uneducable (Wearmouth, 2009, p 19).

Further labelling of children occurred through identification according to the 10 categories of 'handicap', as set out in the 1944 Education Act. These included the blind and partially sighted, the delicate, educationally subnormal and the maladjusted (Hodkinson and Vickerman, 2012, pp 3–4). While in 1945, there were no children labelled as 'maladjusted', by 1960, there were 1,742 children labelled in this way, and by 1975, there were 13,000 such children (Wearmouth, 2009, p 21). The label of maladjustment enabled professionals to segregate children into special schools, while the responsibility for children with severe mental handicaps remained with the health authority not education. It was not until the 1970 Handicapped Education Act that the responsibility for children with severe handicaps was transferred to education authorities, and along with this came an entitlement to a school-based education (Wearmouth, 2001, pp x–xi).

The term 'handicap' was replaced by the concept of 'special educational needs' in the Warnock Report of 1978. This report abandoned the previous categories of handicap and promoted the view that a child's educational provision should be given priority rather than an emphasis on disability or impairment (Hodkinson and Vickerman, 2012, p 4). As a result of the Warnock Report, the term special educational need was introduced.

While this might be a convenient term for teachers, my experience as a teacher and SENCo showed that parents often expressed resistance to the term SEN, referring to the stigma they thought this carried. This is seen in the scenario above. Parents commented on the lowering of self-esteem the label had created for their child and resented the out-of-class support given, as it identified them as different and isolated them from the rest of the class, even though this was seen by the teacher as making additional provision for the child's needs.

The use of labels in current practice

Labelling does not need to be related to children with SENs alone. In talking with trainee teachers, I hear them using common classroom shorthand for children such as HAPs (higher ability pupils) and LAPs (lower ability pupils). Teachers group their children into ability groups and give them names which thinly disguise the level of ability of the children within them. While teachers sometimes think the children are not aware of the significance of the name their group is given, it does not take much imagination to identify which children are in the 'gold group' and which might be in the 'brown group'. I once heard of the ability groups within a class being given the names of insects, this included the 'butterflies' at one end and the 'slugs' at the other.

For some, however, labels can be seen as something to be welcomed. Research by Riddick (1995) showed that children who had been diagnosed with dyslexia were positive about receiving this label. Over 90 per cent of children in the study accepted that this explained why they found reading difficult and were relieved that this was not because they were 'thick' (p 463). Perhaps this raises the question as to whether some labels are considered to be more socially acceptable than others.

In the scenario, Kyle's class teacher thinks that he may be on the autistic spectrum. She is keen for him to be assessed further by professionals from outside of the school to consider this possibility. Some teachers feel that finding a diagnosis for a child will help them to support the child better as they will understand the child's needs more fully. While this may be helpful, there is nothing that can replace the understanding a teacher can gain from knowing the child individually. No two children with autistic spectrum disorder are the same. While they may have similar difficulties, they may need different provision to remove their barriers to learning. Kyle's heightened sense of touch drove him to lick the metal pillars in the classroom, whereas another child might be hypersensitive to noise or bright lights. This can only be discovered by spending time with these children and getting to know them, rather than reading about their named disability or difference. The SENCoP is quite clear that:

> the key to meeting the needs of all pupils lies in the teacher's knowledge of each pupil's skills and abilities and the teacher's ability to match this knowledge to identifying and providing appropriate ways of accessing the curriculum for each pupil.
> (DfES 2001, p 51)

Critical questions

» *How many labels can you think of that you have heard or seen used on your placements? What do they all mean?*

» *What benefit do you think labels bring to (a) the teacher and (b) the child?*

» *How does the use of labels affect the identity of a child?*

» *What difference will the use of a label make to the provision the class teacher offers Kyle?*

Barriers to learning

As a teacher, you must be alert to the barriers to learning that some children face. This includes how you manage your classroom, your attitudes and the way you teach and provide resources. Children may have particular learning requirements which if not met could create barriers to learning. The new National Curriculum Inclusion Statement (DfE, 2013, p 8) recognises this and requires teachers to:

• set suitable challenges;

• respond to pupils' needs and overcome potential barriers for individuals and groups of pupils.

Furthermore, the SENCoP recognises that *some difficulties in learning may be caused or exacerbated by the school's learning environment or adult/child relationships*. It goes on to urge the teacher to look *carefully at such matters as classroom organisation, teaching materials, teaching style and differentiation in order to decide how these can be developed so that the child is enabled to learn effectively* (2001, p 44). This means that the onus for providing appropriate access to learning for the child lies with you. Ways in which this can be put into practice in the classroom are discussed in more detail in Part 3 of this book.

Fully including a child with SEN in mainstream classrooms can be a challenge to the class teacher and particularly so for you as a trainee on placement. While a child may be physically present in the school, they may be segregated from their classmates by the work they are given, who they work with, the position they are given within the class or even whether they are in the class at all. I recently spoke with a trainee who confidently told me that there were no children with SEND in their class. On investigating this further, I found that the children with SEND were taken out of class each morning by the TA. While this was meant as a generous gesture to the trainee in enabling them to teach the class more easily, this denied them the opportunity to gain experience of managing children with SEND. It also denied the children concerned the opportunity to be part of the social and academic community in the classroom. The DfES (2004) states:

> *Inclusion is about much more than the type of school that children attend: it is about the quality of their experience, how they are helped to learn, achieve and participate fully in the life of the school. (p 25)*

It is therefore important to consider what children's experiences of school are like for them and to bear in mind the child's social and emotional development as well as their academic progress.

Models of disability

As discussed earlier in this chapter, educational provision for children with learning difficulties has previously been tied to identification and categorisation of children's difficulties or deficits. The following section considers two different models of disability which have previously been touched on in Chapter 1. Both models have implications for the teacher's professional practice.

The medical model of disability

The medical model is where a person is identified as having a deficit or medical condition which hinders their ability to function. The treatments or strategies employed are intended to cure or ameliorate the disability (Hodkinson and Vickerman, 2012, p 20). With this model the centre of attention lies with the disease or disability rather than the person themselves. Diagnosis is key, so that appropriate interventions can be employed. However, these interventions are largely concerned with requiring the disabled person to change to fit in or become *normalised* (Farrell, 2004, pp 68–69). In the scenario, it could be argued that the class teacher is adhering to the medical model. She is keen for further assessment and wants to know whether Kyle is on the autistic spectrum. She arranges for the TA to take Kyle out of the classroom each morning to work on writing skills, but there is no evidence of an understanding of his wider barriers to learning. Indeed, the class teacher ignores Kyle's discomfort in working in the corridor and does not seem to provide alternative recording opportunities for him to be able to show his understanding of the work. An alternative way of approaching Kyle and his barriers to learning would be through the social model of disability.

The social model of disability

The aim of the social model of disability is to promote an understanding that it is the environment which disables people. Many people with disabilities do not consider themselves to be disabled within their own homes as their environment is equipped to enable them to be independent. However, this is not the case outside of the home, thereby suggesting that the environment restricts mobility and function by placing barriers to accessibility in the way (Hodkinson and Vickerman, 2012, p 23). These barriers may not be physical barriers, but social and organisational attitudes; structures and practices may also inhibit participation. Glazzard et al. (2010) contend that the social model sees disability as *the result of economic, social and cultural oppression rather than the impairment itself being viewed as disabling* (p 9). Furthermore, the social model does not rely on the categorisation of pupils, but rather recognises difference (Farrell, 2004, p 84).

Critical questions

Taking the social model of disability into account, consider the following questions.

» *Imagine you are a trainee teacher in Kyle's class. What aspects of the environment would you consider 'disable' Kyle?*

» *What attitudes do you hold which might need to be challenged in adopting a social model of disability?*

» *How would adherence to the social model of disability impact on the provision you make for Kyle?*

Returning to the scenario, it can be seen that Kyle has been identified as having SENs, that he is being given an individualised programme and that the class teacher and SENCo consider he should be assessed by outside agencies, despite the misgivings of his mother. This next section considers the term *special educational need*, how children are identified as having SENs, how they might be supported through the new single school-based SEN category and possibly beyond this to receiving a statement of educational provision. It also outlines what the parent and child can expect from the school in terms of provision to meet the child's needs.

Special Educational Needs Code of Practice

The SENCoP (DfES, 2001) provides guidance for teachers and SENCos concerning the learning needs of children. While the DfE has indicated that this guidance will be revised in the future in order to promote more consistent identification of SEN, for now the 2001 guidance remains. The underpinning principles of this guidance state that children with SENs should have their needs met normally within a mainstream school and that the wishes of parents and children should be taken into account. This immediately provides a tension between the people in the scenario, as Kyle's mother thinks very differently about the educational provision and processes from the teacher and SENCo. The SENCoP reminds us that *parents hold key information and have a critical role to play in their children's education* and urges all professionals to seek out ways to work with parents, valuing their contribution (p 16). The relationship with parents is therefore vital, and as a trainee teacher, it is important for you to develop effective partnerships, even though you would not be expected at this stage to engage in the kind of negotiating and discussion that the class teacher and Mrs Robinson might need to have. Further discussion on parents as partners is developed in Chapter 9.

Difficulties encountered by pupils with SENDs

While Kyle's behaviour is particularly unusual and therefore obvious, there may be other children that you encounter on placement who have SENDs. Some of the difficulties these children encounter include:

*   reading, writing, understanding information;

*   expressing themselves or understanding others;

*   making friends and relating to adults;

*   behaving appropriately in school;

*   organising themselves and their work;

*   attempting or completing any school work;

*   a sensory impairment or physical need.

Identifying children with SENDs

A child with SENDs may be identified because their level of achievement is less than their peers in most areas of learning, or they may find the acquisition of basic numeracy and literacy skills difficult. It is possible they will have low self-esteem, immature social skills, poor verbal and non-verbal skills, limited auditory or visual memory, poor motor co-ordination or difficulty with acquiring and retaining new learning. While the class teacher on your placement is likely to have already identified such children in the class you will be working in, it will be your responsibility to plan flexibly in order to meet the needs of all children. This is to ensure progression, relevance and differentiation (DfES, 2001, p 47).

The DfE considers that there may be an over-identification of children with SEN. Therefore, in the Green Paper (DfE, 2012a) there is a commitment to support training for teachers and other school staff to enable them to be more confident in identifying and overcoming barriers to learning as well as to deliver effective teaching and provide early interventions (p 38). This focus is also supported in the new standards for qualified teacher status (QTS) (DfE, 2012b), while training materials on severe learning difficulties, produced by the then Teaching Agency, are available to support initial teacher training. Additionally, SENCos in schools have until recently been provided with funding to complete a mandatory Master's level award to strengthen and develop their professional understanding and practice (DfE, 2012a, p 40). It can therefore be seen that teachers are being required to become skilled at identifying and providing for children with SEN who will be in their class.

Definition of SEN

The SENCoP (DfES, 2001) provides a definition of special educational needs as follows.

> *Children have special educational needs if they have a learning difficulty which calls for special educational provision to be made for them.*

> *Children can be considered to have a learning difficulty if they:*

> **a)** *have a significantly greater difficulty in learning than the majority of children of the same age; or*

> **b)** *have a disability which prevents or hinders the child from making use of local educational facilities for children of the same age. (p 6)*

Where a teacher is concerned about a child's progress within school this should be monitored. A teacher's regular observation and assessment of a child will enable knowledge and evidence about the child's progress to be built up and suitable strategies to remove barriers to learning implemented. Where these strategies do not result in the child learning as effectively as possible then special educational provision should be made (DfES, 2001, p 51). Within the proposals of the Green Paper (DfE, 2012a), this would be through the single-school-based category.

While the key test for the need for action is evidence that the child's progress is inadequate, the class teacher should not assume that all children will progress at the same rate. Adequate progress might mean that the attainment gap between the child and their peers is closing, or at least that the gap is not growing wider. Adequate progress might also be related to improvement in self-help skills, social or personal skills or in behaviour. However, where progress is not adequate, then some *additional or different* action should be taken (DfES, 2001, p 52). This will be part of what is provided by the school within their differentiated curriculum.

The SENCoP (DfES, 2001) currently outlines a graduated response for meeting children's needs. This means that some children may need to receive more support than is usually available in school alone. However, the school is expected to employ all the resources available internally before contacting outside agencies (Glazzard et al., 2010, p 20).

Within the new single-school-based SEN category recommended by the DfE (2012b), the class teacher or SENCo should gather appropriate information about the child and this should guide how future support is planned and implemented. Previously, the effectiveness of this support was required to be constantly monitored through the construction and regular review of an Individual Education Plan (IEP) (DfES, 2001, p 53). However, there is no mention of IEPs within the Green Paper, despite the stated intention that the focus for SEN will be on outcomes rather than processes (DfE, 2012a, p 45). Many schools choose to make use of a TA to provide additional support for a child with learning difficulties; however, other interventions such as differentiated work, additional resources, special equipment or group support should also be considered.

Where children are still not making adequate progress despite the action taken by the school, then the SENCo can seek external support from outside agencies. This is the discussion that the class teacher and SENCo are attempting with Kyle's mother. The external agencies that can be called on are varied and differ according to the needs of the children concerned.

For Kyle, an assessment by the local authority (LA) Learning Support Service (LSS) or from other, possibly private, companies offering learning assessments would be appropriate as he is considered to have learning needs related to his writing. However, Kyle also exhibits behaviour which might place him on the autistic spectrum. The SENCo therefore might want to request an assessment by an educational psychologist (EP), which would give a broader profile of his needs and thereby enable more specific provision to be made to remove barriers to learning.

Involvement of an EP also provides a bridge to other professionals who may be able to offer advice or further assessment. These could include members of the health professions, such as paediatricians, who are able to assess children and make a diagnosis such as ADHD, dyspraxia, developmental delay, autism and so on. Other health professionals might include speech and language therapists, physiotherapists, occupational therapists and specialist nurses (ADHD, asthma, diabetes), among others. They are also able to carry out assessments and offer advice on teaching strategies and interventions. A new IEP or plan for learning may be drawn up which reflects new information from assessments and details fresh strategies which should be carried out as far as possible within the class. The delivery of these strategies remains the responsibility of the class teacher (DfES, 2001, p 55). All of this should be done with the consent of the parent.

Statement of educational provision

A small proportion of children do not make adequate progress within the categories of special educational needs despite outside agency advice and intervention. If this is the case, then, currently, the school may request a statutory assessment with a view to gaining a statement for the child. A statement is a legal document which describes the child's needs and the special educational needs provision which will be made to meet those needs. It is reviewed annually.

Within the terms of the 2001 SENCoP, children are considered to have needs which fall into one or more of the following four areas:

• communication and interaction;

• cognition and learning;

• behaviour, emotional and social;

• sensory and/or physical.

However, it is also recognised that children's needs may be interrelated and that the combined effect of these complex needs should not be overlooked (DfES, 2001, p 85). The Green Paper, however, states the intention to reconsider the category of behaviour, emotional and social difficulties, believing it to be over-used and leading to confusion over the kind of support required (DfE, 2012a, p 45).

By 2014, the statement of educational provision will be replaced by an Education, Health and Care Plan (EHCP) brought about through a single assessment process. The EHCP will bring together all the services across education, health and social care and will bring about the same benefits as the previous statement of educational provision, carrying with it a legal obligation for all agencies to provide the services which feature on the plan (DfE, 2012a, p18).

According to government figures in 2012, the number of children with statements is small. The DfE indicates the following.

• 2.8 per cent of all pupils in England have statements. This is 226,125 children nationally.

• 53.7 per cent of pupils with statements were placed in mainstream schools.

• 39.0 per cent of pupils with statements were placed in maintained special schools.

• The incidence of boys with a statement is 2.0 per cent, but for girls is 0.8 per cent.

• 17.0 per cent of pupils across all schools are considered to have SEN but without statements. This is 1,392,215 pupils nationally.

• The incidence of boys with SEN without a statement in state-funded primary schools is 22.8 per cent; for girls it is 12.2 per cent.

• 28,190 new statements were issued in 2011. This is 97 per cent of all statements requested. Of these, 62 per cent were issued to pupils in mainstream schools. (DfE, 2012c)

This data shows that in your placement class of 30 children, you are likely to encounter at least five children with SENs, the majority of whom will be boys. It is also likely that you will have a child in your class with a statement and that this will also be a boy. Given this likelihood, it is essential that you are well acquainted with the SENCoP and with strategies and personal and professional resources to enable all children to reach their potential. This is also important for you in being able to achieve TS 5.

Individual education plans

The 2001 SENCoP states that all children deemed to have SENs should have an IEP which describes the targets and strategies that are put in place to enable that child to progress. The IEP should only record what is *additional to* or *different from* that which is offered as part of the differentiated curriculum available to all children. The IEP should be *crisply written*, with three or four targets which match the child's needs. As well as the short-term targets, it should include the teaching strategies to be employed, the provision to be put in place, when the plan is to be reviewed, the success criteria and outcomes (DfES, 2001, p 54).

The CoP requires the IEP to be reviewed at least twice a year and that this should involve parents as well as the child where possible. Research by Goepel (2009) showed that where children with SENs were not involved in the IEP process their understanding of the targets and expectations was reduced, resulting in lack of progress in learning and sometimes disengagement. Similarly, where parents had a different understanding of the targets, there was confusion about what was being worked on in school and therefore whether progress had been made. This led to misunderstanding and sometimes strained relationships. It is therefore important for the teacher to consider the views of both parents and the child in constructing and monitoring an IEP and to make sure it is relevant and appropriate, with all parties able to give it their allegiance.

More recently there has been a move away from IEPs in some schools with different forms of monitoring and tracking children's progress. This may be shown through provision mapping or the teacher's detailed planning showing differentiated provision. On your school placements you may encounter children who have IEPs and it is important that you adhere to the provision included on this document. Whether or not children in your class have targets identified in the form of an IEP, you must make personalised provision for all children who are considered to benefit from it.

Critical questions

» *Imagine you were Kyle's class teacher. What personalised provision would you make for him? What would your targets be? What strategies would you put in place?*

» *How would you obtain Kyle's view and that of his parents and incorporate these into his personalised provision?*

» *If you were Kyle's class teacher, what would your justification be for wanting him to be assessed by outside agencies?*

» *What evidence would you gather to support this request and what other professionals do you think would be appropriate to consult or involve?*

New government – new initiatives

The coalition government is undertaking the most sweeping overhaul of the provision for children with SENs for 30 years. As has already been stated, the DfE document *Support and*

Aspiration (2012a) replaces the previous two categories of School Action and School Action Plus by a single-school-based category. Additionally, by 2014, the Statement of SEN will be replaced by an EHCP, which will be from birth to age 25 years.

The new approach to SEN and disability will give parents control over the budget for their child, allowing them to choose who should provide for their child. Local authorities and health services will be required to work together to plan and provide for children with SENDs, and LAs will be required to publish a clear local offer of services available so that parents can make informed choices. Furthermore, parents will be given a greater say in the choice of school for their child. While these new approaches are yet to be implemented, clearly as a trainee teacher you will need to become familiar with the requirements, as they will become part of your practice. Additionally, a new SENCoP will be published which will outline a stronger emphasis on the training and development of all school staff in identifying and making provision for children with SEN (DfE, 2012a, p 42).

International perspectives

Armstrong et al. (2010) argue that discussions about education for children with SENs have become more controversial due to the underpinning assumption that some children are 'normal' while others are not. This medical-model approach leads to an exclusion of a significant number of children worldwide who are marginalised, excluded from education and discriminated against as young people and adults (p 45).

However, key international organisations such as the United Nations (UN) and the United Nations Educational, Scientific and Cultural Organization (UNESCO) have committed to supporting the development of quality education for all learners. The Salamanca Statement (1994) recognises the uniqueness of each child and their right to an education. Schools are encouraged to take a child-centred approach which provides for diversity and SENs. The Salamanca Statement acknowledges that children have differences and advocates that learning should be adapted to include those differences, rather than trying to make the child fit the learning (Armstrong et al., 2010, pp 44–45).

The 1990 World Conference on Education for All (EFA) placed mass schooling on the global primary agenda for education systems and policy makers, and in 2000, the World Declaration on Education stated the determination to change education systems from being mostly for the elite to a comprehensive mass-education system. While this is laudable, it also raises the issues of resources and capacity for improvement and change (Armstrong et al., 2010, pp 45–46).

In 2006, the UN Convention on the Rights of Persons with Disabilities emphasised that international co-operation is necessary in implementing its aims, which include raising the aspirations and achievements of children with SENs. The convention accepted the social model of disability rather than the medical model, promoting the ideal that no child should be discriminated against due to their disability (Hodkinson and Vickerman, 2012, p 93). While such conventions and statements are important, the challenge is in how they become practice worldwide.

Special educational needs provision in the European Union

The European Agency for Development in Special Needs Education states its aim as being to develop policy towards the inclusion of children with SEN into mainstream provision and providing teachers with relevant training and resources. The countries in the EU can be grouped according to the categories of provision offered for such children. These are as follows.

1. One-track approach. These countries make provision for almost all children to be included in mainstream education. Countries with this approach include Spain, Greece, Italy, Iceland, Sweden and Norway.

2. Multi-track approach. Countries with a multi-track approach have a variety of systems between mainstream settings and special needs education settings. Countries with this approach include Denmark, France, Finland, the UK, Poland, Estonia and Slovakia.

3. Two-track approach. This is where there are two distinct and separate education systems, sometimes with different legislation for each. Pupils with special education needs do not follow the same curriculum as their counterparts in mainstream education. Two countries operating this system are Switzerland and Belgium.

Even within these three approaches, there are huge differences between countries in terms of the numbers of children considered to have SENs. For example, in the one-track approach countries, Iceland considers 15 per cent of pupils to have SENs, with 0.9 per cent of them in special provision, whereas Italy considers only 1.5 per cent of pupils to have SENs, with less than 0.5 per cent of them in specialist provision. Similarly, in multi-track provision, Finland considers 17.8 per cent of pupils to have SENs, with 3.7 per cent in segregated provision, while the UK considers 3.2 per cent of pupils to have a statement of SENs, with 1.1 per cent in segregated provision.

The number of types of SENs identified also varies from country to country. Denmark identifies only one or two types of special need, while Poland recognises ten categories. Most EU countries recognise between six and ten types of need. All countries recognise the value of an individual education plan or similar individualised provision (European Agency for Development of Special Needs Education, 2003).

Special educational needs provision in Asia

The World Bank works alongside the UN to provide loans to developing countries to improve children's access to education, including those with SEN. Countries such as Bangladesh, India, Japan, Korea, Malaysia, Pakistan, Sri Lanka and Thailand are some of those receiving support. These countries tend to provide education for all children in the same environment; however, this is driven more by financial expedience than a conviction about inclusive education, and it places a greater emphasis on the teacher to provide differentiated strategies and to be responsive to individual children's needs (Hodkinson and Vickerman, 2012, p 102).

Since 1994, Nepal has committed to integrating children with mild or moderate learning difficulties into mainstream primary education. India has increased the budget for children with SEN significantly and supports a national development programme for the integration of children into mainstream schools. The Philippines and Sri Lanka are both integrating children with SEN into mainstream schools and ultimately into the community, while Korea, Malaysia, China, Indonesia and Thailand have pioneered individual learning programmes to support children with SEN. Therefore it can be seen that some Asian countries are responding to the call for greater inclusive education (Hodkinson and Vickerman, 2012, pp 102–103).

Special educational needs provision in Uganda

Hodkinson and Vickerman (2012) note that the main objective of the Ugandan education system is to provide quality education for all learners in order that they can contribute meaningfully in society (p 107). However, special schools are not meeting the minimum standards as set by the Ministry of Education, and it is considered that many children are being educated in special schools who could be successfully included in mainstream settings. Free education is offered to all children; however, those with severe disabilities such as deafness are not included.

Special educational needs provision in America

The United States of America (USA) is seen as one of the most inclusive countries worldwide, with 96 per cent of all children with disabilities being educated in mainstream settings and almost half spending most of their time within general classrooms rather than being withdrawn for specialist lessons. All children with SENs have an entitlement to the same activities and programmes as other children and there is an expectation that such children will make appropriate progress and be prepared for employment.

Special educational needs provision in Australia

Australia espouses a full-inclusion ideology where schools are expected to cater for all children's needs within mainstream settings. Lindsay (2004) points out that inclusive education is not law in Australia, unlike in the USA (p 367). She also observes that while there are an increasing number of pupils wanting to access inclusive environments, social inclusion for such pupils ranges between *inadequate and completely non existent* (p 377). Furthermore, there would appear to be a discrepancy between the skills of teachers of children with SENs and those of children in mainstream schools, with a certain amount of anxiety attached to those required to carry out inclusive practice (p 378).

However, on a visit to Australia in 2005, I visited a school with a strong inclusive philosophy, which was carried into action. There was a programme for children with *high intellectual potential*, as well as facilities for children with severe multiple disabilities. I witnessed children with physical difficulties strapped into standing frames to support them in a standing position while undertaking maths lessons, and also children undertaking Conductive Education, a specialist programme for children with a neurological movement disorder. In addition to this, there were policies and initiatives to address matters of poverty, those from non-English-speaking backgrounds, Aboriginal pupils and itinerant or abused pupils.

It would seem that Australia has strong inclusive ideals, but the carrying out of inclusive practice is not universal.

Critical reflections

» *Identify three things you could do to remove barriers to learning while on placement.*

» *What is your response to the statement* All teachers are teachers of children with SEN *(DfES, 2001)?*

» *How would you ensure a child's educational provision is relevant to their needs and is 'owned' by everyone involved with the child?*

» *What is your response to the different approaches to SEN provision globally? Which country would you like to work in and why?*

Taking it further

Books and journals

Crowther, D., Dyson, A. and Millward, A. (2010) Supporting Pupils with Special Educational Needs: Issues and Dilemmas for Special Needs Coordinators in English Primary Schools. *European Journal of Special Needs Education*, 16(2): 85–97.

This research is concerned with the role of the SENCo. It shows how although SENCos are increasingly expected to take on roles of leadership, there are frequent other demands on their time and resources. As a trainee teacher it will provide you with a helpful insight into the role of a significant colleague in school and enable you to understand more fully how they can support you but also drive forward inclusive policies and practice within your school or setting.

Davis, P. and Florian, L. (2004) *Teaching Strategies and Approaches for Pupils with Special Educational Needs: A Scoping Study*, Research Report 516. Nottingham: DfES Publications.

This is a hefty volume. It undertakes a study of the strategies which are being used for children with SEN. There is an extensive review of the literature, both national and international, and the approaches for children with SENs were evaluated in the light of the evidence from this reading. It is possible to dip into this review and gain a good overall view of strategies to support children with SEN, how they are being carried out in schools and how effective they are. Although this was written at the time of the previous government and policy has changed since then, many of the findings are of value to you as a trainee teacher.

Frederickson, N. and Cline, T. (2009) Autistic Spectrum Disorders, in *Special Educational Needs, Inclusion and Diversity*, 2nd edn. Maidenhead: Open University Press.

In this chapter, Frederickson and Cline consider what autism is, how it can be identified and its prevalence in society. The authors provide an understanding of autistic spectrum disorders and also discuss approaches to education. These include decisions about what educational placement is best for the child, good practice, language and communication, and socialisation, including circle of friends and social stories and behaviour management.

Glazzard, J. and Overall, K. (2012) Living with Autistic Spectrum Disorder: Parental Experiences of Raising a Child with Autistic Spectrum Disorder (ASD). *Support for Learning*, 27(1): 37–45.

This is a piece of research carried out into the parental views of children diagnosed with autism. These children attended special schools. The research shows that parents felt they had limited involvement with professionals and other agencies and that communication was poor. It shows how parents found a range of coping strategies to support themselves and their children.

Wolfendale, S. and Robinson, M. (2007) Meeting Special Needs in the Early Years: Inclusive Stance, in Pugh, G. and Duffy, B. (eds) *Contemporary Issues in the Early Years*, 4th edn. London: Sage.

Sheila Wolfendale and Mary Robinson consider inclusion in the Early Years. They also outline the importance of effective relationships with parents and the professionals involved in the Team Around the Child. Helpful diagrams and charts are included and a case study shows how the principles they outline can work in practice. This is a very readable chapter and is clearly of particular relevance to you if you want to be an Early Years teacher.

References

Armstrong, A.C., Armstrong, D. and Spandagou, I. (2010) *International Education: International Policy and Practice*. London: Sage.

Department for Education (DfE) (2012a) *Support and Aspiration: A New Approach to Special Educational Needs and Disability. Progress and Next Steps*. Cm 8027. London: The Stationery Office.

Department for Education (DfE) (2012b) *Teachers' Standards*. Online: http://media.education.gov.uk/assets/files/pdf/t/teachers%20standards%20information.pdf (last accessed 4 October 2013).

Department for Education (DfE) (2012c) *Special Educational Needs in England: January 2012*. Online: www.gov.uk/government/publications/special-educational-needs-in-england-january-2012 (last accessed 4 October 2013).

Department for Education (DfE) (2013) *The National Curriculum in England: Framework Document*. Online: www.gov.uk/government/uploads/system/uploads/attachment_data/file/210969/NC_framework_document_-_FINAL.pdf (last accessed 4 October 2013).

Department for Education and Skills (DfES) (2004) *Removing Barriers to Achievement: The Government's Strategy for SEN*. Nottingham: DfES Publications.

European Agency for Development of Special Needs Education (2003) *Special Needs Education in Europe: Thematic Publication*. Online: www.european-agency.org/publications/ereports/special-needs-education-in-europe/sne_europe_en.pdf (last accessed 4 October 2013).

Farrell, M. (2004) *Special Educational Needs: A Resource for Practitioners*. London: Paul Chapman.

Field, D.J., Dorling, J.S., Manktelow, B.N. and Draper, E.S. (2008) Survival of Extremely Premature Babies in a Geographically Defined Population: Prospective Cohort Study of 1994–9 Compared with 2000–5. *British Medical Journal*. Online: www.ncbi.nlm.nih.gov/pmc/articles/PMC2405852/pdf/bmj-336-7655-res-01221-el.pdf (last accessed 4 October 2013).

Glazzard, J., Hughes, A., Netherwood, A., Neve, L. and Stokoe, J. (2010) *Achieving QTS Teaching Primary Special Educational Needs*. London: Sage.

Goepel, J. (2009) Constructing the Individual Education Plan: Confusion or Collaboration? *Support for Learning*, 24(3): 126–32.

Hodkinson, A. and Vickerman, P. (2012) *Key Issues in Special Educational Needs and Inclusion*. London: Sage.

Lindsay, K. (2004) Asking for the Moon? A Critical Assessment of Australian Disability Discrimination Laws in Promoting Inclusion for Students with Disabilities. *International Journal of Inclusive Education*, April: 133–52.

Riddick, B. (1995) Dispelling the Myths. *Disability in Society*, 10(4): 457–73.

Wearmouth, J. (2001) (ed) *Special Educational Provision in the Context of Inclusion: Policy and Practice in Schools*. London: David Fulton.

Wearmouth, J. (2009) *A Beginning Teacher's Guide to Special Educational Needs*. Maidenhead: Open University Press.

Part 2
Developing partnerships

8 Working with children

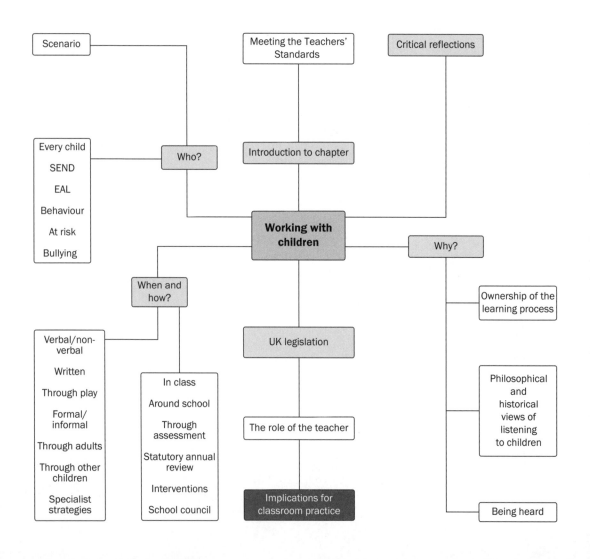

Introduction

Listening to the children you teach sounds like an obvious strategy and part of classroom practice. However, the reality of establishing a learning environment in which every child is encouraged to express their views and needs can be challenging. It can also be difficult to ascertain the feelings of children who have difficulties in communicating their feelings, such as those with special educational needs or a disability, those who have English as an additional language, children who are at risk or who are frightened to share their concerns, or Early Years children who may find it difficult to articulate their thoughts and needs. This chapter considers the *who, what, why, when and how* aspects that need to be understood in relation to listening to children in your school and your class. It also reflects on your role as a trainee teacher and the implications that listening to children will have on your practice.

Throughout the chapter, the 'child's voice' will be referred to. This reflects the terminology used by the Department for Education and many authors: *'voice' refers to ways of listening to the views of pupils and/or involving them in decision-making* (DfE, 2012a, p 1).

Critical questions

»   *Consider your own experiences in primary or secondary school. Were you encouraged to share your views or concerns about your education and welfare? How did you feel about speaking out?*

»   *Think about how you view your role in relation to the children in your class. Do you consider it to be one in which you provide learning opportunities and deliver knowledge? Is it one in which the teaching and learning is a shared experience between yourself and the children? Do you think the children's views can help you be a better teacher? Explain your answers.*

MEETING THE TEACHERS' STANDARDS

Links to Department for Education Teachers' Standards, May 2012.

TS 2; 4; 5

Part 2

In working towards the DfE Teachers' Standards (2012b) you will need to treat *pupils with dignity, building relationships rooted in mutual respect* (p 10) and effective listening strategies will help you to develop these relationships. You are required to *be aware of pupils' capabilities and their prior knowledge* (p 7) and *have a clear understanding of the needs of all pupils* (p 8), and by encouraging children to share their experiences from in and out of school, you will be better informed and more responsive in your planning and teaching. By knowing children in your class well you will be able to *promote a love of learning and children's intellectual curiosity* (p 8); by taking into account their interests and what motivates them to learn and develop when you teach, they will be engaged and enthusiastic. By creating and encouraging a mutually beneficial dialogue, you will have a better understanding of the children and their needs and experiences; this will contribute to a shared understanding and collaborative approach in supporting their physical, social, emotional and intellectual development.

Who am I listening to?

This seems like an obvious question and your answer will probably be *the children, of course!* However, consider the many different backgrounds and experiences that shape each child's identity. These influences mean that each child will have something different to share with you, and by listening to them you will be better informed and more successful in responding to their different needs and different voices.

Critical questions

»   *Think about the children in one of the classes in which you have completed a placement. Consider the different personalities you encountered: confident, shy, eager, reluctant, and so on. Imagine that each of those children wanted to tell you about a holiday – how many different ways can you think of that they might share this information with you?*

»   *Consider the range of additional needs you will work with in a typical class. Imagine that you are about to take the children on a walk around the school. What kinds of things will you need to find out from the children in order to be sure that the walk is enjoyable and accessible for each of them? What kinds of information do you need from them to ensure that the walk is successful?*

Special educational needs and disability

Children who have been identified as having special educational needs or disabilities (SEND) will have their own views about their abilities, skills and needs. While health and education professionals can provide information and strategies to help you plan for and teach the children, only each individual child can tell you what it is like for them on a day-to-day basis. Each child will be able to tell you about, and demonstrate, strategies they have developed that help them to access the learning environment that they share with you, and they should be encouraged to work alongside you to identify any barriers they encounter. These barriers may be physical or intellectual, or might be social or emotional, such as how they work and play with their peers or how they feel about having particular needs which are different from those of other children. It is also helpful to maintain a dialogue with children who have developmental or progressive additional needs so that you can ensure your planning and teaching is appropriate for the child.

English as an additional language

Encouraging each child who has English as an additional language (EAL) to have a voice will have a positive effect on your provision. It is rewarding to listen to children who are developing their English skills and it will reassure you that the support strategies you have put in place are effective. You may find it difficult in the early stages to fully comprehend or grasp what the child is trying to tell you if you are not familiar with their first language; however, visual and non-verbal clues are often used successfully to help with conversations. There may also be children who have recently moved to the community and school who have refugee status due to conflict in their country of origin. They will have particular needs that you will need to be sensitive to, and listening to their experiences will help with this.

Children with social, emotional or behavioural difficulties

This may be an aspect of teaching that you feel apprehensive about. Children who behave inappropriately in the class and school may be doing so because they have social or emotional difficulties and find that they need to express themselves or make you aware of their needs through certain types of behaviour because they cannot articulate how they feel. It is important to be aware that behaviour is a form of communication and that their feelings are being shared with you through their actions, even if they are undesirable.

SCENARIO

Jordan, aged 7

Jordan lives in difficult circumstances. His father died of cancer eight months ago and his mother is finding it difficult to cope with the bereavement. She has limited financial means and very little support from her relatives, who live a long way away. Jordan has been observed hitting and pushing other children and trying to run out of the classroom, and he frequently seeks refuge under a table when he feels overwhelmed with activities or interactions with others. He often shouts at adults and children and has torn or damaged his drawings and work books. His mum is reluctant to go into school to discuss the situation as she finds it very upsetting. She has told Jordan that he has to be a big boy, look after his Mum and that big boys do not cry.

Critical questions

»   What do you think are the social and emotional difficulties that Jordan encounters?

»   Consider the behaviours described in the scenario and match them to the difficulties you identified.

»   What are some of the approaches you could consider to help Jordan choose more appropriate behaviour when he is upset?

Jordan's teacher recognised that his attempts to cope with the traumatic event and aftermath of his father's death meant that he was not able to focus on typical learning activities and the social aspects of being in school. It became clear that Jordan had pent-up emotions that he could not control at particular times, such as when the children talked about family activities they participated in or when he was tired or challenged by tasks. In response to this, she sought guidance from a bereavement counsellor at the local authority and encouraged his mother to contact them to ask for family bereavement support. His teacher also made sure that the teaching support assistant was given activities, approaches and time so that one-to-one and small-group work could be put in place. This helped Jordan to talk about how he felt and identify some ways in which he could share his frustrations in a safe way rather than through violence or by ignoring them.

There will be many different reasons why children have social and emotional difficulties and it is helpful to consider each child's basic needs for possible causes. By developing a sensitive and encouraging dialogue with the child, you will be able to identify possible causes and then work with your colleagues and the child's family to put interventions in place to address the issue.

Children at risk

Children who live in an environment where their needs are not met and where they may be at risk of being hurt or neglected must be assured that there is a safe way for them to speak out. As the person who spends many hours each week with the children in your class, a child at risk may identify you as being a safe and trustworthy person in whom to confide.

There are specific and formal safeguarding procedures in place in every school that must be followed should a child choose to confide in you. You must make it a priority to find out who is responsible for safeguarding at the beginning of every placement in a school or Early Years setting. This person and the class teacher will be the people you talk to about any disclosure. Further guidance about what to do if a child does tell you that they are at risk can be found later in this chapter.

Victims of bullying

Children who are identified as having additional needs, who are at risk or who have EAL may be more likely to experience bullying by other children or by adults. It can be particularly difficult for children who are being bullied if they have limited communication skills and are not able to respond or defend themselves. These children may already have low self-esteem or confidence levels due to the nature of their additional needs and they may have been threatened if they tell another person that they are being bullied, so will find it very difficult to share their worries and fears with another person. If you create a supportive, encouraging and positive learning environment, the child will be more likely to feel empowered to talk to someone they can trust and seek help to stop the bullying.

When and how can I listen to children?

There are many ways in which to listen to children's views, ideas and feelings. Each approach must take into account the child's level of communication skills and any particular additional needs they may have. Children who are unable to express themselves verbally, perhaps due to their age, or who have difficulties in relation to speech and language, hearing or specific learning and expression must be given alternative opportunities to 'talk'. You may also find that what is an effective approach for a particular child on one day will not be as effective on another day, so it is helpful to be prepared to keep trying different ways until you find the one that works for the child you are listening to. Listening and observation skills need to be finely tuned to ensure that implicit or cautiously shared information from the child is noticed and understood. By providing many different opportunities for each child to express thoughts and feelings, you will be able to build up a picture of each child and then apply this to your planning and teaching. It is important to remember that encouraging each child to share information with you does not have to be a negative or worrying thing. While you may learn about concerns, worries or issues that cause the child distress, you can also learn more about the child's interests, passions, skills and motivations.

Possible ways in which you can encourage an effective dialogue are outlined in the table below. Every approach may be appropriate for every single child at some point. Depending on the focus of the dialogue and circumstances, however, some will be particularly effective for a child with specific additional needs and these are also identified.

Ways to encourage effective dialogue with children

Type of communication	Examples of approaches	Specific additional needs	Points to consider
Verbal	• Typical conversation • Through questions and answers • Voluntary sharing of information • During group or whole-class activities	This approach may be particularly effective for children who are able to put their thoughts into words or who are considered gifted or talented.	This approach may not be relevant or appropriate for any child with difficulties in speech or articulation. Expressing thoughts and feelings can also be difficult for the Early Years and children who have limited vocabulary. It relies on the skill and focus of the teacher to listen carefully to what is being said, which can be challenging when many children are trying to share their views.
Non-verbal	• Observation of body language • Observation of interactions with other children and adults • Observation of particular behaviours or approaches to activities	This approach may be particularly suitable for any child who has difficulties with verbal expression. Children with English as an additional language. May also be appropriate for a child who is distressed and unable to articulate their current feelings.	The way in which children interact with their peers and adults may indicate skills or concerns which you can then investigate further. Body language is an important indicator of levels of confidence or apprehension and will indicate how comfortable the child feels in the learning environment.

Type of communication	Examples of approaches	Specific additional needs	Points to consider
Written	• In work produced during taught activities • In notes or letters completed during self-directed learning sessions	This approach may not be appropriate for all children, particularly those with fine motor control difficulties (such as those unable to hold mark-making implements) or those with limited writing skills.	The amount, or lack of work produced can indicate levels of understanding. Children may produce pieces of writing in which they indicate how they feel or what they need. An area in the classroom in which children can write or mark-make freely is an effective strategy for encouraging self-expression.
Creative approaches	• Mark-making • Painting • Drawing • ICT • Clay/dough • Music/singing • Drama	All children will be able to participate in creative approaches, providing they have support and appropriate resources where necessary. Children with specific learning difficulties or complex needs may find that creative approaches are the only ones they can use comfortably to fully demonstrate their levels of knowledge, understanding, feelings or needs.	Taking time to talk to the child about the work they have completed can help you develop your understanding about their feelings or interests. A child who is unable to talk about their feelings may express themselves creatively and they may indicate particular issues or skills in this way.
Play	• In class • In the playground • Role play • Outdoor learning	All children will be able to participate in play, providing they have support and appropriate resources where necessary.	Children with limited mobility or fine or gross motor skills should be supported to ensure they can access the learning environment or the resources available to them. Use of child observations is particularly effective for understanding children during play. It is useful to keep a record of these observations over time so that comparisons and analyses can be made.

Type of communication	Examples of approaches	Specific additional needs	Points to consider
Formal and informal	• Statutory annual review for children with Statements of Special Educational Needs • Through summative and formative assessments • During safeguarding reviews for children identified as 'at risk'	Every child who has a Statement of SEN should be consulted prior to each annual review to ascertain their views about the support they are given and about any needs they have. This must be shared at the review, either by them, if they are able, or by their teacher, support assistant or another adult who can act as an advocate.	Formal meetings can be difficult and scary events for children. It is unlikely that they will feel confident enough to share their innermost thoughts or concerns and this should be addressed. An adult with whom they feel comfortable should be included in the meeting to support and encourage them to share their views. Assessment processes can be difficult for many children and it should be recognised that the work they complete may not be a true indication of their ability, skills or potential. Combining ongoing teacher assessments with the summative results will give a more in-depth and indicative view of progress.
Through other adults	• Parents • Learning support assistants • Lunchtime supervisors • Other professionals involved in the child's care and learning	Children who have difficulties in particular relationships with certain adults will not be able to access this approach. This may be relevant to issues of safeguarding where the child is at risk from an adult or if they are finding a relationship with an adult particularly difficult. Parents will be an important route by which you can learn more about the child and their views and needs. Conversations between the child and parent out of school hours will sometimes be shared with you by the parent.	While the views of other adults can be very helpful in developing a greater knowledge and understanding of the child, it must be remembered that this is not always the child's view; it may be the adult's interpretation. Specific information about a child's particular needs such as SEN or EAL can be ascertained from the specialist professionals involved, although this may not provide information about how the child feels about their care.

Type of communication	Examples of approaches	Specific additional needs	Points to consider
Through other children	• Siblings • Children in the class or school	This approach will be appropriate for most children. Some children with specific social difficulties, such as those on the autistic spectrum may find it very difficult to form relationships with their peers and so may not be able to access this approach.	Brothers and sisters will be aware of home-life experiences and may find it helpful to share this with you on behalf of the child. This will make you aware of feelings or concerns the child has and will enable you to initiate a conversation with the child; it might help to have the sibling present as well to encourage the child to feel confident to speak. Other children in the class may have information about a child that you are not aware of; depending on the information shared, you can then decide how to approach the situation.
Specific strategies	• Mosaic Approach (Clarke and Moss, 2011) • Circle Time (Mosley, 1996) • Diary entries or video rooms • Suggestion or worry boxes • Graffiti walls • Further approaches and ideas can be found on the internet, such as www.sheffkids.co.uk/adultssite/pages/consultationtechniques.html	Each child will be able to access these approaches at different levels depending on their particular needs. By making several approaches available, the level of access is increased.	The Mosaic Approach is a multi-method means for gaining children's views through talk, photography and tours of the learning environment. It is an excellent way to delve into children's views and feelings in a safe and comfortable way. Circle Time is used widely in schools and provides opportunities for children to talk and be heard. Not all children will feel comfortable sharing sensitive or very personal information, but it is a useful way for you to identify aspects that you might wish to follow up at a more appropriate time.

Critical questions

» *Consider the ways in which children have been encouraged to share their views and concerns with you or their class teacher while on placement. Make a list of the ways in which children were encouraged to share their views or have a voice.*

» *Identify the ways in which you feel some children were unable to share their views. What were the barriers and how would you change or develop the approach to make it more appropriate for the children's needs?*

» *Look at the list of different approaches in the table above, which do you feel you could implement while on your next teaching practice? What positive impact would the approach have?*

Why is it so important to listen to children?

Rinaldi (2006) refers to the Italian Reggio Emilia provision, an education approach designed for Early Years children in which a *pedagogy for listening* (p 14) is fundamental to creating high-quality learning opportunities for children. While this approach is recognised as being appropriate for very young children, the principles should be regarded as highly relevant for all children in all our schools. She refers to the *space* (p 68) in which children learn, meaning the physical, emotional, intellectual and social environment, and identifies that teachers should strive to *construct and organise spaces that enable children:*

• *to express their potential, abilities and curiosity;*

• *to explore and research alone and with others, both peers and adults;*

• *to perceive themselves as constructors of projects and of the overall educational project carried out in the school;*

• *to reinforce their identities, autonomy and security;*

• *to work and communicate with others;*

• *to know that their identities and privacy are respected.* (p 68)

This list captures the benefits for children when they are able to learn in an environment where their views, ideas and feelings are actively sought and encouraged. Longley and Sharma (2011) also list the benefits they feel are to be gained from *developing a listening culture in an organization working for children* (p 121).

As a teacher, you will want to ensure that your provision is informed, meets the needs of all the children in your class and takes place in a learning environment where everyone feels valued, important and confident. The strategies, examples and guidance in this chapter will help you develop your practice and create effective ways to listen to children.

Critical questions

» *Think of a time when you have tried to talk to another person when you know they have not been listening to you. How did you know that you were not being listening to? Think about the body language, eye contact or verbal responses demonstrating that the person was not interested in what you had to say. How did this affect what you said and how you said it?*

» *Now consider the opposite situation where your comments have been warmly received and where the listener makes it apparent that they are interested in what you have to say. How do the body language, eye contact and verbal responses differ from the situation above?*

» *Consider how your body language, eye contact and responses can be used in the classroom to demonstrate to a child that you are genuinely interested in what they are telling you.*

Philosophical and historical views of listening to children

You will be aware that every child in your class, whether or not they have additional needs, deserves to be given opportunities to be heard. Billington (2006) considers the issues and challenges inherent in relationships between children and professionals in *Working with Children*. He refers to a societal view of children in which they have very little power and where *they are subject ultimately to any adult in their family, school or other government agency who seeks unreasonably to impose their will upon them* (p3).

While there is no doubt that a priority for adults working with children is to ensure their social, emotional, physical and intellectual needs are met, it is important to question your own philosophy as a trainee teacher. Is teaching something that you do *to* children? How do you view the historical perspective that children should be *seen and not heard*?

> *Cultural assumptions about what children are and how adults should be in relationship to them play a significant part in how easy it is for practitioners to work collaboratively with them. If children are regarded as 'innocents to be protected' or 'wild beasts to be tamed' ... there is little room for partnership. (Todd, 2007, p 40)*

Critical questions

» *Think of a time when you have held a conversation with someone you considered to be more in control, more powerful or more important than you. How did this inequality in the relationship affect what you said?*

» *Consider the dynamics in a relationship or interaction which would make you feel comfortable to share your views, ideas or concerns. How could you incorporate these dynamics in your interactions with the children you teach?*

UK legislation

The United Nations Convention on the Rights of the Child (UNCRC, 1990), an internationally agreed set of rights and standards, was agreed by signatories from 140 countries from around the world. A total of 54 Articles were produced which outline the basic rights that all children should be afforded and these include non-discriminatory rights and the need for every child to be heard and their opinions sought in matters that relate to them. Articles 12 and 13 are particularly relevant to this chapter: *assure [to] the child who is capable of forming his or her own views the right to express those views freely in all matters affecting the child, the views of the child being given due weight in accordance with the age and maturity of the child* and *The child shall have the right to freedom of expression; this right shall include freedom to seek, receive and impart information and ideas of all kinds, regardless of frontiers, either orally, in writing or in print, in the form of art, or through any other media of the child's choice.*

The current coalition government clarifies that although the UNCRC is not considered statutory because it has not become part of national law, it will take into account the recommendations when legislation is written and that *schools are strongly encouraged to pay due regard to the Convention* (DfE, 2012b, p 2).

The SENCoP (DfES, 2001) was approved by Parliament to ensure that schools and local authorities provide effective care for children with SEND. Section 3, entitled 'Pupil Participation', builds on the rights agreed by the Convention on the Rights of the Child (1990) and identifies how these rights are applicable to children's participation with parents, in schools, with the local education authority and in assessment and decision-making processes.

It is anticipated that the current CoP will be replaced in 2014 by a new Code which is currently going through the consultation process. The SEN and Disability Green Paper *Support and Aspiration* (DfE, 2011) does not have an explicit section on promoting the voice and participation of pupils, although it does give much greater focus on the needs of parents, which will impact on their children and families.

The role of the teacher and the trainee

Your role as a teacher will require you to organise and manage the learning and progress for large numbers of children, and although control is important, it is possible to achieve a balance between the level of control and the amount of shared ownership and responsibility you have with the children. Providing each child with a voice in which they feel valued and encouraged to share their views, ideas and concerns will contribute to this shared approach and will enhance learning opportunities. A relationship between a child and their teacher in which the child feels they have no control and where the teacher is explicitly powerful is not conducive to promoting the child's voice; it is more likely to encourage the child to say what they think the teacher wants to hear or not to speak out at all.

Implications for practice

Consider the learning environment

- Look around your classroom. Where could you add opportunities for children to express their views, feelings and needs?

- Think about some possible activities that children with additional needs or who speak English as an additional language could participate in, such as creative approaches, or by using specialist equipment. How might these improve their opportunities to communicate with you?

- Identify opportunities within the timetable for each day and week where you encourage children to be heard. Consider some of the activities such as the Mosaic Approach

(Clark and Moss, 2011) or circle time (Mosley, 1996) that you could include in the timetable of sessions.

- Consider the outdoor play and breaktime sessions. These are often times when children feel comfortable in talking to adults and children; could you include an area in the playground where children can go to seek support or a friendly ear?

Ensure you are fully aware of the safeguarding procedures

- You must know who the person responsible for safeguarding or child protection is in every setting in which you are placed.

- Follow the guidelines carefully should any child disclose sensitive information to you.

- Do not ask any further questions as these may influence the child's responses and may affect any future investigations by the safeguarding team or the police.

- Do not promise the child confidentiality or say that you will keep their information a secret. Assure them that you will need to talk to their teacher or the person responsible for safeguarding so that they can make sure that they are safe.

Develop your verbal and non-verbal interaction skills

- In order to create an encouraging and supportive communication culture, develop your responses so that you demonstrate an effective rapport with the children.

- Concentrate on your body language, eye contact and verbal responses so that children are more likely to feel they can approach you and share their thoughts and feelings.

Use the information you gain to inform your future practice

- Think about how your knowledge and understanding about each child can influence your planning and teaching.

- You may have identified approaches that motivate and encourage children to engage in the learning. How can you include these approaches in your teaching?

Create a balance between control and classroom organisation and shared learning

- Ask the class teacher or your tutor to observe your interactions with the children in relation to behaviour management and the way in which you control the sessions and the children.

- Are there examples where the children have been encouraged to take responsibility for some of the organisation?

- What is the ratio of teacher talk and child talk? You should aim to create sessions in which the children have approximately 80 per cent of the talk time. This supports your aim to develop greater talking opportunities for children.

- Give children time to think about their comments and responses. If there are only a few seconds between your question and your expected response, many children may find it difficult to consider the question, formulate their response and then reply in the time allowed.

- Reflect on the types of questions you ask the children. Do you ask many closed questions in which the children can only reply with one- or two-word answers?

- *... teachers who have participated in experimentally contrived classroom sessions, in which they have modified their style of talking to children by asking fewer questions ... have commented that they found out things about the children's experiences, views and ideas that they did not know.* (Wood, 1998, p 173)

- Sharing aspects of learning and classroom organisation with the children will enhance their feelings of ownership. This will in turn influence the levels of interest, engagement, motivation and enthusiasm, all of which will enhance the learning.

Critical reflections

» *Identify three children who you have worked with while on placement. Choose children who have very different needs, such as one with a disability, one who speaks English as an additional language and one who has social, emotional or behavioural difficulties, if possible. List ways in which each of these children may find it difficult to express their thoughts and feelings.*

» *Consider ways in which you could develop your practice to ensure that each of the three children is able to communicate effectively with you. What changes could you make to the learning environment to enhance interactions?*

» *Try and imagine the types of information they might share with you and think about how this would make a difference to your planning and teaching.*

Taking it further

Books and journals

Hoogsteder, M., Maier, R. and Elbers, E. (1998) Adult-Child Interaction, Joint Problem Solving and the Structure of Cooperation, in Woodhead, M., Faulkner, D. and Littleton, K. (eds) *Cultural Worlds of Early Childhood*. London: Routledge in association with The Open University.

This chapter looks at different types of relationships and interactions between children and the adults in their classroom. It is useful to consider your own practice in relation to the descriptions identified.

Macintyre, C. (2005) *Identifying Additional Learning Needs*. Abingdon: Routledge.

Chapter 2 of this book, titled 'Listen to the Children Explain Their Difficulties', provides some interesting case studies which will help you identify examples of children's voices.

Wood, D. (1998) Aspects of Teaching and Learning, in Woodhead, M., Faulkner, D. and Littleton, K. (eds) *Cultural Worlds of Early Childhood*. London: Routledge in association with The Open University.

David Wood in Chapter 9 reflects on the way in which the questions asked by the teacher and types of language used can affect the level of response by children.

Web-based material

Involving Children and Young People in Decisions About Their Education (report produced by Enquire, the Scottish advice service for additional support for learning): www.enquire.org.uk/pcp/pdf/involving-young-people.pdf (last accessed 4 October 2013).

Listening to and Involving Children and Young People (guidance and advice by the Department for Education): http://media.education.gov.uk/assets/files/pdf/l/listening%20to%20and%20 involving%20children%20and%20young%20people.pdf (last accessed 4 October 2013).

Listening to Children's Perspectives: Improving the Quality of Provision in Early Years Settings (useful research report by Coleyshaw, Whitmarsh, Jopling and Hadfield commissioned by the Department for Education): www.gov.uk/government/uploads/system/uploads/attachment_data/file/183412/DfE-RR239b_report.pdf (last accessed 4 October 2013).

UNICEF (information explaining each Article in The Convention on the Rights of the Child at www.unicef.org/crc/index_understanding.html (last accessed 4 October 2013).

References

Billington, T. (2006) *Working with Children*. London: Sage.

Clark, A. and Moss, P. (2011) *Listening to Young Children: The Mosaic Approach*, 2nd edn. London: National Children's Bureau.

Department for Education (DfE) (2011) *Support and Aspiration: A New Approach to Special Educational Needs and Disability*, a consultation (Green Paper). London: HMSO.

Department for Education (DfE) (2012a) Listening to and Involving Children and Young People. Online: http://media.education.gov.uk/assets/files/pdf/l/listening%20to%20and%20involving%20 children%20and%20young%20people.pdf (last accessed 4 October 2013).

Department for Education (DfE) (2012b) *Teachers' Standards*. Online: http://media.education.gov. uk/assets/files/pdf/t/teachers%20standards%20information.pdf (last accessed 4 October 2013).

Department for Education and Skills (DfES) (2001) *Special Educational Needs Code of Practice*. London: The Stationery Office.

Longley, M. and Sharma, S. (2011) Listening to Voices of Children and Families, Together, in Trodd, L. and Chivers, L. (eds) *Interprofessional Working in Practice: Learning and Working Together for Children and Families*. Maidenhead: Open University Press.

Mosley, J. (1996) *Quality Circle Time in the Primary Classroom: Your Essential Guide to Enhancing Self-Esteem, Self-Discipline and Positive Relationships*. London: LDA.

Rinaldi, C. (2006) *In Dialogue with Reggio Emilia: Listening, Researching and Learning*. New York: Routledge.

Todd, L. (2007) *Partnerships for Inclusive Education: A Critical Approach to Collaborative Working*. Abingdon: RoutledgeFalmer.

United Nations (1990) *Convention on the Rights of the Child*. Office of the High Commissioner for Human Rights: www.ohchr.org/EN/ProfessionalInterest/Pages/CRC.aspx (last accessed 4 October 2013).

Wood, D. (1998) Aspects of Teaching and Learning, in Woodhead, M., Faulkner, D. and Littleton, K. (eds) *Cultural Worlds of Early Childhood*. London: Routledge in association with The Open University.

9 Working with parents

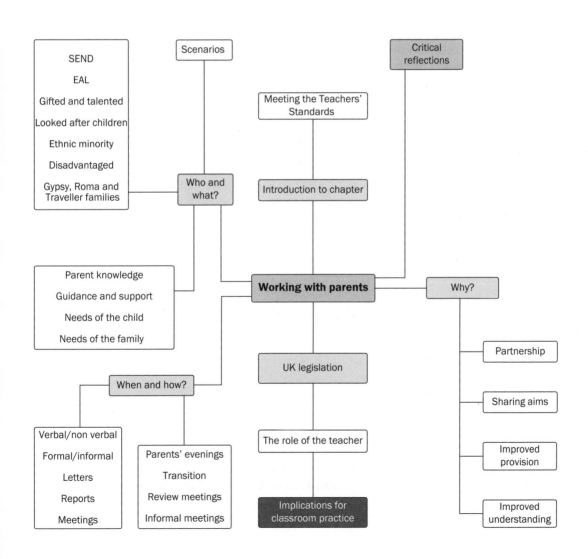

SEND
EAL
Gifted and talented
Looked after children
Ethnic minority
Disadvantaged
Gypsy, Roma and Traveller families

Scenarios

Critical reflections

Meeting the Teachers' Standards

Who and what?

Introduction to chapter

Parent knowledge
Guidance and support
Needs of the child
Needs of the family

Working with parents

Why?

Partnership

UK legislation

Sharing aims

When and how?

Verbal/non verbal
Formal/informal
Letters
Reports
Meetings

Parents' evenings
Transition
Review meetings
Informal meetings

The role of the teacher

Improved provision

Implications for classroom practice

Improved understanding

Introduction

As you will have discovered from reading other chapters in this book, supporting children who have additional needs can be a challenging process which requires many strategies and approaches to ensure progress. There will be occasions when you need to consider and try out different approaches until you find the ones that meet each individual child's needs. Knowing where to begin can sometimes be difficult, particularly if the child is new to your school or Early Years' setting, as you will not be able to build on the interventions already in place. Alternatively, the barriers to learning, and therefore the needs, may develop and change over time and so a previously used approach may become inappropriate. Whatever the case, there is an important partnership you should use to help you learn more about the child and identify possible approaches: this is your partnership with the parents and/or carers. Note that throughout this chapter the term 'parents' is used; this encompasses other adults with parental responsibility, including relatives from the child's extended family, or carers such as foster parents.

Parents will know their child better than anyone else and will have developed ways to support the child and help him or her address and cope with many of the barriers faced in day-to-day life. This chapter considers the aspects that need to be understood in relation to listening to parents. It also reflects on your role as a trainee teacher and the implications that listening to parents will have on your practice.

Critical questions

»   *Consider your own experiences of primary or secondary school. Make a list of the ways in which parents were encouraged to play a part in your education.*

»   *Consider the needs of pupils in the settings you have worked with while on placement. Make a list of the ways in which parents were encouraged to take part in the school life.*

»   *Compare your experiences as a learner with those as a trainee teacher. Do you feel provision in schools for children and their parents has changed?*

MEETING THE TEACHERS' STANDARDS

Links to Department for Education Teachers' Standards May 2012

TS 1; 2; 5; 8

In working towards the DfE Teachers' Standards (2012), you will need to *set goals that stretch and challenge pupils of all backgrounds, abilities and dispositions* (p 7) and *be aware of pupils' capabilities* (p 7). Effective and informative discussion with parents can help you begin to address these aspects. You are required to ensure you consider the *strengths and needs of all pupils* (p 8) by teaching appropriately and to *communicate effectively with parents with regard to pupils' achievements and well-being* (p 9). By forming working partnerships with the parents of the children you teach, you can ensure you have a better understanding of the child, his/her strengths and needs and home-life experiences; this will contribute to a shared understanding and collaborative approach in supporting physical, social, emotional and intellectual development.

Who am I listening to and what can I learn?

In Chapter 2: Understanding identity and gender, you considered the many different backgrounds and childhood experiences that shape a child's identity. The familial influences (parents, siblings and extended-family members) contribute greatly to these experiences, and parents will usually raise their children in an environment that reflects their own culture, beliefs, religious choices and lifestyle preferences. By encouraging a partnership with parents, you will be able to gain an insight into the child's home life and how they are supported to grow and develop.

Special educational needs and disability

Parents of a child with an identified special educational need or disability (SEND) will have already had contact with other professionals to discuss the child's barriers to learning and making progress. In the case of a physical disability, it is possible that the parents are the first to notice that the child may not be developing as they expect and so will arrange the first of many visits to the doctor or other health professional.

SCENARIO

Molly, aged 4

Molly's parents noticed that Molly did not lift her head, sit up or crawl during her first year and became worried when she did not seem to be doing the same things that her older brother had done at a similar age. They took Molly to the GP at the local doctor's surgery and were referred to a specialist for tests at the hospital. After four months of consultations, Molly was diagnosed with cerebral palsy. Molly and her parents have received a lot of guidance and resources (such as a walking frame) to help them support Molly. They know how to encourage Molly to be as independent as possible and how to overcome the barriers related to her poor mobility. They recognise when Molly is very tired and needs to rest and also how her disability can impact on her social and emotional development. Sharing their knowledge with Molly's Early Years' teacher has allowed the teacher to quickly learn effective strategies to use in the classroom to enhance the settling-in process in Molly's new school.

Critical questions

» *What are the barriers that you think Molly will face in the classroom?*

» *Make a list of questions that you could ask Molly's parents to help you plan for her learning in your classroom.*

Molly's parents have been able to draw on their experiences of supporting her at home and have found ways to make the day-to-day living more accessible and manageable. Sharing strategies such as moving from one place to another, what kinds of specialist cutlery Molly can use independently, or knowing her physical limits, all provide her teacher with insights into how to continue her support at school. This means that many aspects of Molly's daily experiences do not need to be re-established by the teacher, which can be time consuming and may slow down Molly's progress. As Macintyre (2005) points out, *without this communication, valuable time can be lost and much energy wasted in reinventing the wheel or trying out things that do not work* (p 37).

It is important that all those supporting Molly ensure she is able to concentrate on starting school and to enjoy the social, emotional and intellectual aspects of each day in the same way that her peers do. Eliminating as many of the mobility and motor control challenges that might arise in school by implementing already-identified strategies from the home reduces some of these barriers.

Ethnic minority or different religious backgrounds and preferences

There may be children in the classroom who have different ethnic or religious backgrounds from their peers. It is not always possible to have a full understanding of what each of these backgrounds and practices are like for each child. However, by creating an open and effective dialogue with the parents, it is possible to have an insight into how the cultural, traditional or religious practices may impact on each child's life.

SCENARIO

Qasir, aged 8

Qasir's grandparents moved to the north of England from the Kashmir region of Pakistan when Qasir's father was 11. His father returned to Pakistan and married when he was 22 and the couple returned to England and have since had three children. Qasir is the eldest child. Qasir's father is an engineer and his mother is a housewife. The family follow the Islamic faith, which includes attending the local Mosque, wearing appropriate clothing, such as the shalwar kameez (men and women) and the hijab (women), and eating appropriate foods. Qasir attends Mosque school to learn about the Islamic faith, the Qur'an, and to learn to read Arabic. His lessons are on Wednesdays, Thursdays and Fridays from 6.30–8pm and from 10am–1pm on Saturdays and Sundays. Qasir's teacher at school and his parents have discussed how these expectations may impact on his school life.

Critical questions

» *Consider a typical Thursday for Qasir. Make a timetable of his day, including meal times, schools and opportunities to play and be with his family.*

»   *How can you ensure that any homework you set can be completed without putting*
    Qasir under undue pressure?

Teachers in the school understand how attending Mosque school can limit the amount of
time Qasir and other Muslim boys have to complete their homework and attend after-school
clubs in the evening. They are also sensitive to the need for dressing modestly, particularly
during physical education lessons. Staff who provide school lunches ensure a vegetarian
menu is available. Qasir's parents are happy to meet with his teacher to discuss aspects of
his cultural and religious practices and this ensures that expectations are shared and that
he experiences no disadvantage to either his home or school life.

Gypsy, Roma and Traveller families

You may need to be aware of cultural expectations and experiences distinct to Traveller families. Children may attend the school for short or long periods, depending on whether their
families are living permanently in the area or visiting for a few weeks or months before they
move on. These families are protected by the Equality Act (UK Government, 2010) as being
a distinct ethnicity and may have Roma, Gypsy, circus or New Traveller backgrounds. One
particular challenge for the class teacher is being unaware of the child's current attainment
or whether they have any identified additional needs. Due to the transient nature of the family lifestyle, it is likely that school records and assessment information is not immediately
available from the previous school and so transition to the new school may not be as seam-
less as it could be. Therefore, by being welcoming and encouraging to the parents, you can
gain much of the vital information needed during the first few days and weeks. Derrington's
(2011) comments are helpful in recognising that this relationship may take some time to
develop, though: *Traveller parents do tend to be very child-centred and highly protective, and
it may take time and effort for a trusting relationship to develop between home and school*
(p 47).

English as an additional language (EAL)

You will need to be aware of children in your class who speak English as a second, third or
even fourth language. They are not considered to have SEN, but additional support in the
classroom is often vital in supporting their social, emotional and intellectual progress. While
it is possible that these children's cultural or religious needs may also be different from many
of the other children in the class, this is not always the case. If you have a child in your class
who is in the very early stages of learning English, you may find that they benefit from the
support of another person (adult or child) who also speaks their first language to aid with
inclusion and integration. It may also be possible that one or more members of the child's
family have limited understanding and use of English and so communication with parents is
likely to be challenging and something at which you will need to persevere.

Gifted and talented

There may be some children in the class who are working at levels above those expected for
their age. An effective relationship between the parents and the class teacher is helpful in
ensuring that support is provided for the child, both at home and school, that expectations

are shared and that aims are realistically identified. It is important to make sure that each child who is identified as being gifted and talented in one or more curriculum areas is provided with learning objectives and tasks which are interesting, promote progress and encourage engagement. Children who are not engaged or enthused to learn can sometimes behave inappropriately due to boredom or not feeling challenged by the learning activities. It is therefore helpful if the teacher and parents can identify the child's areas of interest and provide stimulating learning experiences to encourage a depth and breadth of knowledge and skills. It is not always appropriate only to encourage progression through the attainment levels, but also to help the child understand how their knowledge can be applied to other activities and curriculum areas.

Looked after children

A child who is in foster care, a children's residential home or going through the adoption process is considered to be in the care of the local authority, and their well-being, care and education is monitored by the Looked After Children (LAC) team at the Department of Social Services. In the same way that an effective relationship needs to be established with parents, the partnership between carers and the class teacher is equally important. A child who is no longer looked after by their biological parents may have experienced traumatic events which have led to them being in care, and a holistic approach to their social, emotional, physical and intellectual development needs to be established. Updated guidance from the Department of Education (2010) based on the Children Act (UK Government, 1989) identifies that looked after children should be allocated a social worker and designated teacher (often the teacher responsible for safeguarding children) to oversee their care. This includes ensuring that children are given opportunities to attend after-school clubs, go on school trips and receive appropriate induction and transition support. They also track assessment and attendance and ensure that possible problems such as transport to and from school, getting funding for extra activities or school uniform, and liaison with the biological parents and siblings, where appropriate, are addressed. The class teacher will be able to contribute to these aspects and may also need to be aware of who brings the child to and from school, particularly if custody for childcare is an issue.

As you can see, there are many situations that you and the class teacher need to be aware of when supporting the diverse needs of the children in the class. These can be addressed by building an effective dialogue with the parents. To ensure this partnership is given the time and opportunity to develop and be maintained, specific meetings need to be arranged.

Critical questions

» *For each of the case studies above, create a spidergram showing the range of diverse approaches that you need to adopt when supporting each of the parents.*

» *What positive aspects of school–home partnership can you identify in the sections above? Consider how you could implement these positive aspects in your own relationships with parents.*

» *Consider ineffective home–school partnerships from your own or others' experiences. Consider why they were ineffective and how they could be improved and developed.*

When and how can I listen to and meet with parents?

There are several meetings identified throughout the school year in which the class teacher and Special Educational Needs Co-ordinator (SENCo) meet with parents. As a trainee teacher, it may be that some of these meetings take place while you are in school. Asking if you can be involved in or observe these meetings would be beneficial to your understanding of provision and may help you identify specific targets for the child when you are planning and teaching. It is important to remember, however, that these meetings are confidential and may include discussions that are sensitive and, as a result, your presence may not be appropriate. Some meetings will be arranged for all children and their parents, such as termly or annual parents' evenings, class talks when the teacher may be introducing new information, or during transition periods when parents are invited to the school to meet their child's new teacher. There will also be meetings specific to a child's needs and circumstances, such as SEND review meetings or child protection/safeguarding meetings. An overview of each of these is discussed in the table below.

Types and purposes of meetings with parents

Meeting	Attendees	Focus	Things to consider
Parents' evenings	Parents Teacher	• To discuss the child's progress • To explain and reflect on the learning that has taken place • To discuss social and emotional well-being • To consider the targets for the next stage	This can be a difficult event for parents who have negative memories of their own education or those who have to discuss concerns such as behaviour issues or lack of progress.
Transition meetings	Parents Current and new teachers Support staff where relevant	• To introduce children and parents to their new class or school and teacher • To support children who have part-time education in a specialist setting or unit • To support Travellers' children who are moving between schools and areas	Early Years and Year 6 teachers tend to be most closely involved with formal transitions, though any transition from one year group to another can be improved by providing activities, visits and talks.
SEND review meetings	Parents Teacher SENCo Teaching support staff Other professionals involved in the child's care Child (where appropriate)	• To review and update the education or care plans in place for a child with a Statement of Special Needs • To review local authority provision such as health care • To identify changes to the child's needs and abilities • To set new targets, identify how they can be met and who will be involved in the support process	These meetings are a requirement of the SEN CoP and must take place every year, though many schools carry out interim reviews as well. Due to some SEND diagnoses, the child's needs can change more frequently due to the developmental nature and the child's age, so it is important for parents and teachers to share this information.

Meeting	Attendees	Focus	Things to consider
Child Protection meetings	Parents Social Worker Designated teacher for safeguarding Class teacher Other professionals providing support to the family who are relevant to the current focus targets	• To set and review targets in place to ensure the child's welfare is improving • To identify the appropriate professionals to take part in the process • To support the parents throughout the process so that their parenting and care of the child is effective	Concerns such as inadequate parenting, housing, neglect or the child's exposure to drugs or inappropriate adults are common aspects for discussion at safeguarding/child protection meetings. Partnership between parents and professionals can be difficult at times like this due to the nature of the meetings. As a result, you may find that your involvement as a trainee teacher is limited or discouraged.
Informal meetings	Parents Teacher Other colleagues such as the SENCo or head teacher may be invited depending on the nature of the meeting	• To find a mutually convenient time in which to meet with the parents and respond to their queries or concerns • To invite parents into the classroom to take part in activities with their child • To share their child's achievements through an assembly or open session in class • To take part in fundraising activities • To take part in activities such as Sport's Day	In addition to these sessions being good ways to build a rapport with the parents, most of the informal meetings tend to be times when children can share their achievements with their parents. Some schools also provide sessions in which children and their parents with specific needs can attend support groups such as family learning sessions, family nurture groups or family literacy and English communication programmes.

Critical questions

Think about the body language and consider the verbal communication used between a class teacher and parents.

» *Which aspects of body language promote a good relationship between the teacher and parent? (Consider eye contact, body position, how the furniture is arranged in the meeting, use of hands and arms.)*

» *Think about the verbal language used. Is specific educational terminology used? Is there a shared understanding? How could misunderstandings occur in relation to the types of language used?*

» *Consider parent and teacher meetings from the point of view of parents. What might these meetings be like if the parents are very nervous or uncomfortable with the teacher or school setting? What might these meetings be like if the parents are very angry about something? How could you improve the quality of the communication with parents in each of these situations?*

Why is effective communication with parents so important?

Sharing information

Consideration of the diverse needs of parents must be made in the case of all meetings and sharing of written documents with them. Parents who have limited or no understanding of English, those who have difficulties with reading, or those with visual or hearing impairments will need additional support to access the information to ensure they have a comprehensive understanding of what is being shared. This will help them be aware of what is happening at school, what is expected of them and how they can work with the school to support their child. This consideration applies to all the meetings, letters to parents, school brochures or prospectus, the school website and any forms that parents are expected to complete. It may be possible to arrange bilingual documentation if there is a large number of families who share a language in addition to English, or it may be useful to work with another colleague, pupil or parent to act as translator. It is not uncommon for an older sibling to attend some meetings with a parent with limited English so that they can translate between teacher and their parent.

Sharing aims and expectations

Achieving a partnership in which the parents and the teacher have shared expectations and understanding of their aims for the child is crucial. By clearly defining the targets that are appropriate for the child's progress, everyone can work together to achieve the same goals. There is no doubt that in almost every case, parents want the very best for their child. After all, a child is the most precious thing in their lives and the main concern for them is to ensure that their child is happy, healthy, secure and confident and has the best opportunities to succeed. The class teacher can reassure the parents that this is a shared concern by talking with them and agreeing educational and personal well-being aims while the child is in school.

The use of specialist terminology is common in schools. Many teachers may refer to aspects of learning by using such terminology or abbreviations; for example, teachers are familiar with SSP (systematic synthetic phonics) but this may be unfamiliar to many who are not involved in education, including the parents. Therefore it is important for you to take care when using such terminology and to ensure the parents understand what is being referred to. This is equally important when referring to aspects of disability, such as diagnoses, to cultural or religious terms or to terms that are specific to particular families. Parents may talk about aspects of their child's life which the teacher is unfamiliar with and by having an open and friendly teacher–parent relationship with them it is much easier to ask 'Can you explain what you mean?'

Sharing expectations between parents and the teacher is important. These expectations may range from levels of parental involvement in school, appropriate behaviour, completion of homework, uniform or levels of progress and achievement. Any parent who is unsure about how much support they should give their child with their homework, what uniform should be worn, or how much they are expected to go into school can be easily reassured and the expectations clarified. However, it can be more challenging for parents and teachers to have shared expectations in relation to behaviour or progress targets, particularly if the child is identified with SEN or a disability or who comes from a different cultural background. Discussing the aims and expectations, why they are important and how they will be beneficial to the child is more likely to result in a shared approach than merely producing a list of targets.

Being very clear about who is responsible for aspects of the child's learning will help promote a more effective partnership. Macintyre (2005) states, *both parties can feel inadequate, not sure of the role they have to play, and be left wondering about how the other is assessing them* (p 37).

If there is any doubt in the minds of the parents or teacher regarding who is responsible for particular elements of the child's learning or care, then uncertainty can develop; feelings of resentment could even occur if one person feels the other has either neglected to address, or taken over, an area of responsibility they thought they had. Possible aspects specific to the pupil's additional needs might include administration of medicines, provision of resources, or certain learning or care strategies. This issue of who is responsible, and for what, should be discussed and clarified at the review meetings and the support, guidance and experience of the SENCo is often helpful.

Parent Partnership support groups

Being a parent can be a difficult, worrying and sometimes lonely process. Building effective partnerships with staff in the school may be daunting for parents. They may feel apprehensive about building relationships with a new professional, particularly if they have had negative experiences of visiting medical practitioners or members of the social services team, or they may have memories of unsuccessful relationships with teachers when they were at school. Whatever the circumstances, the National Parent Partnership Network is in place to work with parents and give them advice, support and strategies to promote good partnerships with schools and local authorities. It is recommended that the SENCo or class teacher give the parents the contact details of the service. The Parent Partnership Service will provide support by putting the parents in touch with other families in similar circumstances, by guiding them through the SEN or disability identification and review processes and by acting as an intermediary where the partnership with the school or local authority has broken down. Every local authority is required by law to provide a Parent Partnership Service and parents and teachers will find the impartial advice and documentation they provide useful.

UK legislation

In 2010 the Equality Act was published. This Act has consolidated and updated earlier legislation found in the Race Relations Act, the Disability Discrimination Act and the Sex Discrimination Act. The Equality Act (2010) states that schools cannot discriminate against children with a protected characteristic such as disability, race or religion. It also clearly defines discrimination by association, in which anyone with a link to that person with the protected characteristic, such as a parent, carer or sibling, should also receive the same legal protection.

The Special Educational Needs Code of Practice (DfES, 2001) was approved by Parliament to ensure that schools and local authorities provide effective care for children with SEND. The Code provides definitions, policies and regulations that schools must follow. It also provides guidance on the identification, provision and review processes for Early Years, primary and secondary providers. The Code also identifies the partnership between parents and schools as a fundamental and vital aspect of the support for children. It states:

> *Parents hold key information and have a critical role to play in their children's edu-cation. They have unique strengths, knowledge and experience to contribute to the shared view of a child's needs and the best ways of supporting them ... All parents of children with special educational needs should be treated as partners. (2001, p 16)*

It is anticipated that the current Code of Practice will be replaced in 2014 by a new Code which is currently going through the consultation process. The SEN and Disability Green Paper *Support and Aspiration* (DfE, 2011) continues the previous Code's intentions for ensuring parents play a key role in the SEND process. The Green Paper states that many parents did not feel that provision reflected their needs in the past. The new code aims to *give parents more control over support for their child and family ... ending the frustration, complexity and confrontation inherent in today's system* (2011, 2:3, p 41).

You will need to be aware of the legislation and changes to the Code of Practice for support-ing the diverse needs of learners in your classroom and you need to understand how the expectations, aims and law impact on your practice.

The role of the teacher and trainee

... the onus is on the school staff to initiate, encourage and support parental involvement (Westwood, 2013, p 86).

To foster effective relationships with parents, regardless of the diverse backgrounds and needs of the children, it is necessary to be positive and understand how beneficial they can be to your teaching role. If you can create an open, friendly and welcoming school and class-room, parents are more likely to feel comfortable in the setting and will therefore be more likely to engage in discussions with you. While your primary role is to plan, teach, assess and support the progress of the children in your class, finding time to develop the parent partner-ship is also very important. Being able to listen to parents' concerns, ideas and practices in relation to their child will help you to provide appropriate support for children with additional needs or from diverse backgrounds. It will also enable you to reassure parents and be more proactive in your classroom organisation or provision.

A useful approach to use when considering if your partnership with parents is effective is to try to look at it from their perspective. Imagine how it might feel if you were the parent, and think about how the meetings and visits to the school might make you feel. It might also help to talk to friends or relatives who are parents and consider how they feel about the partner-ships with teachers they have experienced.

Implications for practice

As the trainee teacher, you should be keen to ensure that your practice encourages and maintains good working relationships with all parents of the children you support while on placement. There are a number of specific approaches and strategies that you can use to enhance the partnerships you have with parents.

Good communication skills with parents are vital

- Make sure that you find an appropriate time and place in which to meet; somewhere where you can concentrate on your conversation and where you are not going to be disturbed or distracted by other people or events.

- Be aware of your body language and tone of voice.

- Listen carefully to what the parents are telling you and if you do not understand what they say, ask for clarification or for them to explain again.

- Aim to reiterate to the parents what they have just told you so that they are reassured that you understand what they are saying.

- Work together to agree strategies and approaches that can be used at home and at school; this will create a shared responsibility and understanding.

- Be sure that you explain to parents what you are hoping to achieve, why it is relevant and how it will support their child. This may include homework tasks that you set, information about extracurricular activities or school trips; the more parents understand, the more likely they are to work in partnership with you.

Liaison with colleagues in school is also something you need to consider

- Sharing information with the SENCo, designated teacher for LAC, Safeguarding Co-ordinator and/or bilingual support teacher will help the effectiveness of the partnerships; and this is a two-way process – you will provide as well as receive information.

- Sharing formative and summative assessment data with classroom support colleagues, other classroom teachers and the SENCo will enhance the target-setting process.

- The greater depth and knowledge you have of the child's understanding and skills, the more informed you and the SENCo can be in review meetings and this will be reassuring to the parents.

Ask for advice, further information and guidance if you are not sure

- You cannot have in-depth knowledge of all the additional needs that children will have in relation to their SEN, disability, race, religion or culture, so you must be prepared to ask for advice.

- Other teachers who have also taught a child in your class will be able to share the strategies and approaches they have used, and the SENCo will be able to give guidance or make contact with another professional for advice.

- People in the community or older siblings will be happy to talk to you about their race, religion or culture if you ask them and explain your desire to know more.

- In addition to asking for advice about specific needs, it is also useful to talk to your teaching colleagues about effective ways to build good partnerships with parents; find out what has worked for them and be prepared to try them out.

Keep a journal or diary

- Regular notes about each child's welfare can help to identify further needs, as well as strategies that are or are not successful and to comment and give evidence of concerns.

- This is particularly important when working with children for whom you may have safeguarding concerns or for whom attendance and punctuality is an issue. By keeping a record, the cumulative evidence will support the next steps in provision.

Critical reflections

» *When you are on placement, a parent confides in you that they find reading the school documents and letters difficult and that they are worried that they might miss a meeting or open morning because of this. What can you do about this?*

» *Consider the diverse needs of the children who could be in your class. What kinds of approaches might you consider to develop the partnerships with their parents?*

» *How would you justify these to your class teacher or SENCo?*

Taking it further

Books and journals

Digman, C. and Soan, S. (2008) *Working with Parents: A Guide for Education Professionals.* London: Sage.

> This book considers the home–school links and the role of the professional who works with parents. Chapter 4 'Special Educational Needs: Learning Difficulties' broadens the view of home–school partnership and the range of interventions available to parents of children with SEND.

Moore, M. (2011) Including Parents with Disabled Children, in Richards, G. and Armstrong, F. (eds) *Teaching and Learning in Diverse and Inclusive Classrooms: Key Issues for New Teachers.* Abingdon: Routledge.

> Moore's discussion of 'social model thinking' in Chapter 12 demonstrates how this approach can be used to reduce the extent of exclusion for disabled children. Her viewpoint as a parent of a disabled child as well as an academic and professional is insightful and helpful.

Richards, G. and Armstrong, F. (eds) (2010) *Teaching and Learning in Diverse and Inclusive Classrooms: Key Issues for New Teachers.* Abingdon: Routledge.

> This book is a useful resource for any new or trainee teacher. Chapter 4 gives comprehensive information and guidance for teachers working with Traveller families.

Westwood, P. (2013) *Inclusive and Adaptive Teaching: Meeting the Challenge of Diversity in the Classroom*. London: Routledge.

> Chapter 8 'Accessing and Utilizing Support' provides useful information for trainees who seek further information and guidance about supporting learners and their parents. There are also chapters providing further information on aspects mentioned in this chapter such as gifted and talented, culture, disability and language.

Web-based material

Children in Care (guidance and advice): www.education.gov.uk/childrenandyoungpeople/families/childrenincare (last accessed 4 October 2013).

Ethnic Minority support (guidance and advice): www.education.gov.uk/schools/pupilsupport/inclusionandlearnersupport/mea/a0013246/ethnicminorityachievement (last accessed 4 October 2013).

National Parent Partnership Network: www.parentpartnership.org.uk (last accessed 4 October 2013).

Parental involvement (guidance and advice): www.education.gov.uk/schools/pupilsupport/parents/a0014567/parental-involvement (last accessed 4 October 2013).

References

Department for Children, Schools and Families (DCSF) (2010) *Promoting the Educational Achievement of Looked After Children*. Nottingham: DCSF Publications.

Department for Education (DfE) (2011) *Support and Aspiration: A New Approach to Special Educational Needs and Disability*, a consultation (Green Paper). London: HMSO.

Department for Education (DfE) (2012) *Teachers' Standards*. Online: http://media.education.gov.uk/assets/files/pdf/t/teachers%20standards%20information.pdf (last accessed 4 October 2013).

Department for Education and Skills (DfES) (2001) *Special Educational Needs Code of Practice*. London: The Stationery Office.

Department for Education and Skills (DfES) (2004) *Every Child Matters: Change for Children*. Nottingham: DfES Publications.

Derrington, C. (2011) Supporting Gypsy, Roma and Traveller Pupils, in Richards, G. and Armstrong, F. (eds) *Teaching and Learning in Diverse and Inclusive Classrooms: Key Issues for New Teachers*. Abingdon: Routledge.

Macintyre, C. (2005) *Identifying Additional Learning Needs*. Abingdon: Routledge.

UK Government (1989) *The Children Act 1989*, Chapter 41. London: The Stationery Office.

UK Government (2010) *The Equality Act 2010*, Chapter 15. London: The Stationery Office. Online: www.legislation.gov.uk/ukpga/2010/15/pdfs/ukpga_20100015_en.pdf (last accessed 4 October 2013).

Westwood, P. (2013) *Inclusive and Adaptive Teaching: Meeting the Challenge of Diversity in the Classroom*. Abingdon: Routledge.

10 Working with colleagues

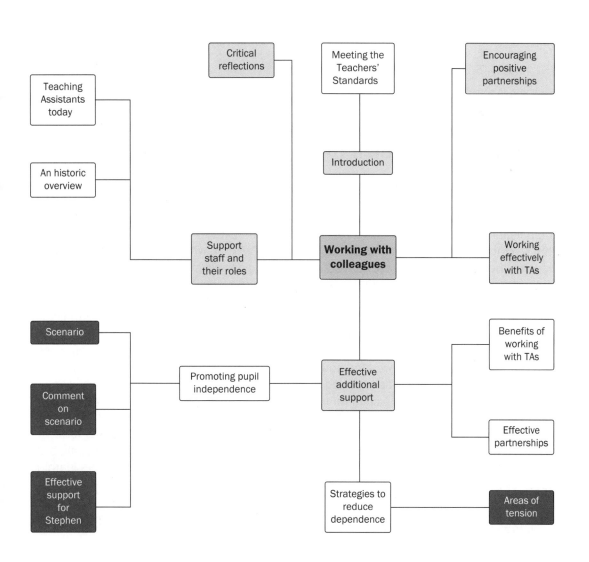

Introduction

This chapter highlights the necessity for good working relationships with colleagues, in particular TAs. Teachers and TAs work together to support the learning development of all pupils and this chapter focuses on the quality of the working relationship and the benefits of working together in a successful partnership.

The introduction of effective support begins with an emphasis on good communication. The discussion of successful communication strategies outlines the benefits to children and the potential pitfalls. There are links to recent studies, and the impact of TAs' support on pupil progress is examined. An assessment of the possible tensions and dissonances that are linked to the historical working practices of TAs emphasises the contradiction between the medical and the social model of inclusive working practices.

MEETING THE TEACHERS' STANDARDS

Links to Department for Education Teachers' Standards May 2012

TS1: 1 & 2; TS 8: 2; TS8: 3; TS 8:4

Part 2 Personal and Professional Conduct

Support staff and their roles

An historical overview

TAs began to make an appearance in schools in the 1960s, mostly in a voluntary role, but more inclusively in the 1980s, as a result of the Warnock Report (1978) recommendations that were incorporated into the 1981 Education Act. Children with special educational needs began to be educated in mainstream schools with supportive statements of need and close support from TAs for children with complex learning and behavioural needs. Teaching assistants were attached to and only worked with specific children, giving rise to the term 'velcroed' TAs. TAs who had a more general role in class were initially used to provide assistance for all non-teaching activities. These classroom assistants were regarded as a useful extra pair of hands. They were also nicknamed the 'mums' army' because the workforce was mostly female and wanted suitable working hours to accommodate their family's needs. No teaching was expected: that role was reserved for trained teachers. Classroom assistants were on hand to wash paint pots, help children into coats and shoes, provide support with displays and they soon became adept with sticky-backed plastic! Gradually the role has changed, and after the remodelling of the workforce in 2002 there is now a higher ratio of TAs to teachers, with a clearer understanding of duties and responsibilities and much greater availability of formal training. It is now customary for all teachers to have a TA to support the learning needs of the pupils, if not on a daily basis, then at least for some part of the week.

The DfEE (2002) produced a good practice guide for working with TAs, recommending that the role should encompass four dimensions of:

- support for teachers;

- supporting the curriculum;

- support for particular pupils;

- supporting the whole school.

This firmly established a role that went beyond 'helping' in the classroom and support for children with special educational needs. The recommendation gave clarity to the role and underlined the intention that TAs were in class to support pupils' learning.

The number of full-time TA-equivalent posts in schools in England increased from 61,000 to 162,900 over a ten-year period from 1997 to 2006 (DfES, 2007). This was mainly due to the Labour government's policy of modernisation and remodelling of the school workforce. The increased use of TAs was seen as a way of reducing teacher workload. It was at this time that the term 'classroom assistant' changed to 'teaching assistant', with later addition of the term 'learning support assistant', which is more commonly used in schools to refer to those TAs who work with students who have the label of special educational needs.

Blatchford et al. (2012), reporting on their large-scale study, The Deployment and Impact of Support Staff (DISS) Project, cite government statistics that show an increase in the number of full-time-equivalent TA posts in all mainstream schools in England since 1997 to a total of 170,000 in 2010.This represented 24 per cent of the workforce in mainstream schools overall, and, more specifically, 32 per cent of the workforce in mainstream nursery and primary schools. This study also found that, by 2010, TAs comprised 44 per cent of the primary school workforce in Wales, and 24 per cent in Scotland.

Teaching Assistants today

There are now many different types and categories of teaching assistant but, for the purposes of this chapter, the abbreviation TA is used generically. Some TAs may have undergone training for the delivery of a specific intervention, for example, a phonics programme, which results in a particular expertise. Some TAs may still be used specifically for pupils who have the label of special educational needs and others may have an extra qualification such as the higher level teaching assistant (HLTA).

Most TAs fall into the following categories.

- **Teaching assistants** (TAs) work alongside teachers, helping with pupils' learning on an individual or group basis; some specialise, eg literacy, numeracy, SEND, music, EAL, and creative arts learning.

- **Learning support assistants** (LSAs) refers to those TAs who work in small groups or one-to-one with students who have special educational needs.

- **Higher level teaching assistants** (HLTAs) are experienced TAs who plan and deliver learning activities under the direction of a teacher, and assess, record and report on pupils' progress. They may also supervise a whole class if required. The government no longer funds the training for HLTAs, but it is planned that the National College of Teaching and Leadership will continue to maintain and review the HLTA professional standards.

- **Nursery nurses** work in co-operation with teachers and are concerned with children's social and educational development; they may plan and supervise activities and inform parents about a child's progress. Many nursery nurses have a level 3 qualification in Childcare or Early Years and Education (previously known as NNEB).

- **Cover supervisors** are 'suitably trained' staff who supervise pupils when teaching staff are absent.

- **Learning mentors** are suitably trained adults who motivate and challenge pupils who are underachieving. They help pupils overcome barriers to learning caused by social, emotional and behavioural problems.

- **Bilingual teaching assistants** share a language and cultural heritage with pupils and are uniquely able to build on forms of knowledge and cultural experience brought from pupils' homes.

- **Student teachers** may either be on placement or on school-based teacher training programmes such as Schools Direct.

Critical questions

TAs are treated as low-paid 'minders' coaxing pupils to comply with an otherwise undifferentiated and often inappropriate curriculum *(Gross, 2000, p 127)*.

» *In what ways do you think this statement is justified?*

» *List the benefits of working with TAs:*

  - *for the teacher;*
  - *for the child;*
  - *for the teacher assistant.*

The role of the TA is varied and diverse. It very much depends on how the school wishes to deploy its assistants. But this list encompasses most of the required support for children's learning. TAs may take on one or several of these tasks:

- ensuring access to the curriculum;
- pre-tutoring;
- helping to manage behaviour;
- observing particular pupils;
- group work on structured intervention programmes;
- preparing differentiated resources;
- working with pupil/s on ICT programmes;
- helping with self-assessment;
- supervising the class while the teacher works with a group/individual;
- revisiting earlier part of session;
- working in home language.

Critical questions

» *Which of the above activities do you think are most suited to the role of TA and why?*

» *Which of the support roles do you think might cause possible tensions and why?*

» *How could these possible tensions be avoided?*

Encouraging positive partnerships

Butt and Lance (2005) emphasised *the need for sensitivity of approach* when partnering TAs because of the nature of the imbalance of power between that of teacher and TA. Lowe and Pugh (2007), in their study of morality, power and leadership, asked questions of TAs relating to their feelings about their own power and identity. Highlighted in this study was the TA's notion of powerlessness. One TA revealed:

> *As a teaching assistant I am told what my role is and what to do for each day. My role can change several times throughout the day and my role is to follow orders and instructions. (Lowe and Pugh, 2007, p 28)*

Lowe and Pugh's study also recognised that the power status was the TA's own choice. However, it was felt that if they were to gain qualifications then their individual power would increase.

Mills and Mills (1995) highlighted the need for *each partner ... to respect the integrity of the other* (p 125). Hayes (2003), on the other hand, has written of the need for teachers in training to treat fellow workers with *utmost courtesy* in their respective roles. As a professional, it would be unthinkable for you not to be respectful and courteous to your colleagues. Hayes (2003) emphasises that, *many assistants willingly give their time over and above their hours, but it is important not to take what they do for granted* (p 9).

The necessity and availability of training for TAs was recommended with the move away from a focus upon care and ancillary support for teachers to one of additional responsibility in relation to classroom pedagogy. It was recognised that simply providing additional adults in classrooms would not necessarily have a positive impact upon pupil progress unless it was accompanied by opportunities for accredited training and the establishment of a framework of good practice. As a consequence, an expansion in professional development opportunities has been seen as a positive force.

There is now a range of recognised qualifications for support teachers:

* Level 3 Diploma in specialist support for teaching and learning in schools;

* Level 3 Certificate in supporting teaching and learning in schools;

* NVQ 3 in supporting teaching and learning in schools;

* NVQ 3 for TAs;

* Level 3 Certificate for TAs;

* NVQ 3 in Early Years Care and Education;

- Level 3 Diploma for the Children and Young People's Workforce;

- NVQ 3 Childcare and Education;

- NVQ 3 in Children's Care, Learning and Development.

Balshaw (2010) suggests that the opportunities given to TAs to study for qualifications makes a real difference to their confidence and skill in their roles and that TAs are less likely to *close down* pupils' talk for reasons of behaviour management.

There is a need for teachers to form and sustain effective partnerships with TAs, but this can only happen with support from the senior management. Balshaw (2010, p 338) suggests that school leaders who create opportunities for TAs to plan effectively with teachers will see the benefits in successful classroom strategies, with a shared approach to teaching and learning leading to an improvement of the quality of curriculum experience for all pupils.

Difficulties may arise due to the working contracts of some TAs, particularly those who are part time, and due consideration should be given to this when planning meetings. Again this can be helped by senior management providing non-contact time for meetings.

Potential pitfalls and how they may be overcome when working in partnership with TAs

Pitfall	Strategy to overcome
• Confusing variety of job titles, contracts, remits, experience and qualifications. • Confusion as to specific roles and responsibilities of TA and teacher. • Expertise and usefulness of TA under-utilised – feelings of powerlessness. • No allocated protected time to talk or to plan sessions.	• Communication between teacher and TA to clarify TA's role. • Clear lines of communication between teacher and TA. • Valuing of TA's contribution, effective liaison, involvement of TA in planning, IEPs and assessment. Practical and creative ways to enable this to happen. • SMT to arrange for allocated time for planning.

Working effectively with TAs

The question of how much a TA can be involved in planning is a difficult one. Given the differentials in pay between a teacher and a TA, there needs to be a fair allocation of the workload. An in-depth understanding of pedagogy and knowledge of progression within the curriculum is an expectation of teacher training, and the difference in remuneration reflects an expectation of a different knowledge base. However, Moyles and Suschitzky (1997) felt that TAs were functioning *from an inadequate knowledge base* if they were not involved in the planning. Goddard and Ryall (2002) were also of the view that *teachers and teaching assistants should plan and discuss activities in order to ensure understanding and so maximise benefit and efficiency* (p 31). They also suggested that it was essential for teachers to receive feedback from the TA to report back on pupils' progress. There is good reason for TAs to be fully informed and to have some ownership of planning; however, teachers should really bear the overall responsibility for children's learning.

Critical questions

»   *Why do the teacher and TA need to agree on ground rules, ie who does what and when?*

»   *Identify some ground rules for an effective working relationship by considering the expectations of*

a)   *the teacher;*

b)   *the TA.*

»   *How would you manage the following?*

• *overall responsibility for pupils' learning;*

• *recording pupils' progress;*

• *behaviour management: approaches; rewards and sanctions;*

• *pupils' leaving the room on completing work;*

• *marking work and feedback;*

• *role if supported pupil is absent.*

Effective additional support

There have been some interesting and far-reaching longitudinal studies about the effectiveness of TA support on pupils' learning. These studies have produced some surprising and contradictory findings. Blatchford et al.'s (2009) major research report on the deployment and impact of support staff in English schools covered a broad range of areas, including the characteristics of support staff, their conditions of employment, their training, deployment and impact. In relation to their impact, one of Blatchford et al.'s (2009) key and disturbing findings concerned the negative relationship between the amount of support a pupil received and the progress they made in core National Curriculum subjects. The findings were a shock and surprise because, contrary to the expected outcome – that support assistants improved pupil performance – the opposite was found: *the more support pupils received, the less progress they made* (Blatchford et al., 2009, p 135). This finding raised various questions about the future employment and deployment of TAs in mainstream schools.

However, Farrell et al.'s (2010, p 447) study suggests that TAs can have an impact in raising the academic achievement of *specific* groups of pupils with learning difficulties, provided they are trained and supported in this process. This was true of support given to pupils with literacy and language difficulties, although the findings were less positive for pupils with numeracy difficulties. Farrell states that this finding is particularly welcome in view of the less encouraging outcomes from the more general non-targeted intervention studies of Blatchford et al. (2009) and Gerber et al. (2001).

One suggestion for these findings given by Moyles and Suschitzky (1997) is that, where TA support is of a more general nature, assistants may put more focus on completing work set than on learning outcomes. Or, as Giangreco and Doyle (2007) suggest, increased pupil dependence on adults reduces the opportunity for pupil interaction, which can aid learning.

TA support was most effective in situations where the outcome of the tasks was clear. The recommendations from Blatchford's study suggest that schools need to explicitly and rigorously set out the quality of provision and support in relation to anticipated academic outcomes. There were other suggestions for schools about changing the routine deployment of TAs to support lower attaining pupils and those with special educational needs.

The stark statement: *We suggest that pupils in most need should get more not less of a teacher's time* (Blatchford et al., 2009, p 12) is a reminder to all senior management who make the decisions about deployment of school staff that all teachers have a responsibility to teach children with special educational needs.

The studies just discussed were looking at benefits to pupil attainment and academic progress, but there are other benefits to staff and pupils when viewed from a wider perspective. Webster et al.'s (2011, p 13) study suggests that *TAs had a positive effect in mainstream classrooms in terms of reducing off-task behaviour and disruption, and allowing more time for the teacher to teach.*

Benefits of working with TAs

The following list emphasises a few of the positive aspects of working with TAs:

- increased ratio of adult: pupil support;
- flexibility in tailoring support to meet needs (personalised learning);
- another adult with whom to share perspectives, expertise, successes and concerns – it can be lonely in the classroom;
- additional support to enhance attainment, positive behaviour and pastoral care of pupils;
- the undoubted specialist expertise and knowledge of some TAs;
- the opportunity to target support more effectively through specific interventions, eg Early Literacy Support, Additional Literacy Support, Further Literacy Support, Springboard maths, etc.;
- benefits of working in a shared partnership with clear goals about pupils' attitudes to learning and behaviour.

Effective partnerships

Successful partnerships do not just happen; they have to be worked at, redefined and renegotiated. The most successful partnerships have at their core a good working relationship with clear goals. In order to achieve this, there needs to be clearly agreed and defined roles with allocated tasks and clear boundaries. If the teacher and TA know each other's expectations then the relationship in the classroom will achieve 'mutual engagement'. The process of teaching and learning will then be a satisfying one, for both the pupils and the adults.

The school is the main community of learning but each class base is a microcosm of that community with its own identity. Within this small learning community, there should be shared and clearly defined ways of working, giving a sense of purpose and meaning to the learning opportunities that take place. For the teacher and the TA there is a shared account-ability towards the pupils with well-organised and established modes of communication. In this way, you can build a good working relationship with your TAs and value and respect the qualities that they bring to the partnership.

Critical questions

»   *In what ways can you as a class teacher support and develop the skills of a TA assigned to your class for general support of pupil learning?*

»   *How can you ensure that there is a shared approach to behaviour management?*

»   *What is the best way to utilise the TA in the whole-class teaching element of the session?*

Strategies to reduce dependence

One of the criticisms of the practice of assigning TAs to small groups of pupils with special needs while the teacher concentrates on the main body of the class is, as Balshaw (2010) points out, that the *most vulnerable pupils are being further isolated from the teaching their peers experience* (p 337). Although the studies of Blatchford et al. (2009) have suggested that this has proved to be the most successful use of TAs, it can have a negative effect upon the pupils' confidence and self-esteem, knowing that they are in the *slow learners group*. It is a very *medical model* (Mittler, 2000) of practice and is the legacy of the original way funding was organised for the support of children with the label of special educational needs. There is also an argument that this practice of withdrawing children can create dependency on the TA and in some cases further barriers to learning for the child/ren within the groups. A variety of strategies can be used to avoid this.

*   Consider alternative access strategies – the teacher could take the groups.

*   Plan for TAs to work with different groups at different times.

*   TA should remain with pupil/s only as long as takes to ensure understanding of task.

*   Discuss reducing dependence.

*   Model good practice – teachers can share their own higher-order skills and knowledge.

*   Help TAs to develop questioning techniques that open up interactions with pupils.

*   Teachers should model how to provide quality feedback.

Areas of tension

Areas of tension can build up between teachers and TAs through the management and util-isation of the support for children's learning. We have seen that studies of the effectiveness of TAs in school have provided unexpected revelations and exposed a dissonance of practice which questions the overall effectiveness of TAs.

There are opposing views about whether TAs should support targeted interventions or widen their role and support the more universal 'learning environment'. This may be a more inclusive way of using the support so that it goes to the majority rather than the minority. We have seen tensions evolve between the need for TAs to support the pastoral care of pupils and the more pressing need for achievement of targets. All of this is played against a back-drop of managing the distribution of finite resources, where senior management teams have to make some very difficult budget choices. The role of the TAs is very much driven by the ethos and values of the school, but there are other outside agendas imposed upon schools that have to be met, such as targeting and achieving academic progress for every child.

The success of TAs in their support of children's learning carries uncertainties, risks and dilemmas. As Webster et al. (2011) conceded, there remains the fundamental question of whether TAs should continue to have a pedagogical role, teaching, supporting and interacting with pupils in a tightly defined role with support by better training and monitoring or whether TAs should have a non-pedagogical role.

Critical questions

» *Discuss your own experience of working with (or as) additional support.*

» *In what ways does it reflect research findings on the impact of additional support on pupils' learning?*

Promoting pupils' independence

SCENARIO

Stephen

Stephen, Y2, cannot be hurried. He is slow and deliberate in his movements and approaches most tasks with the same slow pace. He is usually the last out of the dining hall at dinner time and he is always last to get undressed for PE.

Stephen takes time to think about his response to questions and can get left behind in the quick pace of some lessons. He will sometimes answer a question a few minutes after it was asked. The exception to this is in music, which he loves – he can pick up and hold a tune easily and remembers the words to songs.

He goes to the special reading group with the same learning support assistant on a daily basis, which he enjoys. He can read and write his name and recognises labels positioned around the classroom. He has some knowledge of phoneme–grapheme representation and is beginning to write some CVC words successfully. He likes to dictate his ideas to the learning support assistant, which he will then copy. He is proud of his work.

He can do basic add on 1 and simple maths with the help of apparatus such as unifix cubes.

He is popular with the girls, who try to mother him and help him to tie his shoe laces. He likes to tidy the cloakroom and, although there is a rotation of monitors, he sees himself as the permanent cloakroom monitor. If he is away from his work table for any length of time he is usually found tidying the cloakroom.

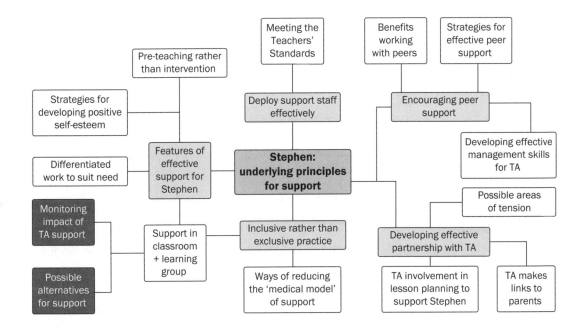

Effective support for Stephen

Critical questions

»   *Consider the profile of Stephen given in the scenario and suggest possible inclusive strategies that will support his literacy development in the classroom and foster more independence.*

»   *What support will Stephen need in order to*

   a)   develop his literacy skills?

   b)   begin to foster some independence in his own learning?

»   *Decide what you think would be a suitable use of a TA's skill and time in developing a programme of support.*

Comment on scenario

Your choice of strategy is not necessarily either the medical model of inclusion or the social model. As Mittler (2000, p 3) suggests, *it is important to avoid polarising these models as though they are mutually incompatible*. It may be necessary, for the benefit of the child, to work within the parameters of both the social and the medical model of inclusion. For example, it will be necessary to assess Stephen's capabilities using a variety of modes of assessment. This will help you achieve a starting point for your plan of support and possible choice of interventions. Once his general capabilities are known, you need to provide a carefully devised plan of action which will support Stephen's literacy needs while giving him some independence. Your plan should enable Stephen to feel a sense of belonging in class, to be able to participate in whole-class learning and to feel a sense of achievement with his own learning.

Your TA will be invaluable in helping to achieve the most suitable learning plan for Stephen. S/he can help in the initial assessment and provide details and information that provide an accurate picture of Stephen's capabilities. This will also give a sense of ownership for the TA of the education plan. Together, you can plan a forward course of action incorporating both small-group work and in-class support.

You will need to consider the best use of the TA's skills. Pre-teaching is a strategy that could help strengthen Stephen's self-esteem and enable him to participate more in the session, but you need to question what is the best way forward for Stephen, for you as the teacher and for the most effective use of the TA's skills.

Time for planning may need to be negotiated with the senior management team if it is not already an accepted use of TA's time in the current situation. You may have to balance what time you have with the TA and carve out some planning time. This will indicate how much you value the partnership and that you do not expect a TA to give hours that are outside their contracted hours.

You need to consider the use of the TA in supporting differentiated work. The aim is to support Stephen in independent work and to move away from copy writing. There needs to be planned opportunities for Stephen to use the knowledge that he has accrued from his phonic sessions. He could use the support of a voice recorder in order to tell stories, but he should also be given the opportunity to compose his own very short sentences with a known vocabulary. He should be given practice in using his knowledge of phonics to encode his ideas for himself.

In order to move away from TA support the use of structured peer support should be considered. It is noted that the girls mother him, but this sense of care could be harnessed in a more positive way in order to give Stephen an opportunity for supported achievement. Stephen could participate in mixed-ability learning-group work where the roles are allocated according to skill development. In this way, the outcomes will be more structured to the pupils' needs.

Stephen needs to feel a sense of belonging in the class. Although his self-appointed cloakroom attendant duties gives him some satisfaction, he really requires other areas of responsibility to give him a sense of belonging.

The other consideration for the TA is to encourage a closer relationship with the parents. Although, as the teacher, the overall responsibility is yours, Stephen's parents may welcome some informal daily contact with the TA when reporting progress.

Critical reflections

» *What government guidance and reports should you be aware of with regard to working with TAs? How will these enable you to fulfil the Teachers' Standards?*

» *Think about how, as a trainee teacher on placement, you can enable a strong working partnership to develop with the teacher assistant.*

- *What steps will you take to ensure that the TA feels valued?*

- *In what ways can you involve the TA in planning and assessment?*

Taking it further

Books and journals

Anderson, V. and Finney, M. (2008) I'm a TA not a PA': Teaching Assistants Working with Teachers, in Richards, G. and Armstrong, F. (eds) *Key Issues for Teaching Assistants*. London: Routledge.

> A useful and informative chapter that records the findings of a study of the role of the TA in school. The study reiterates the problematic role of the TA and records the thoughts and feelings and some of the frustrations of TAs working with teachers.

> The authors suggest that there should be a revised pay structure with a system of management and structures for appraisal to allow TAs to identify strengths and areas for development so they can move on an identifiable career path. There are strong hints at the benefits of valuing colleagues.

Hancock, R., Hall, T., Cable, C. and Eyres, I. (2010) 'They Call Me Wonder Woman': The Job Jurisdictions and Workplace Learning of Higher Level Teaching Assistants. *Cambridge Journal of Education*, 40(2): 97–112.

> This paper reports on an in-depth interview study of the roles and associated learning of higher level TAs (HLTAs). The role of the HLTA is examined in the contexts in which they work. The expectations are that HLTAs can cover for teachers to be released for planning, preparation and assessment (PPA). The individual job boundaries are described and discussed, as are implications for their knowledge and practice. The HLTAs are found to have wide-ranging job domains and, sometimes, unexpected involvements that mean they have to improvise practice. The study acknowledges that these HLTAs are being creatively managed and deployed by head teachers for the sake of teachers and schools. However, they are, at times, required to take on planning and cover duties which are beyond their knowledge and training, with a likely impact on children's learning. Given their training and experience, it is asked if covering classes to release teachers is the most effective use of their abilities and time. Although they were doing their best to respond to the expectations of head teachers and teachers, the HLTAs within the study seemed at times out of their depth. The authors suggest that the HLTAs were sometimes unavoidably diluting the practice of qualified and experienced teachers, with implications for children's learning. The article concludes that for all their dedication and willingness to teach themselves new class-teaching skills and the required curriculum knowledge, deploying HLTAs to cover classes in order to release teachers seemed not to be the best use of their training, abilities and time.

Web-based material

> Context for learning support – identify features of good practice from these OU videos:

www.open.edu/openlearn/education/educational-technology-and-practice/educational-practice/ teaching-assistants-support-action/content-section-1.5 (last accessed 4 October 2013).

> This Open University Unit focuses on the role of the TA and the variety of working contexts. There are nine short videos and in them you should be able to identify the features of good practice. Consider the working practices of each TA, note how they interact with the children in ways to promote self-esteem and enhance children's learning.

Rose, R. and O'Neill, A. (2009) Classroom Support for Inclusion in England and Ireland: An Evaluation of Contrasting Models. *Research in Comparative and International Education*, 4(3): 250–26.

Online: www.wwwords.co.uk/pdf/validate.asp?j=rcie&vol=4&issue=3&year=2009&article=3_ Rose_RCIE_4_3_web (last accessed 4 October 2013).

This comparative study of the deployment of TAs in England and Ireland illustrates the importance of the role of TAs in supporting inclusive education in mainstream schools. The article considers how two distinctive models of classroom support have emerged and the different ways in which they impact upon inclusion. The changes in practice which were taking place at the time are discussed and the possible impact upon the current and future inclusion agendas is considered.

Wilson, E. and Bedford, D. (2008) New Partnerships for Learning: Teachers and Teaching Assistants Working Together in Schools – the Way Forward. *Journal of Education for Teaching: International research and pedagogy*, 34(2): 137–150. Online: http://dx.doi. org/10.1080/02607470801979574 (last accessed 4 October 2013).

This paper was in part a response to Ofsted's call in 2002 for more research into the partnership between teachers and TAs. The article describes a three-year project named 'New Partnerships for Learning' (NPfL) that was centred on the delivery of a professional development programme which equipped teachers with the skills needed to work in partnership with TAs. This research posed the question: What are the issues to address in enabling teachers to work in effective partnership with teaching assistants? The findings include the different experiences of teachers working with TAs across the primary and secondary phases. It reports on variable training opportunities; variations in needs, aspirations, roles and responsibilities of TAs; unevenness of resourcing and remuneration; and tensions between leadership and partnership practice. Significant issues emerged surrounding the roles and responsibilities of TAs, and directly related to these is the question of the pay differentials. The varied needs and aspirations of TAs also emerge, and none of these issues can be seen in isolation from the tensions around whether the relationship between teacher and TA is a hierarchical one or a genuine partnership between two equal adults in the classroom.

References

Balshaw, M. (2010) Looking for Some Different Answers About Teaching Assistants. *European Journal of Special Educational Needs*, 24: 4.

Blatchford, P., Bassett, P., Brown, P., Koutoubou, M., Martin, C., Rubie-Davies et al. (2009) *Deployment and Impact of Support Staff in Schools: The Impact of Support Staff in Schools (results from Strand 2, Wave 2)* Institute of Education, University of London, DCSF RR148.

Blatchford, P., Russell, A. and Webster, R. (2012) *Reassessing the Impact of Teaching Assistants: How Research Challenges Practice and Policy*. London: Routledge.

Butt, G. and Lance, A. (2005) Modernizing the Roles of Support Staff in Primary Schools: Changing Focus, Changing Function, a School of Education. *Educational Review*, 27(2):139–49. Published online 2010, DOI: dx.doi.org/10.1080/0013191042000308323 (last accessed 4 October 2013).

Farrell, P., Alzborz, A., Howes, A. and Pearson, D. (2010) The Impact of Teaching Assistants on Improving Pupils' Academic Achievement in Mainstream Schools: A Review of the Literature. *Educational Review*, 62:4. DOI: 10.1080/00131911.2010.486476 (last accessed 4 October 2013).

Gerber, S.B., Finn, J.D., Achilles, C.M. and Boyd-Zaharias, J. (2001) *Teacher Aides and Students' Academic Achievement. Educational Evaluation and Policy Analysis*, 23(2): 123–43.

Giangreco, M.F. and Doyle, M.B. (2007) Teaching Assistants in Inclusive Schools, in Florian, L. (ed) *The Sage Handbook of Special Education*. London: Sage.

Goddard, G. and Ryall, A. (2002) Teaching Assistants: Issues for the Primary School. *Primary Practice*, 30: 29–32.

Gross, J. (2000) Paper Promises? Making the Code Work for You. *Support for Learning*, 15(3): 126–33.

Hayes, D. (2003) *A Student Teacher's Guide to Primary School Placement. Learning to Survive and Prosper*. London: RoutledgeFalmer.

Lowe, M. and Pugh, J. (2007) Teaching Assistants' Perception of Power. *Management in Education*, 21: 25.

Mills, J. and Mills, R.W. (eds) (1995) *Primary School People. Getting to Know Your Colleagues*. London: Routledge.

Mittler, P. (2000) *Working Towards Inclusive Education: Social Contexts*. London: David Fulton.

Moyles, J. and Suschitzky, W. (1997) *'Jills of All Trades?' Classroom Assistants in KS1 Classes*. London: Association of Teachers and Lecturers Publications.

Webster, R., Blatchford, P., Bassett, P., Brown, P., Martin, C. and Russell, A. (2011) The Wider Pedagogical Role of Teaching Assistants. *School Leadership and Management*, 31(1): 3–20.

11 Working with outside agencies

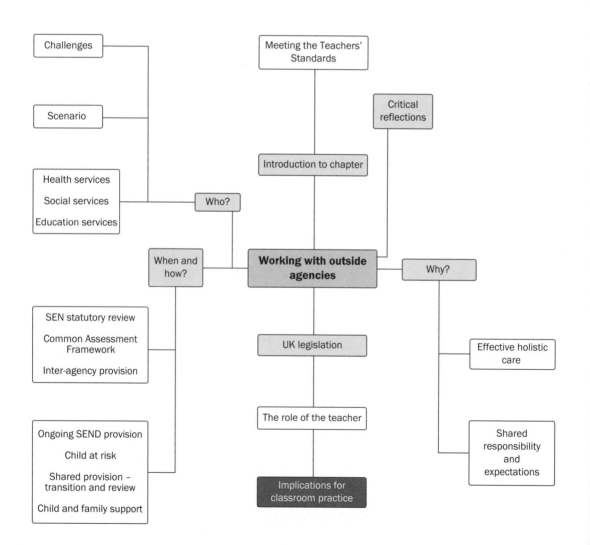

Challenges

Scenario

Health services
Social services
Education services

Who?

Meeting the Teachers' Standards

Critical reflections

Introduction to chapter

When and how?

Working with outside agencies

Why?

SEN statutory review

Common Assessment Framework

Inter-agency provision

UK legislation

Effective holistic care

Ongoing SEND provision

Child at risk

Shared provision – transition and review

Child and family support

The role of the teacher

Shared responsibility and expectations

Implications for classroom practice

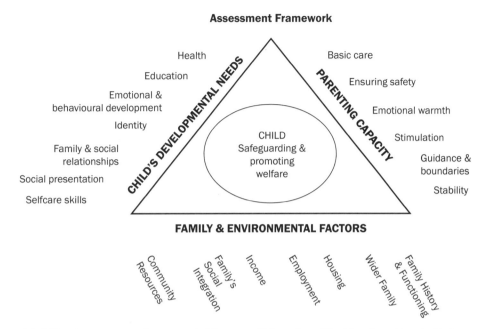

Figure 11.1 The Assessment Framework Diagram. Taken from *Working Together to Safeguard Children* (HM Gov, 2013, p 20) Crown Copyright / Department for Education.

Introduction

As a teacher you will be required to work with other professionals to ensure that children in your class receive the support they need. These professionals will come from different disciplines and will vary depending on the intervention required. Professionals from outside agencies such as health care and social services may know as little about your education field as you know about theirs, but in order to provide the best care and support for children and their families it is important that effective professional relationships and ways of working are formed. It is recognised in the Children Act (UK Government, 1989) that children can benefit from the wider support given to their families when concerns and issues are identified. The Assessment Framework diagram (Figure 11.1) demonstrates why professionals and families need to work together to identify issues, develop strategies to improve opportunities for progress and ultimately ensure that the child has the best possible education, health and social care.

You will come across different terminology in relation to working with outside agencies in this chapter and in other books. Terms such as interprofessional, collaborative, multi-agency and interdisciplinary working, integrated services or the Team Around the Child (TAC) all refer to the range of professionals who work together, or, as Wigfall and Moss (2001) clarify, *a range of different services which have some overlapping or shared interests and objectives, brought together to work collaboratively towards some common purpose* (p 71). Though, as discussed later in this chapter, the challenges, benefits and levels of collaborative success may vary.

This chapter provides you with a greater understanding of the who, how, why and when aspects of working with outside agencies. It also reflects on your role as a trainee teacher and the implications that interprofessional and collaborative working will have on your practice.

Critical questions

» *Reflect on placements you have experienced and make a list of professionals from outside agencies that you have been aware of, or worked with, in order to enhance the support provided for children.*

» *Consider the different disciplines that other professionals may come from and how they can support your role as a teacher when working with children.*

MEETING THE TEACHERS' STANDARDS

Links to Department for Education Teachers' Standards, May 2012

TS 5; 8

Part 2

In working towards the DfE Teachers' Standards (2012a) you will need to *develop effective professional relationships with colleagues, knowing how and when to draw on advice and specialist support* (p 9). This will entail improving your own understanding of the needs of particular children and how your interventions and support can be enhanced by incorporating other professionals' guidance and interventions. You also need to have *regard for the need to safeguard pupils' well-being* (p 10), and working with outside agencies is an important aspect of this. The benefits of effective interprofessional and collaborative working partnerships will have a direct impact on your planning, teaching and general provision and so will help you to *have a clear understanding of the needs of all pupils* and *have a secure understanding of how a range of factors can inhibit pupils' ability to learn, and how best to overcome these* (p 8).

Who might I work with?

Stanley (2007) states that *Each team member needs to have sufficient knowledge of all the services on offer and a shared vision, so the service can be used to its full potential, and parents and children can receive continuity and progression* (p 132).

This section identifies the three main areas of provision – education, social and health services – and many of the professionals working within these areas that you are most likely to come into contact with during your career as a teacher. It is possible that the children you teach will never need this level of intervention, or perhaps their level of complex needs will lead to significant and sustained collaborative working partnerships. Whichever is the case, it is helpful to be aware of who you might work with.

Specific groups of children considered to be at potential risk are identified in *Working Together to Safeguard Children: A Guide to Inter-Agency Working to Safeguard and Promote the Welfare of Children* (HM Gov, 2013). It states that, *Professionals should, in particular, be alert to the potential need for early help for a child who:*

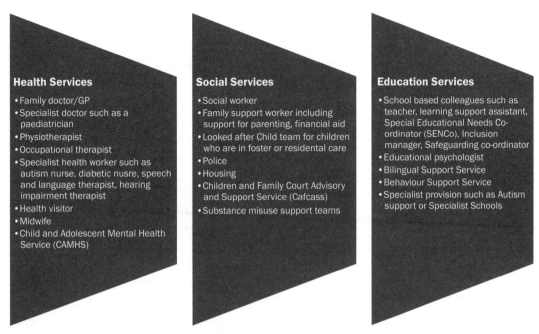

Health Services

- Family doctor/GP
- Specialist doctor such as a paediatrician
- Physiotherapist
- Occupational therapist
- Specialist health worker such as autism nurse, diabetic nusre, speech and language therapist, hearing impairment therapist
- Health visitor
- Midwife
- Child and Adolescent Mental Health Service (CAMHS)

Social Services

- Social worker
- Family support worker including support for parenting, financial aid
- Looked after Child team for children who are in foster or residental care
- Police
- Housing
- Children and Family Court Advisory and Support Service (Cafcass)
- Substance misuse support teams

Education Services

- School based colleagues such as teacher, learning support assistant, Special Educational Needs Co-ordinator (SENCo), Inclusion manager, Safeguarding co-ordinator
- Educational psychologist
- Bilingual Support Service
- Behaviour Support Service
- Specialist provision such as Autism support or Specialist Schools

Figure 11.2 Key professionals from different services

- *is disabled and has specific additional needs;*

- *has special educational needs;*

- *is a young carer;*

- *is showing signs of engaging in antisocial or criminal behaviour;*

- *is in a family circumstance presenting challenges for the child, such as substance abuse, adult mental health, domestic.* (p 12)

Many of the services identified will be co-ordinated by the local authority and local council. However, with the introduction of academy schools, who are not obliged to seek service intervention from the local authority and have greater freedom in how they spend their budget for outside agency support, it is possible that schools may choose to access independent and privately run companies or providers. You will find it useful to discuss the situation of the schools in which you complete your placements and qualified teaching roles as to their status.

Some of the key professionals from each of the services who you may collaborate with are shown in Figure 11.2.

Supporting a child with special educational needs or disability

When working with a child who is identified as having a special educational need or disability that you and your colleagues are unfamiliar with, it is important that you seek further information and guidance from specialists. They will be able to tell you more about the

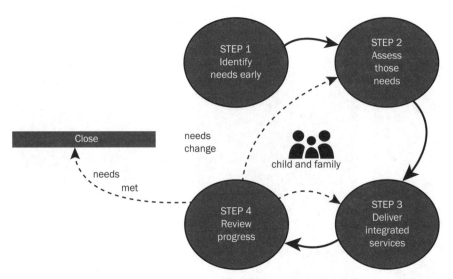

Figure 11.3 Diagram showing the Common Assessment Framework process, taken from the Department for Education website (2012). Crown copyright / Department for Education.

barriers to learning that the child may face, any specific support that they need and to provide information about successful interventions other teachers have used in other settings. This information will influence and shape your planning, teaching and interactions with the child. You may find it particularly helpful to arrange a meeting with the specialist and the child, if appropriate, and the child's parents at the beginning of the school year or when the diagnosis is made so that ongoing objectives, targets and reviews take account of the information shared.

Supporting a child who is at risk

If a professional has concerns about a child in their care who they feel may be at risk as a result of their living circumstances or from another person that they know, it is their duty to make their concerns known to the appropriate colleagues in school and professionals from other agencies.

If there is concern that a child is at immediate risk or where action needs to be taken straight away in order to prevent potential or further harm, then the teacher in the school who is responsible for safeguarding must be informed immediately. They will then follow the appropriate process for notifying the duty officer at the social services department, who will co-ordinate the safeguarding procedures with professionals in school and with the police if necessary.

In a case where there is concern due to a lack of social, emotional, physical or intellectual progress and where neglect may be an issue, then the Common Assessment Framework (CAF) process can be used. The CAF is in place to support all professionals to work together to identify the child's needs and to share the responsibilities for putting in place interventions relevant to their roles and responsibilities. The CAF was introduced as part of the Every Child Matters agenda (DfES, 2003). This identified gaps in provision between different services and was designed to ensure that a shared approach was achieved. Further information about the CAF process and a copy of the CAF form can be found in Figure 11.3

and at www.education.gov.uk/childrenandyoungpeople/strategy/integratedworking/caf/a0068970/the-pre-caf-and-full-caf-forms

The scenario below demonstrates how the CAF process can be used by professionals from different agencies to support a family in difficulty in which it was felt that intervention was needed to prevent the children becoming at risk.

SCENARIO

The Smith family

Family members:

- Ben Smith, aged 43
- Jenny Smith, aged 37
- Joshua Smith, aged 9
- Bethan Smith, aged 6
- Daniel Smith, aged 5

Mr and Mrs Smith and their three children moved into a local authority home in an area of the city that is recognised as being of low socio-economic status, six months ago. The children seem to have settled well, though all are working below the age-expected levels in the core subjects.

There are concerns about the welfare of the children as they regularly attend school in dirty clothes and complain that they are hungry. Bethan has been teased by the other girls in her class as her clothes smell of stale urine and she has confided to her class teacher that she has wet the bed a few times since moving house. Joshua and Daniel are sharing a bed due to lack of funds to buy a third single bed. Daniel has significant hearing loss and attends the hearing-impaired unit which is opposite the school.

Ben Smith is a mechanical fitter who works on an oil rig and works 15 days on the rig and then has 10 days off at home. Mum says that this is making life difficult as he spoils the children during these 10 days and then leaves her to try and get the children's behaviour back on track after he has gone back to the rig. This is affecting their relationship and Daniel has told the therapist from the hearing-impaired unit, *I don't like it when Mummy hits Dad and shouts at him a lot.*

Jenny Smith is 32 weeks pregnant with her fourth child and is beginning to wonder how she is going to cope when the new baby arrives. She is feeling increasingly tired and is struggling to keep up with the housekeeping, particularly when this involves a two-mile walk to and from the laundrette with the washing because they can afford neither a car nor a washing machine.

The SENCo (who is also the deputy head teacher) has been approached by each of the class teachers due to their concerns and has completed an initial pre-CAF assessment form, which identifies the need for a full CAF meeting. Several professionals have been identified who may be able to support the family and these have been invited to the initial meeting.

Critical questions

» *Identify the needs of the family. Which professionals would be able to provide relevant help to address each of these needs?*

» *Make a list of all the professionals you think should be invited to the initial meeting.*

» *Consider the actions that need to be identified in order to support the family. Which actions do you feel should be prioritised in the short term and which could be considered as longer-term actions?*

Comment on scenario

In this scenario, the professionals invited to the initial meeting were:

• Mr and Mrs Smith;

• SENCo (acting as Chair for the meeting);

• school secretary (acting as scribe for the meeting);

• Year 5 class teacher;

• Year 2 class teacher;

• Reception/Foundation 2 teacher;

• Reception TA;

• social worker;

• family support worker;

• midwife;

• hearing-impaired unit therapist;

• housing welfare officer.

The purpose of the meeting was to work collaboratively with these professionals to complete the CAF form and identify actions that the professionals could complete with the family. The initial actions agreed were:

• for the housing welfare officer to support the family to find a larger home so that it could be ready before the new baby was born;

• for the family support worker to work with Mrs Smith to address the issues in relation to washing and dressing the children in clean clothes and to ensure that they are given regular, healthy meals;

• for the SENCo to work with Mr and Mrs Smith to identify shared behaviour-support strategies to use in the home to ensure consistency of expectations with the children;

• for the midwife to arrange to meet with Mr and Mrs Smith to identify their concerns about the arrival of the new baby;

- for the social worker to support the family to complete the relevant forms entitling them to free school meals for the children;

- for the hearing-impaired unit therapist to work with Daniel's class teacher to review his progress and identify strategies, next-step suggestions and any resources that may be needed in school.

A review meeting was arranged to take place three weeks before baby Smith was due to be born. At this meeting, the actions were reviewed, progress identified and new targets set. This then involved inviting any additional professionals from the different services who could provide continuing assistance for the family.

Seven months after the initial CAF meeting was held, it was agreed at the final review meeting that the Smith family had made significant progress in relation to their circumstances, that the teachers had no further concerns about the children's welfare and that the CAF intervention could be stopped. The intervention was considered successful by the family and all professionals who had been involved.

Challenges of working with professionals from outside agencies

Many professionals, regardless of the service they represent, can find it difficult when working interprofessionally. As each service will have different purposes and aims to achieve in relation to care and support for the family, there can sometimes be challenges in recognising and working with these different expectations. Social service professionals may view their roles as being focused primarily on the welfare, safety, and care of children and their families. Health service professionals may consider the physical development, diagnoses, medical interventions and support for improving health and well-being as being their major focus. Education service professionals will have educational progress, inclusion and intellectual development as their priority focus. While these aspects are vital to the holistic care and development of each child and their family, not all professionals will consider them to have equal weight or relevance. Therefore it is not unusual for meetings between professionals from different services to encounter some disagreement in identifying priority targets or levels of perceived importance in professional status. Fitzgerald and Kay (2008) state that *individual practitioner identity can be challenged by becoming part of an interdisciplinary team. Staff may face threats to their identity through 'homogenisation' of roles and tasks, or they may be concerned about their own disciplinary background being less valued or seen as less useful than others* (p 80). In order to address this potential issue, it is important to be clear about each professional's purpose and involvement in the care for the child or family and to identify their expectations for the outcome of the process in which they are involved.

Critical questions

» *Consider your own identity as a teacher in relation to other professionals, such as doctors, social workers or members of the police force. Do you consider your role as being equally important to theirs? How might this perception of your professional status impact on how you relate to them?*

» *Your training and experiences on placement provide a depth of knowledge and understanding in relation to educational provision. You will also have formed profiles of children and identified their learning needs. How might this information be important to other professionals in developing a comprehensive and holistic support package?*

» *Think about a child you have worked with while on placement that had additional needs. What kinds of information do you think you might need to know from other professionals in order to support your provision in school?*

When and how will I work with outside agencies?

Working with other professionals who support families and children can be a complex process with many aspects and elements to be taken into consideration. Different systems may be put into place, depending on the needs of the child and family. This will involve different levels of involvement for the class teacher. The extent to which you are expected to attend meetings, reviews, or produce reports of progress will also vary with the circumstances.

As a trainee teacher on placement, you may find that you are able to talk with other professionals about aspects of care and intervention for a child in your class and you may be able to attend the child's SEN annual review or other meetings. However, in situations where intervention by other professionals is due to more complex or sensitive concerns, such as a child being at risk, it is unlikely that you will be able to have any in-depth involvement. This will be due to the confidential nature of the intervention and the difficulties professionals and families can face in working together. It can take several meetings to establish trusting and effective relationships between parents and professionals, particularly if neglect or poor parenting is a concern, and so you will need to be guided by your class teacher and SENCo as to whether you will be able to observe any meetings that take place.

Possible ways in which you will be expected to work with outside agencies are shown in the table below. You will have varying degrees of involvement, depending on the needs of the children and their families; in every case, however, you will have support from colleagues in school, such as the SENCo, the Safeguarding Co-ordinator, the Inclusion Manager and head teacher.

Critical questions

» *Consider a child you have worked with while on placement who had SEN in relation to health or learning difficulties that you had limited understanding and knowledge about. What were the child's barriers to learning?*

» *Make a list of questions that you would like to have asked another professional from an outside agency about the needs of that child.*

» *Imagine that you have a child in your class who has social and emotional difficulties which impact on their behaviour. The child spends mornings in a behaviour support unit at the Education Development Centre, which is run by a behaviour support therapist. What would you need to know about the child's experiences in the unit to support your planning for the child when they are in your class in the afternoons?*

Ways of working with outside agencies

Focus	Professionals involved (this should be read in conjunction with the list of professionals shown earlier in the chapter)	Format for involvement with outside agencies	Points to consider
Child with SEN receiving support from external provider	Health and Education services – any professional involved in supporting the child and family with specific educational or health needs related to their SEN or disability. Such professionals may include nurses, therapists and educational psychologists	• Ongoing support process – meetings with specific professionals • Annual statutory review for Statement of SEN	Shared understanding of the child's needs and expectations for their progress is vital in this relationship. The views of the parents and child are fundamental to ensure professional decisions and actions are appropriate and meet the child's needs.
Another provider involved in part-time care/ education for a child	Teachers, learning support assistants and colleagues based at the alternative provision that the child attends on a part-time basis, such as a specialist school or unit	• Transition meetings and discussions to support child and professionals involved • Planning of support and review of progress meetings	A child who experiences shared provision, such as spending the morning in school and the afternoon in a special school or unit (such as an autism support setting) will need consistent care, approaches and expectations. Transition between the settings is vital to ensure that progress is achieved and maintained. You will find that you need to take into account the alternative provision in your planning and teaching.
Child with EAL	Bilingual support teacher, assistant or learning mentor	• Planning of support and review of progress meetings	While this provision is part of the education service, it is possible that you and your colleagues will need to access support from a centrally located Bilingual Support Service. A member of the service will assess the child and provide strategies and resources that you and the learning support assistants can use to help the child's English speaking and writing skills.

Focus	Professionals involved (this should be read in conjunction with the list of professionals shown earlier in the chapter)	Format for involvement with outside agencies	Points to consider
Child or family at risk – CAF	Any professional considered to be relevant to the complex care of the family during the Common Assessment Framework process. This will include areas such as health, social services, education, police, housing and substance misuse support	• Pre-CAF assessment • Initial and ongoing CAF process involving identification of actions and review • Specific meetings between the family and professionals in order to complete the actions identified in the CAF	This is probably one of the most complex examples of interprofessional working and will include several professionals from different services. This process will have the child as the main focus but will identify ways in which support for family members can enhance the child's circumstances, welfare and safety. Involvement by trainee teachers is rare due to the sensitive nature of the concerns; however, understanding the needs of the child will influence your teaching.
Other short-term involvement with the family and child	There may be other professionals who support the child or their families on a short-term basis. This will not necessarily be linked to SEND	• Temporary involvement of professionals such as bereavement counsellor, doctor, police	You may identify circumstances where a child in your class is unable to temporarily access the learning opportunities. This may be due to the death of a family member or friend or where the child has broken a bone and needs short-term support to cope with their difficulties.

Why is it so important to work with professionals from outside agencies?

You will already have begun to understand that a child's educational progress is affected by many factors from reading other chapters in this book. Identity, culture, background, social, emotional and physical development and needs, and prior experiences will all impact on the way in which learning opportunities are approached and embraced by the child. You are responsible for understanding these experiences and for ensuring your provision reflects these. Any child who is affected by their additional needs or who is living in circumstances where they are at risk will not be able to concentrate on the learning opportunities you strive to provide. When these needs or circumstances are significant it is not possible to put them right on your own in the limited learning environment. The wider circumstances of home life, relationships and human needs must be addressed, and this is achieved through partnerships with other agencies by creating a holistic support process. Your involvement in this collaborative teamwork is essential. By sharing your knowledge and concerns about the child and by clarifying the educational needs (social, emotional, physical and intellectual), all professionals involved will be able to benefit from the larger, shared vision and respond appropriately. The ultimate goal is to improve the circumstances and opportunities to succeed for the child and, where appropriate, their family.

Critical questions

»   *Consider a time when you have had personal concerns or challenges which have prevented you from focusing on your learning, work or relationships. Think about your feelings during this time and how it affected your ability to focus or concentrate on your day-to-day activities.*

»   *Think about how a child with worries or concerns not directly related to their education might find it difficult to engage with the learning taking place in the classroom. What might the child do to demonstrate to you that they are not able to focus or concentrate?*

»   *Reflect back on Chapter 8 'Working with children'. What kinds of strategies or approaches might you consider to support this child and provide him or her with opportunities to share their worries and feelings?*

UK legislation

The Every Child Matters agenda, introduced in 2003 by the UK government, sought to place the child at the heart of provision. The death of Victoria Climbié in 2000 and the subsequent public inquiry led by Lord Laming (2003) into her murder by the adults she lived with, identified, among other things, that the agencies involved did not work together effectively to put in place the interventions needed to ensure her safety. The Children Act 2004 (UK Government, 2004) followed the agenda and legislated to promote children's health, safety and well-being. The Government elected in 2010 have reduced funding, prioritisation and focus for the Every Child Matters agenda and the most recent documentation to be published in relation to safety and well-being for children is *Working Together to Safeguard Children: A Guide to Inter-Agency Working to Safeguard and Promote the Welfare of Children* (HM Gov, 2013). This document used in conjunction with *Safeguarding Children and Safer Recruitment in Education* (DfES, 2007) and *Safeguarding Disabled Children: Practice Guidance* (DfES, 2009) provides all relevant guidance and legislation for teachers in schools. There are also a significant number of government and local authority publications for professionals working in other disciplines.

The *Special Educational Needs Code of Practice* (DfES, 2001) was approved by Parliament to ensure that schools and local authorities provide effective care for children with SEND. Section 10 'Working in Partnership with Other Agencies' provides the principles and objectives schools must follow to ensure interprofessional working is effective. It states:

> *The objective should be to provide integrated, high quality, holistic support focused on the needs of the child. Such provision should be based on a shared perspective and should build wherever possible on mutual understanding and agreement. Services should adopt a flexible child-centred approach to service delivery to ensure that the changing needs and priorities of the child and their parents can be met at any given time. (DfES, 2001, 10:4, p 135)*

It is anticipated that the current Code of Practice will be replaced in 2014 by a new Code which is currently going through the consultation process. The SEN and Disability Green Paper *Support and Aspiration* (DfE, 2011) continues the previous Code's intentions for inter-professional working. Section 5 of the paper, 'Services Working Together for Families' (p 93), reflects that many parents have felt frustrated that support provided by agencies did not meet their expectations or needs. It suggests that reducing the levels of bureaucracy the complexity of funding systems will give professionals greater freedom to develop effective and innovative interprofessional working practices.

You will need to be aware of the legislation and changes to the Code of Practice for support-ing the diverse needs of learners in your classroom, and you need to understand how the expectations, aims and law impact on your practice.

The role of the teacher and the trainee

In order to be an effective teacher, support each child to make progress and meet your professional responsibilities, you should be prepared to use a breadth of approaches, strat-egies and knowledge in your practice. The diverse needs of children in your class will make it almost impossible for you to know every need, barrier to learning, diagnosis or living circum-stance of every individual. Therefore you should be prepared to work in partnerships with colleagues in school and from outside agencies. Your primary role is to plan, teach, assess and support the progress of each child; positively acknowledging and embracing support, knowledge and guidance from others will help you to be effective in this.

You are a trusted adult that a child will feel comfortable with and feel confident to talk to. Your role is to respond appropriately to the information the child shares with you and to ensure they are safe and secure. This may require you to follow safeguarding procedures or to seek ways of removing barriers to learning. You should consider yourself an advocate for the child and be prepared to represent their views, feelings or concerns when they are unable to do so. Therefore, representing them, alongside their family members and other professionals, in interprofessional meetings is something you may need to do.

Another aspect of your role is to represent yourself and your profession at multi-agency meet-ings. You may feel unconfident, hesitant, shy or uncomfortable during your first experiences of these meetings. If you are well prepared and clear about what you know and hope to learn and achieve, these meetings are more likely to be successful and will help you to continue to make progress in your role and provision. Be positive, well prepared, listen carefully and be open to suggestions and guidance; you will then be more effective in supporting the diverse needs of the children in your class.

Implications for practice

Ensure you are fully aware of the safeguarding procedures

• You must know who the person responsible for safeguarding or child protection is in every setting in which you are placed.

• Follow the guidelines carefully should any child disclose sensitive information to you.

- Do not ask any further questions as these may influence the child's responses and may affect any future investigations by the safeguarding team or the police.

- Do not promise the child confidentiality or say that you will keep their information a secret. Assure them that you will need to talk to their teacher or the person responsible for safeguarding so that they can make sure that they are safe.

Be prepared to ask for support and help and to share information about the child involved in the intervention

- You will be able to put into practice suggestions and strategies shared with you.

- Keep a record of how the strategies worked and the child's responses so that you can share them at the next review.

- Keep evidence (examples of work, photographs, assessments, observations) to support your record.

Be aware of the wider view and involvement of other agencies

- Having an understanding of the roles and expectations of professionals from other services will help you to see the process from their point of view.

- You may find that a lack of shared expectations can lead to challenges between professionals about what is given priority when identifying actions.

- Try and consider the priorities from a health or social service perspective, does it explain the alternative viewpoints?

Share the information you have and your concerns clearly with other professionals from outside agencies

- Specific terminology, abbreviations or references to certain documentation (such as the National Curriculum) may not be understood by other professionals.

- References to specialist terminology may alienate other professionals or parents at the meeting.

- Keep your information brief, to the point, and free of any terms or educational references to avoid causing confusion, lack of clarity or misunderstanding.

Use the information, guidance and strategies suggested by other professionals from outside agencies to inform your provision, planning and teaching

- The information shared with you should be included in the child's education or care plan.

- Use the guidance to help you identify particular resources or approaches that will support the child.

- Ensure that your reflections and assessments after sessions consider the strategies and resources used; how will these reflections influence your future planning and teaching?

Keep a journal or a diary about the children you teach, particularly if you have concerns

- Any concerns regarding a child's welfare should be shared with the Safeguarding Co-ordinator or SENCo straight away.

- If the child is not considered to be at immediate risk but needs monitoring, then record your concerns with dates and evidence.

- Keep this journal in a safe place and ensure that confidentiality is a priority.

- Reflect on the journal on a regular basis. Does the cumulative information lead you to have new concerns or does it show that the issues you originally had are now resolved?

Appreciate the practicalities of multi-agency working

- In addition to appreciating the necessity for shared expectations and aims and how these can sometimes present challenges, you also need to see the process from a practical point of view.

- Time and availability are factors to consider. The dates and times for meetings may not be mutually convenient. Professionals from health and social services are more likely to be available during the day (when you are teaching) or during school holidays. It is important to negotiate mutually convenient times to meet.

- If you know that you are not going to be able to attend a meeting due to teaching commitments, be prepared to write a report in which you comment on the progress made in relation to each of the actions previously identified.

Critical reflections

» *Reflect on the holistic nature of a child's development. Make a mind map or spidergram for a child you have worked with that shows how each social, emotional, physical and intellectual aspect relates to the others.*

» *Extend this mind map by showing which professionals from other agencies may be involved in each of the developmental aspects.*

» *Research the roles and responsibilities of the professionals mentioned in this chapter. Consider your own role and responsibilities in relation to them and identify overlaps and similarities.*

Taking it further

Books and journals

Siraj-Blatchford, I., Clarke, K. and Needham, M. (2007) (eds) *The Team Around the Child*. Stoke on Trent: Trentham Books.

> This book contains useful insights and information regarding historical perspectives, effective practice and critical analyses of the challenges and benefits of multi-agency working.

Todd, L. (2007) *Partnerships for Inclusive Education: A Critical Approach to Collaborative Working.* Abingdon: RoutledgeFalmer.

Chapter 5 'Integrated Services: An Invitation to Inclusion, or Exclusion' considers the philosophy behind the practices for professionals working in disciplines and will help you to consider the extent to which working with outside agencies supports inclusive practice.

Trodd, L. and Chivers, L. (2011) (eds) *Interprofessional Working in Practice: Learning and Working Together for Children and Families.* Maidenhead: The Open University Press in association with McGraw-Hill Education.

This very accessible book provides research, data and discussion to support your understanding of the complex issues in relation to working with outside agencies. It considers the challenges for teachers who are working interprofessionally and the dynamics that occur within this practice. Chapters 1, 3, 4, 7 and 8 are particularly useful.

Walker, G. (2008) *Working Together for Children: A Critical Introduction to Multi-Agency Working.* London: Continuum.

Chapter 2 'Frameworks for Practice' provides an overview of the benefits and barriers of effective multi-agency work. An awareness of the barriers, in particular, can help you identify how to understand the dynamics in multi-agency meetings and how you can develop your practice as a result.

Web-based material

Multi-agency working: www.education.gov.uk/childrenandyoungpeople/strategy/integratedworking/a0069013/multi-agency-working (last accessed 4 October 2013).

Team around the child: www.education.gov.uk/childrenandyoungpeople/strategy/integratedworking/a0068944/team-around-the-child-tac (last accessed 4 October 2013).

What to do if you're worried a child is being abused: www.gov.uk/government/uploads/system/uploads/attachment_data/file/190604/DFES-04320-2006-ChildAbuse.pdf (last accessed 4 October 2013).

Safeguarding Disabled Children: Practice guidance: www.gov.uk/government/uploads/system/uploads/attachment_data/file/190544/00374-2009DOM-EN.pdf (last accessed 4 October 2013).

References

Department for Education (DfE) (2011) *Support and Aspiration: A New Approach to Special Educational Needs and Disability*, a consultation (Green Paper). London: HMSO.

Department for Education (2012a) *Teachers' Standards.* Online: http://media.education.gov.uk/assets/files/pdf/t/teachers%20standards%20information.pdf (last accessed 4 October 2013).

Department for Education (DfE) (2012b) *The Common Assessment Framework Process* www.education.gov.uk/childrenandyoungpeople/strategy/integratedworking/caf/a0068957/the-caf-process (last accessed 4 October 2013).

Department for Education and Skills (DfES) (2001) *Special Educational Needs Code of Practice.* London: The Stationery Office.

Department for Education and Skills (DfES) (2003) *Every Child Matters: Change for Children.* Nottingham: DfES Publications.

Department for Education and Skills (DfES) (2007) *Safeguarding Children and Safer Recruitment in Schools*. Nottingham: DfES Publications.

Department for Education and Skills (DfES) (2009) *Safeguarding Disabled Children: Practice Guidance*. Nottingham: DfES Publications.

Fitzgerald, D. and Kay, J. (2008) *Working Together in Children's Services*. Abingdon: Routledge.

HM Gov (2013) *Working Together to Safeguard Children: A Guide to Inter-Agency Working to Safeguard and Promote the Welfare of Children*. Online: http://media.education.gov.uk/assets/files/pdf/w/working%20together.pdf (last accessed 4 October 2013).

Lord Laming/Her Majesty's Government (2003) *The Victoria Climbié Inquiry*. London: HMSO. Online: http://webarchive.nationalarchives.gov.uk/20130401151715/https://www.education.gov.uk/publications/eOrderingDownload/CM-5730PDF.pdf (last accessed 4 October 2013).

UK Government (1989) *The Children Act 1989*. Chapter 41. London: The Stationery Office.

UK Government (2004) *The Children Act 2004* Chapter 31. London: The Stationery Office.

Stanley, F. (2007) Investigating the Practical Challenges of Integrated Multi-Agency Work, in Siraj-Blatchford, I., Clarke, K. and Needham, M. (eds) *The Team Around The Child*. Stoke on Trent: Trentham Books.

Wigfall, V. and Moss, P. (2001) *More Than the Sum of Its Parts? A Study of a Multi-Agency Child Care Network*. London: National Children's Bureau.

Part 3
Developing inclusive environments

12 The inclusive classroom

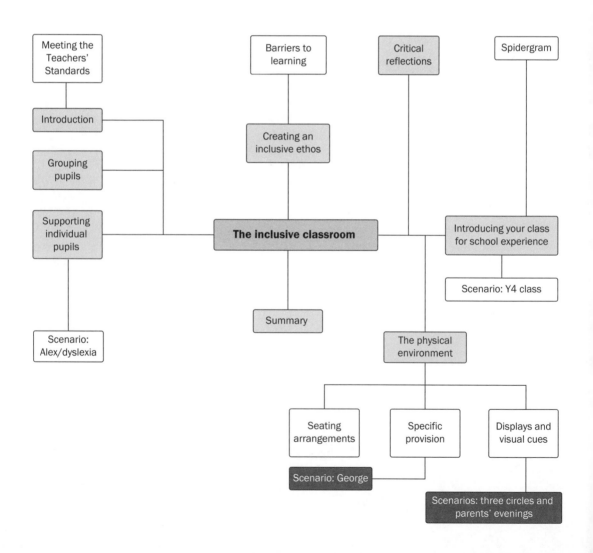

Introduction

All primary schools have their own distinct character and atmosphere. The ethos of the school is often apparent as soon as you walk through the door. Many schools are very welcoming. The reception area is brightly decorated, pictures of children and exciting activities are evident and the staff are friendly and keen to share their practice. There are the usual formalities of signing in and wearing name badges, but despite appropriate safety concerns, schools are usually places of richness, colour and fun and promote enjoyment in learning.

It is important that our classrooms are also places of exciting teaching and confident learning and that this is the experience of all children, not just those for whom learning seems easy. It is important that the class teacher is aware of what makes a good learning environment for all children and that provision is made for all to succeed in their learning. Hand in hand with an inclusive learning environment is an inclusive curriculum. In many ways there is a false division between the two as each impacts on the other; however, this chapter considers how you as a trainee teacher can create an inclusive learning environment within your classroom which will benefit all learners.

MEETING THE TEACHERS' STANDARDS

Links to Department for Education Teachers' Standards May 2012

TS 5

Introducing your class for school experience

During your training, you will be expected to work in a school environment where you will be exposed to a range of different educational cultures and learning environments. The following is typical of a placement that you may experience and where you will be expected to create a positive and inclusive learning environment.

SCENARIO

You have been placed in an inner-city school in a suburb of a large city. There are 30 children in your Year 4 class. The parents of the children are largely professionals, although some of the children come from a neighbouring area where most of the parents are working class. There can be some tension between children from different backgrounds and, on occasions, the parents of the children from the more affluent background object to some of the friendships that are formed with children from the working-class area. Some of the children have parents who are studying at the local university and have come from non-English-speaking countries. You have four such children in your class. Some are from China and some are from Pakistan. There are also two children in your class who have come from Slovakia. Their parents are working in a local factory.

There are eight children in your class who are considered to have SENs. These include one child with a statement for autism, one child who is considered to have ADHD and one child with dyslexia. The other children are not working at expected levels in literacy or numeracy. You have a TA working in the class during the mornings and a specialist teacher for EAL visits twice a week working with the children from non-English-speaking backgrounds.

Critical questions

Consider how you would manage the classroom environment for the scenario above.

» *What is the priority for this class in terms of socialisation and gaining a sense of common purpose and identity?*

» *What provision would you make for children with English as an additional language to be fully included in the classroom?*

» *How would you balance specialist provision for children with SENs or EAL with the needs of the whole class?*

» *How would you group children so they can learn most effectively?*

» *How would you deploy additional adult support in order to bring about effective learning for all children?*

The following spidergram provides an overview of some of the issues which are raised in the scenario.

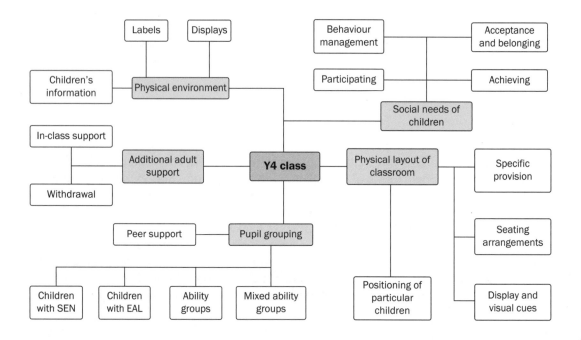

Creating an inclusive ethos

Each classroom has its unique ecosystem which is an interplay of the teaching and learning environment. Conway (2005, pp 107–108) suggests there are four main factors that contribute to what happens in the classroom. These are:

1. teacher factors;

2. student or pupil factors;

3. curriculum and resources factors;

4. the physical environment.

All of these interact throughout the day and influence learning outcomes. While the curriculum and resources factors are discussed in the following chapter, this chapter concentrates on teacher and pupil factors and the physical environment.

Conway (2005, p 108) goes on to outline how the attitudes of teachers, as well as their knowledge and confidence in teaching children with special educational needs, influences the classroom ecosystem. He states that the teacher's acceptance or otherwise of a child with additional needs acts as a model to others in the class. Glazzard et al. (2010) challenge all teachers concerning their values and principles in terms of inclusion, stating:

> You surely cannot pretend to believe in inclusion … You have to believe that all children are important and deserve the best education, even those with the most challenging behaviour. This commitment to all learners must be deeply embedded within you so that your practice is true to your values and principles. (p 131)

Therefore, in seeking to improve the learning environment for the children in this class, as a trainee teacher you would need to pay attention to your own attitudes towards each of the children and provide an ethos which is accepting of difference and celebrates diversity.

Glazzard et al. (2010, p 138) go on to state that children working in inclusive environments gain confidence and have high self-esteem. They contend that such children are able to work independently, develop creativity, to feel able to ask for help and to know their attempts at producing work and answering questions will be valued. Teachers who work inclusively value feedback from parents, carers, pupils and colleagues. They are willing to embrace new ways of working, including technology, and make effective use of additional classroom support. Inclusive teachers recognise and celebrate the small steps that some children take and contribute towards a feeling of self-worth for the child.

Social inclusion is vital for all children and is concerned with the interactions between all members of the class, adults as well as children. This includes peer acceptance, friendships and being able to participate in group activities. It is also important to note that being physically present in the school does not necessarily mean a child is included. The experience of Maresa McKeith, who is a non-verbal wheelchair user, was that, although she attended a mainstream secondary school, she was taught in a room on her own as she was considered to be unready for social contact with her peers. At the ISEC conference in 2000, she said:

The most important thing is that I want to be part of ordinary life and I want the same experiences as other kids. Also I want to be allowed to learn things that need thinking about and are challenging. I want to be able to contribute, and to discuss things that are important to me and other kids. We need to be together to do that. When we experience things together, we can learn about what we are each interested in, and about each other's lives. (quoted in Reiser, 2005)

Therefore the importance of social inclusion for all children cannot be overestimated. According to Booth and Ainscow (2002), inclusion involves a process of increased learning and participation for all students. This means learning alongside others and collaborating with them through shared learning experiences.

Barriers to learning

In the class detailed in the scenario, there are potentially several factions which have different social groupings. There are the children from the professional families who form the majority of the pupils in the class. It is possible that their values and expectations will be dominant. It could be that the children from the working-class families feel inferior or different, creating a social divide. There are other children, too, who may not feel comfortable within the classroom environment. The language differences of children with EAL may isolate them from the majority of the class and, even within this group, there are differences, as some of the children come from more academic backgrounds, while others come from families with different expectations and backgrounds. Therefore the children with EAL cannot be seen as a homogeneous group, but are rather a microcosm of the class as a whole. In addition, there are eight children with varying SENs for whom the classroom will present different and particular barriers to learning. The now disbanded TDA (2006) observed that the beginner teacher should understand that *the classroom environment itself can be a barrier to learning* (p 4), and while catering for the diverse needs of all of the children in one class can seem daunting, the TDA also advised that beginner teachers should *concentrate at first on strategies that improve the learning environment and your style of teaching rather than assuming you have to do something different for every individual* (2006, p 10).

In considering how to create an inclusive learning environment it is important to enable children to develop skills which will allow them to interact well with others. The development of good social skills, along with language which facilitates positive interaction with peers and adults, is vital. Siraj-Blatchford (2007, p 115) outlines how social skills are used to begin and develop interactions, to maintain friendships and to manage conflict. She maintains that teachers and other adults should be mindful of the different cultural and socio-economic backgrounds of children and support children in balancing the tensions of being brought up in one way and educated in another. As a trainee teacher faced with the class in the scenario, you would need to be aware of the different backgrounds, cultures and educational expectations of the different individuals and groups in the class and try to bring a sense of common purpose and mutual acceptance.

Jenny Mosley identifies that true learning can only take place where there is an atmosphere of trust and safety. She maintains that a teacher's first task is to unite the class so they can work together as a *cohesive whole* (2001, p 76). She recommends regular circle time sessions as a class in order to tackle such concerns as friendship, resolving conflict, feelings, co-operation and problem solving. Developing emotional intelligence, with the social skills to express it appropriately, would enable the class in the scenario to develop an inclusive ethos, to demonstrate empathy and to work co-operatively. While differences in background and cultural influences will remain, these are no longer seen as a difficulty or cause for division, but an opportunity to recognise and celebrate diversity.

The physical environment

When children come into the classroom, it is interesting to see how they position themselves relative to their teacher. Some children are keen to sit near the front, wanting engagement and interaction, while others sit at the back in tightly knit groups and are resistant to working more widely with others. Almost invariably, left to their own choices, children will sit in friendship groups as this is how they are most secure and comfortable. As a teacher, you can make decisions about how the furniture is arranged so that children sit accordingly. Generally, the furniture is arranged so that discussion and group work can take place easily, giving credence to social theories of learning, such as Vygotsky's zone of proximal development, which involves the construction of knowledge within a social context (Wearmouth, 2009, p 11).

Seating arrangements

Within the classroom, the teacher controls the layout and positioning of the furniture as well as who sits next to whom. The orientation of desks and how close they are to each other impacts on classroom interactions, therefore as the class teacher, you will need to consider which formation of desks best suits the activity and learning needs of the children. Wannarka and Ruhl (2008) carried out a review of empirical research concerning seating arrangements. Most of the eight studies they examined compared seating arrangements in rows with those in clusters, tables or groups. It was reported that for individual work, seating children in rows increased on-task behaviour as interacting with peers was less possible. However, where interactive learning was required, clustered desks or semi-circles were found to be effective. It is interesting to note that on-task behaviours were considered to be hand-raising and complying with requests, while off-task behaviour was considered to be talking out of turn or being out of seat. Therefore, there is little wonder that rows are deemed to be more conducive to work output than clusters of tables, as what is deemed to be off-task behaviour is more likely in a cluster or group.

In considering the most appropriate seating arrangement for an inclusive environment, Wannarka and Ruhl suggest that seating children in rows provides a useful approach for those who have behavioural difficulties, but they recognise that the best approach is for teachers to think about what learning they want the children to gain and configure the seating arrangements accordingly (2008, pp 92–93). Some children, particularly those lacking in confidence or with special educational needs, may find working alone a difficult and daunting task and may find the opportunity to talk with others about the task an important part of their learning and building of self-esteem. Similarly, children with EAL may have the cognitive ability to manage demanding tasks, but lack the vocabulary to express it. Working with others not only helps build co-operative relationships within the class, but enables pupils to be involved in peer-supported learning, giving the opportunity to try out answers and ideas in a mutually supportive environment. Clearly, for this to be effective, the seating arrangements within the classroom need to be organised in such a way as to provide rich opportunities for speaking and listening.

Specific provision

Having considered the general seating arrangements for the class, it is also important to be mindful of children with specific learning requirements.

The following table shows some common impairments or learning difficulties and the barriers to learning that may need to be removed, along with some suggestions as to how they may be overcome. Finally, the table shows how the child's access to learning may be improved by such inclusive practices.

Barriers to learning for some common impairments or learning difficulties with specific provision

Impairment	Barrier to learning	Suggested provision	Outcome
Visual	Inappropriate seating arrangement	Favourable seating position, probably near the front of the class	Improved engagement with work Ability to access whiteboard
Hearing	Acoustics	Carpets, curtains and other soft furnishings to dampen the resonance of the room	Ability to access teacher and peer voice Engagement in collaborative work
Dyslexia	Reading material in inaccessible format	Coloured overlays Print on coloured paper	More independent reading
Dyspraxia resulting in writing difficulties	Position of paper/book	Sloping desk or wedge	Improved writing ability
ADHD	Expectation to remain seated and keep still – no fiddling	Special cushion to aid core stability Stress ball	Greater concentration Improved learning Improved social relationships

Additionally, children with autism may find the social dimensions of a busy classroom particularly difficult, and may display behaviours such as aggression, flapping or making noises. Insisting that such children participate in collaborative learning may be presenting a barrier to learning for that child. Some children with autism respond well to working at an individual work station where noise and stimuli are reduced. As Glazzard et al. comment, some children with autism are very sensitive to lighting, such as the flicker of fluorescent lights, busy patterns and colourful displays, as well as loud sounds, such as the lunchtime or fire bell (2010, p 80). They suggest dividing the classroom into low-stimulus areas and high-stimulus areas, with the children with autism and others who prefer a calmer environment being able to work in the former (p 83).

SCENARIO

George had a statement for autism. He was high functioning, but had routines and high sensory sensitivity. He was capable of working well with other children but only on specific tasks in clearly defined roles and for short periods of time. At playtime he would run up and down in a specific area of the playground by himself. While other children had encouraged him to play with them, he refused, preferring instead to run up and down along a line in the yard. He seemed to need this time to free himself of the tensions of working within the classroom. The busyness of the playground was in itself quite stressful for George, and the jostling of lining up, putting coats in the cloakroom, and filing into the classroom were all stress points for him. Therefore, when George came into the classroom he had a specific chair designated for him in a special area with soft lighting, which he went to in order to settle and prepare for classroom activities. In the special area were some of his favourite books, *Thomas the Tank Engine*, a railway timetable, a seed catalogue and an atlas. He also had headphones with a choice of music which he could select to give him the opportunity to de-stress from playtime and acclimatise to the learning environment of the classroom.

These strategies and accommodations to the physical environment made the day run much more smoothly for George, the teacher and his classmates. He learned to recognise when he was becoming agitated and, instead of flapping and possibly biting other children, which he only did when stressed, he would request time out to sit in his special low-stimulus environment, returning when he was calmer and ready to learn. George's achievement levels in the class were age appropriate or above in literacy and numeracy, therefore it can be assumed that these arrangements provided him with appropriate learning opportunities and did not detract from the learning of other pupils in the class.

Critical questions

» What barriers to learning is the teacher seeking to remove for George?

» What strategies and/or interventions is she providing?

» Looking at the information in the scenario. How well do you think George is included in the classroom and why?

» What do you think is the next step towards further inclusion for George?

Displays and visual cues

Children such as George can benefit from a visual timetable, as this can provide routine. It will enable them to track what lesson is next, to be prepared for change and to signal the structure of the day. Such supports can be helpful for all children and can be referred to throughout the day by the teacher. Visual timetables enable children with EAL to understand the structure of the day and the expectations of lessons and therefore to feel more included in the activities. Similarly, a well-labelled classroom, identifying where resources can be found, provides scope for children to be more independent in their learning. Depending on the age and stage of development of the children in the class, labels can include pictures, and where there are children with EAL, resources and items can be labelled in the language spoken by the children, providing a link to their own culture. These provisions are of benefit to all children and as such should not be seen as only for children with additional needs. It is helpful to be aware that children with additional needs may not appreciate the attention generated by too much individual and specialist attention or the provision of specific resources, as it marks them out as different and runs the danger of creating a stigma. Any provision which benefits the child with additional needs but is also of universal benefit is more likely to be welcomed and used effectively.

In creating displays of children's work, you need to be mindful that all children want to know that their work is valued enough to be displayed. Children's work will be of a variable standard, but there are many ways in which it can be celebrated. Some children may be particularly able in some curriculum areas rather than others. For example, children who are good at sport can be photographed taking part in their sporting activity or demonstrating a particular skill. These can be displayed. Examples of children working collaboratively can be displayed, as can particularly good examples of art work, design and technology, computer-generated work or models. Displays can be created relating to children's different cultural backgrounds, using artefacts which children value, or showing events which they have celebrated, particularly if they relate to any of the curriculum subjects being studied. In this way, all children can provide a contribution towards classroom displays and in doing so will be recognised as valued members of the class.

Displays can also show visual prompts, spellings, class rules and reminders of routines as well as information about the topics being taught at the time. They can include useful vocabulary for literacy, methods and skills for maths, science or design and technology as well as lists of names of children with certain responsibilities or roles for that day or week. These prompts are particularly useful for children whose behaviour is supported by the use of clear structure. A vigilant teacher will become aware when a child needs a reminder and can simply point to the relevant wall display, making eye contact with the relevant child so that they make the connection between the reminder and expected action or compliance.

SCENARIO

I once visited a classroom while observing a trainee in their school-based practice and was confronted with a large diagram of three circles on the wall. The circles were labelled HAPs (higher ability pupils), MAPs (medium or middle ability pupils) or LAPs (lower ability pupils). There was an individual photograph of each child in the class and they were placed in the relevant group. Each group had its own specific set of targets and expectations of work and the children knew which they were working on. This information was also freely available to anyone who came into the classroom.

Critical questions

» *In considering using displays to show how children are grouped, which groupings would you think are appropriate for classroom display and which are best kept for the teacher's private records?*

» *As a class teacher, how would you make sure that the pupils were aware of the groups they should be in and the targets they should be working on?*

» *Classrooms are visited by many different adults. What do you think the parents of the children in the group labelled LAPs felt about their child's ability being displayed publicly? What might you do differently?*

It is vital that in considering what information you choose to display about children in your class, you do not give away information that should not be common knowledge. While it might be useful for you as a teacher to have a readily accessible chart showing children's achievement, you need to remember that classrooms are not private spaces. To illustrate this point further, consider the following example from practice.

SCENARIO

A colleague in school was taken to task one parents' evening by a particularly offended parent as their child's name had been left on the board from the day's teaching. It was the custom of the teacher in question to write the name of any child who had misbehaved on the board and then to mark off up to three chances before the child was sent out of the classroom for a cooling-off period. Unfortunately, the teacher had not removed the child's name before parents' evening, and so not only had the parents of the child in question become aware that there had been some difficulty during the day but, more significant from the parents' perspective, was the fact that other parents could see this information too. This was not information they wanted to have in the public domain.

There are more adults than ever in our schools, so whatever you put on the walls in your classroom can be seen by many and talked about to others. In acting professionally and with respect to the children in your class, you need to protect their right to confidentiality, making sure that you do not give away information which can damage a child's reputation or self-esteem.

Critical questions

Consider the class in the first scenario in this chapter (page 192). You are placed with this class for school-based experience.

» *Draw a plan of the classroom showing how you would arrange the children's seating for a literacy lesson on storytelling. What are your reasons for choosing this layout?*

» *Show how you would place other furniture, equipment or resources. What are your reasons for these choices?*

» *Label your diagram, showing how you would decorate the classroom, bearing in mind the barriers to learning the classroom might present to specific children.*

» *Indicate what specific physical provision you might make for some of the children. What are your reasons for these choices?*

» *How might you use this lesson to provide opportunities for all children to provide an item for classroom display?*

» What visual prompts or reminders would you choose to display in your class and which children do you think would particularly benefit from them?

Grouping pupils

Having considered how you have arranged the furniture in your classroom to take into account pupils' diverse needs and reduce barriers to learning, it is important that you consider how you choose to group pupils in order to provide maximum opportunities for the participation of all learners. As stated by the TDA (2006), the way pupils are grouped within a class can be significant to how they feel about themselves as learners and how they approach learning. The TDA also urged the beginner teacher to ensure that the way pupils are grouped enables positive and confident engagement with learning activities. This chapter has already touched on the grouping of children when considering how furniture might be arranged, and Chapter 7 also contains relevant information in the section on labelling. When you are working in school, it is important that you are aware of the benefits and limitations of different pupil groupings and when they might best be used.

Research by Kutnik et al. for the DfES (2006) into teachers' use of pupil groupings found that while teachers believed that they used setting in order to make specific provision for children's different understanding and achievement, the evidence from the classroom did not support the expected gains in children's achievement. Paired seating arrangements were found to be common, with table-based groupings being the preferred option. However, it was often found that the configuration of the tables did not match the activity that the children were engaged in. For example, they were often expected to complete individual tasks while seated in groups, therefore pupil grouping was more about behaviour management than facilitating learning. Indeed, teachers were found to be wary of using group work as a learning strategy as they were apt to feel that their control of the class was threatened (pp 4–5).

The TDA (2008) suggested that collaborative group work is a very beneficial inclusion strategy. They maintain that when a teacher is not working with a group, mixed-ability groups are better than single-ability groups for children of average and below-average ability. Children who are skilled at working in groups are less dependent on adult input. Pupils can support each other and children with SENs or additional needs can learn from others, try out ideas in a safe environment and be exposed to alternative explanations and ways of problem solving. If children with SENs are always placed together in a 'low ability' group, their opportunity to gain wider vocabulary and knowledge from their peers is reduced.

Just as seating arrangements need to vary according to task and learning, so does pupil grouping. Single-ability groups may be appropriate where all children in the group are working on the same learning objective in that subject, for example, in literacy; however, group composition will need to be re-examined depending on the subject, as children who show ability in literacy may not be as able in other subjects such as science or maths, or indeed art, music or sport, where it is much more common to work in mixed-ability groups. It is not appropriate for children to remain in literacy groupings for all of their learning experiences.

Similarly, when children are given collaborative tasks, the groups need to be carefully organised so that all children are given the opportunity to participate in the learning activities. The TDA (2008) list the following as key features of successful co-operative group work.

- The group has a shared goal.

- Individual pupils are given complementary and specific roles, such as scribe, timekeeper, chairperson and so on. These roles can be tailored to the capacity of the members of the group.

- Everyone in the group relies on the others for the task to be completed.

- Group members work together over a period of time and establish a group identity.

- Pupils are taught the necessary social skills for effective group functioning.

- Pupils are given opportunities to consider how well they work together and what improvements can be made to the way they function.

It can therefore be seen that effective group work requires good preparation by the teacher, the acquisition and practice of social skills by the children, and an understanding of the various roles and how the individual child contributes to the group task.

Critical questions

Consider this list of ways in which pupils may be grouped in the classroom, taken from the TDA (2008):

» *friendship;*

» *ability;*

» *structured mix;*

» *random selection;*

» *single sex;*

» *pair;*

» *small group (three or four);*

» *large group (six or more).*

» *Consider the benefits and limitations of each of these different types of group.*

» *When might you use each of these groups?*

» *Which do you think would be the most effective grouping for the class in the scenario and why?*

Supporting individual pupils

It is common practice for children with special educational needs to be taken out of the class to work with a TA. However, the TDA (2006) cautions that any decision to withdraw a child from the class for regular support should be balanced against the loss of social contact and opportunity to learn from peers (p 4).

The Deployment and Impact of Support Staff (DISS) Project (Blatchford et al., 2009), which investigated the role of TAs, found that many teachers had not had any training in how to work with TAs, they did not share their planning with them nor gain feedback from the work they did with the children. The project also found that TAs seemed to be concerned more with task completion than learning and that they tended to be reactive rather than proactive (p 2). As a beginner teacher, you need to think carefully about how you will work with TAs and how you will deploy them to enhance inclusive practices. Arguably, using a TA for individual, out-of-class support could be considered to be exclusive, even though the child may be deemed to need an individualised approach. Further discussion on how to provide an inclusive environment through additional adult support is given in Chapter 10.

One often overlooked source of support for children with SEN or additional needs is other pupils. While it is sometimes considered that helping other pupils could detract from their own learning, taking on the role of 'teacher' enables a child to explain and consolidate their own learning, which brings benefit. Ways in which peer tutoring can be used are paired reading, paired maths, sharing spellings, tables and explaining concepts or skills (TDA, 2008).

SCENARIO

Alex was a Y6 child with significant dyslexia. He was shy and lacking in confidence and his reading ability was well below that of his peers. However, every morning he took part in a paired-reading activity, where he shared books he enjoyed or liked the pictures in with a hesitant reader in Y3. This began as an experiment for a short time, but the confidence and reading ability of both boys developed considerably, as did their enjoyment of the session and ultimately their enjoyment of books. From being reluctant about reading, Alex became a willing and more confident reader, despite still having problems decoding. This increased confidence spilled over into his other work, built up his self-esteem and improved his relationships with other children in the class.

Summary

Taking all of this into account, in providing an inclusive environment in your class, you should be aware of the choices you need to make regarding the arrangement of furniture and the seating of children, how you organise displays, pupil grouping and how children's individual needs are met. All of this will be guided by your own inclusive ideas. Each new class will provide new and different challenges, but a positive inclusive position will enable you to be creative in your approaches and adapt your working practices to suit the needs of the children in your class.

Critical reflections

» *Think about the last school you worked in as a trainee teacher. How inclusive would you consider the learning environment to have been and why?*

» *As inclusion is a process, what changes would you make to the learning environment of the class you were placed in to make it more inclusive?*

» *What three things would you implement in your own classroom as a beginner teacher to provide an inclusive physical environment?*

» *How will you consider grouping pupils and why?*

Taking it further

Books and journals

Mosley, J. (2001) *Quality Circle Time in the Primary Classroom*, Vol 1. Cambridge: LDA.

> This book offers a rationale for the use of circle time. It reports from teachers and pupils on the benefits of circle time and offers over twelve session ideas, including sessions for Key Stage 1.

Whittaker, J. and Kikabhai, N. (2008) How Schools Create Challenging Behaviours, in Richards, G. and Armstrong, F. (eds) *Key Issues for Teaching Assistants: Working in Diverse and Inclusive Classrooms*. Oxon: Routledge.

> This chapter details one teacher's experience of facing children with challenging behaviour and his response to it. It shows how the school he worked in created barriers to children's learning and how he began to examine his own values and practices in relation to such children.

Web-based material

www.michelinemason.com/ (last accessed 4 October 2013).

> This link will take you to the website of a disabled writer called Micheline Mason. It provides a fascinating insight into how people with disabilities think of themselves and their view of how they are treated by non-disabled people. It also provides details of her book, *Incurably Human*, which is well worth a read. This book is very readable and not only relates her life story, but is shot through with her strong inclusive principles and beliefs.

References

Blatchford, P., Bassett, P., Brown, P. et al. (2009) *Deployment and Impact of Support Staff Project*. Institute of London: DCSF Publications. Online: www.ioe.ac.uk/diss_research_summary.pdf (last accessed 4 October 2013).

Booth, T. and Ainscow, M. (2002) *Index for Inclusion: Developing Learning and Participation in Schools*. Centre for Studies of Inclusive Education. Online: www.csie.org.uk/resources/translations/IndexEnglish.pdf (last accessed 17 October 2013).

Conway, R. (2005) Adapting Curriculum, Teaching and Learning Strategies, in Foreman, P. (ed) *Inclusion in Action*. Melbourne: Thomson.

Glazzard, J., Hughes, A., Netherwood, A., Neve, L. and Stokoe, J. (2010) *Achieving QTS Teaching Primary Special Educational Needs*. London: Sage.

Kutnick, P., Hodgkinson, S., Sebba, J. et al. (2006) *Pupil Grouping Strategies and Practices at Key Stage 2 and 3: Case Studies of 24 Schools in England*. Nottingham: DfES Publications.

Mosley, J. (2001) *Quality Circle Time in the Primary Classroom,* vol 1. Cambridge: LDA.

Reiser, R. (2005) The Struggle for Inclusion, in Nind, M., Rix, J., Sheehy, K. and Simmons, K. (eds) *Inclusive Education: Diverse Perspectives*. London: David Fulton.

Siraj-Blatchford, I. (2007) Diversity, Inclusion and Learning in the Early Years, in Pugh, G. and Duffy, B. (2007) *Contemporary Issues in the Early Years*. London: Sage.

Training and Development Agency for Schools (TDA) (2006) *Special Educational Needs in Mainstream Schools: A Guide for the Beginner Teacher*. Online: http://dera.ioe.ac.uk/8478/1/TDA-04278-2006.pdf (last accessed 4 October 2013).

Training and Development Agency (TDA) (2008) *Special Educational Needs and/or Disabilities: A Training Resources for Initial Teacher Training Providers: Primary Undergraduate Courses.* Online: http://webarchive.nationalarchives.gov.uk/20101007090812/http://www.sen.ttrb.ac.uk/ViewArticle2.aspx?anchorId=17841&selectedId=18436&menu=18297&expanded=False&ContentId=15002 (last accessed 4 October 2013).

Wannarka, R. and Ruhl, K. (2008) Seating Arrangements that Promote Positive Academic and Behavioural Outcomes: a Review of Empirical Research. *Support for Learning*, 23(4): 89–93.

Wearmouth, J. (2009) *A Beginning Teachers Guidance to Special Educational Needs*. Maidenhead: Open University Press.

13   The inclusive curriculum

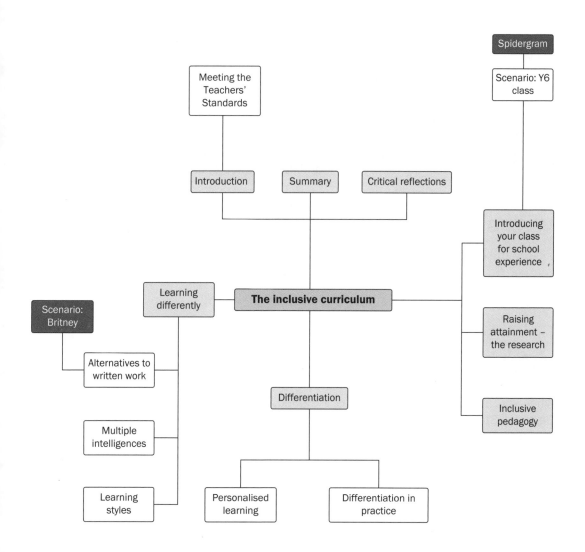

Introduction

The way a teacher organises the physical environment of the classroom, the seating arrangements, the grouping of pupils and specific provision to remove barriers to learning all contribute towards the creation of an inclusive environment. As a trainee teacher, and later as a qualified teacher, you will be expected to create a learning environment which provides rich experiences for children and provides every opportunity for them to develop to their full potential. Ways in which progress towards an inclusive classroom can be made are discussed in the previous chapter. However, another important aspect of developing inclusion is through providing a curriculum which is accessible to all. This is, of course, linked very closely to the inclusive environment, and both stem from the teacher's beliefs and attitudes towards inclusion.

The DfE (2010) states:

> It is unacceptable for educational attainment to be affected by gender, disability, race, social class or any other factor unrelated to ability. Every child deserves a good education and every child should achieve high standards. (p 1)

The DfE Impact Assessment (2010) goes on to outline how studies in America show that the quality of the individual teacher is the single most important determinant in the child's ability to make progress. Furthermore, the Impact Assessment states that, while there is little evidence to suggest that the pedagogy for teaching children from deprived areas is any different from that for other pupils, there is evidence to suggest that children from deprived areas are less likely to experience good-quality teaching. It can therefore be seen that the practice of the teacher and the way the curriculum is made accessible to all children is of vital importance when considering the achievement and participation of all.

MEETING THE TEACHERS' STANDARDS

Links to the Department for Education Teachers' Standards May 2012

TS 1; 2; 4; 5; 6; 8

Part 2

Introducing your class for school experience

When you are working in a school as a trainee, you will be required to work towards the Teachers' Standards (DfE, 2012a) in order to gain qualified teacher status (QTS). Therefore, your understanding of children's abilities, how they learn, as well as factors which inhibit learning, will affect how you plan, teach and assess pupils. The following scenario outlines a typical class that you may experience while working in school. It will provide the opportunity for you to consider how to develop an inclusive pedagogy and adapt the curriculum to become more inclusive.

SCENARIO

You have been placed in a school of average size in a predominantly white culture in an ex-mining town. It is a Y6 class and your placement takes place in January. The school is preparing the children to take the SATs in May.

The community has experienced significant deprivation since the closing of the mines, with unemployment stretching back for three generations. Most of the parents of the children in your class are receiving benefits from the government. However, there has also been an attempt at regeneration, with some new housing on the edge of the community. This has brought some young professionals and their families to the area as the housing is affordable and it is possible to commute to the nearby city for work. This means your class has a range of children, the majority of whom are from deprived backgrounds but including some children who are considered, according to the DfE (2012b), to be *academically more able*. Of the 30 children in your class, 12 of them are working below age-expected levels in most areas of the curriculum, with one of them working at P8 of the P scale. The P scale is used for children who are not yet achieving at Level 1 of the National Curriculum. The boy working at P8 also presents with significant challenging behaviour.

Of the remaining 11 children who are at an earlier stage of development, there is a child with a statement for autism who has a TA assigned to him for most of the day. There is also a child with dyspraxic-type tendencies. Three children have been identified as having dyslexia. However, at least six children have a reading age in advance of their chronological age. There are no children with EAL in your class and there is no experience of people from other cultures in the school or local community. Many of the children and parents do not seem to value education and have little aspiration or hope of employment. However, the children who live in the commuter community have a more positive view of education and employment, seeing it as a way to avoid the deprivation they see in the ex-mining community.

Critical questions

Consider how as the class teacher you would ensure the curriculum is accessible for all learners.

» *How would you make sure the curriculum is accessible for the boy working at P8 while ensuring that the academically more able pupils are also making progress?*

» *What methods of differentiation might you use in this class?*

» *How would you use other adults to make the curriculum more accessible to the children in the class?*

» *How would you take into account different learning styles in your planning, teaching and assessment?*

Some of the issues raised in the scenario are illustrated in the following spidergram.

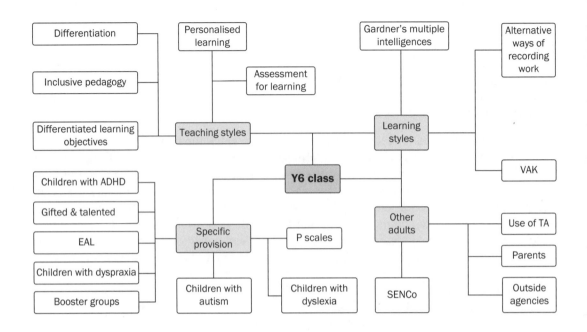

Raising attainment – the research

The revised framework for the National Curriculum (DfE, 2013) makes it clear that it is the teacher's responsibility to ensure the progress of all children through effective teaching, planning and assessment. This document acknowledges that, while teachers should plan *stretching work* for pupils who are working beyond their expected level of attainment, they *have an even greater obligation to plan lessons for pupils who have low levels of prior attainment or come from disadvantaged backgrounds*. It is stressed that there should be *no barriers to every child achieving* and that the teacher should plan accordingly, using assessment to set *deliberately ambitious targets* (p 9). It is the expectation that every child should be able to study the National Curriculum with the skilful use of planning, different approaches and resources.

Cassen and Kingdon's research for the Joseph Rowntree Foundation (JRF) (2007) considers the wider factors of low educational achievement. It found that the factors of disadvantage include the unemployment rate in the locality, the percentage of single-parent households and the proportion of parents with low educational qualifications. They state that poor reading and writing scores in the primary years are strongly tied to low achievement later on and that white British children are on average more likely than other ethnic groups to persist in low achievement. Of all low achievers, nearly half are white British males, outnumbering low-achieving girls by 3 to 2.

Perhaps even more worrying is research by Carter-Wall and Whitfield (2012), also for the JRF, which found that while interventions may be aimed at raising aspiration, changing attitudes and addressing disengaging behaviours (AABs), few are clearly linked to closing the attainment gap. Additionally, their research found that parental involvement in their child's education had a causal effect on the child's readiness for school and subsequent attainment. It is therefore important to recognise that in raising achievement for all pupils, the teacher's role includes developing partnership with others, particularly parents, as well as developing an accessible curriculum. This is particularly important when considering the class in the scenario, as the link between the nature of the class and the research findings are obvious.

Inclusive pedagogy

Pedagogy is concerned with how a teacher teaches. It is the art of teaching or the skill of how the curriculum is delivered. It is not about subject knowledge, although this is important, but about the values that a teacher holds which influence how they carry out their professional practice in the classroom. Armstrong (2011, p 10) considers that an inclusive pedagogy requires a consideration of the values and processes involved in pedagogy which should be measured against the principles of inclusion. This would cause the teacher to examine whether the teaching methods used promoted the inclusion of all pupils or whether some groups or individuals were being excluded, ignored or marginalised.

Corbett (2001) introduces the idea of a *connective pedagogy* (p 35) which is about how the teacher recognises and connects with the individual's learning style and how they learn most effectively. Connective pedagogy is also related to linking the learner with the curriculum and learning activities so as to bring about positive outcomes. Additionally, connective pedagogy links learning styles and the curriculum with community values as well as the values of the teacher. This is in contrast to the transmission model, which sees the teacher as the owner of knowledge with a responsibility to transfer this knowledge to the learner (Armstrong, 2011, p 14).

Corbett's notion of connective pedagogy is consistent with the theories of learning known as social constructivism. Theorists such as Vygotsky believed that children learn through talking and interacting with others and by constructing new learning which builds on existing knowledge (Pound, 2008, p 40). Taking this approach means that teachers should provide children with the opportunity to work with others, perhaps someone more experienced or competent. Other theorists such as Bruner emphasise the importance of cultural influences in learning (Armstrong, 2011, p 15) and consequently the importance of collaborative work within the classroom in building communities of learning. An inclusive pedagogy therefore involves the following:

- recognising individual differences;
- valuing cultural diversity;
- a commitment to inclusive values and practices in the wider school environment beyond the classroom;
- valuing the contribution from the local community in supporting education and inclusion. (Armstrong, 2011, p 10)

Lewis and Norwich (2001) carried out a review of evidence regarding whether children with SENs should be taught with specifically different and distinct pedagogical approaches even though the curricular content might be the same. They recognise that *effective pedagogy is an ideal that the practicalities of the classroom may threaten, or perhaps foster, in unpredictable ways*. Their review showed that there was little evidence that distinctive teaching approaches for children with SENs have a sustainable and transferrable impact. However, it showed that in literacy, for example, *common teaching approaches* needed to be used more carefully and intensely for low-achieving children.

The research showed that teachers tended to move on before mastery of the skill or learning was achieved for some children, and therefore more practice to achieve mastery is required. Additionally, Lewis and Norwich (2001) recommend that common teaching approaches should be used for all children, but for children with different learning needs, additional emphasis is required. This might include:

- more examples to learn concepts;
- more experience of transfer of knowledge to different situations;
- more explicit teaching of learning strategies and the reinforcement of them;
- more frequent and more specific assessment of learning;
- more time to solve problems;
- more careful checking or preparedness for the next stage of learning.

Therefore, it can be seen that *effective teaching for children with SEN shares most of the characteristics of effective teaching for all children* (DfES, 2004, p 52). As such, this does not mean that the teacher is required to teach completely differently to meet the needs of specific children, but more to consider what additional emphasis is required in using common teaching approaches.

Critical questions

Consider the scenario outlined earlier.

» *What teaching methods or approaches might the teacher consider in working towards an inclusive pedagogy?*

» *How would Jenny Corbett's notion of connective pedagogy impact on how you approach teaching this class?*

» *What impact would taking a social constructivist approach to learning have on how you deliver the curriculum? How would the work of Vygotsky and Bruner influence this?*

» *What additional emphasis on the common approaches to teaching do you feel would benefit some of the children in the class?*

Differentiation

The DfES (2001) states that the *key to meeting the needs of all children lies in the teacher's knowledge of each child's skills and abilities and the teacher's ability to match this knowledge to finding ways of providing appropriate access to the curriculum for every child* (p 51). One of the ways of providing access to the curriculum is through differentiation by ability. Many teachers provide differentiated learning opportunities for three different groups within their class, usually the high-achieving pupils (HAPs), the middle-achieving pupils (MAPs) and the low-achieving pupils (LAPs). This is most likely to involve the provision of different tasks or expectations, though the learning objective may be the same. However, Corbett (2001) suggests that differentiation should be linked with effective learning and the valuing of differences of all kinds. Effective differentiation is an evolving responsive process of bespoke provision for individual differences. It requires high-quality teaching skills and can be difficult to achieve. For this reason, Corbett considers many teachers find differentiation daunting (p 49). She proposes a model of differentiation with three stages (p 48).

Stage 1: The traditional model which has grown from the SEN framework. It is a deficit model and involves differentiated worksheets and individual programmes.

Stage 2: The inclusive learning model. This links effective inclusion with effective learning. It involves different levels of tasks, a responsiveness to different learning styles, engaging with a range of teaching styles, the teaching of thinking skills and respect for individual learning styles.

Stage 3: This model values differences. It links inclusive learning to empowerment. It is about meaningful engagement in learning processes which provide tools for the learner throughout their life.

Corbett (2001) sees these stages as opening up wider and more imaginative ways of providing differentiation. Good differentiation is not about planning and making provision for the children in the middle-achieving group and then extending it or providing additional work for the children in the higher-achieving group and dumbing down the work for the children in the lower-achieving group. It is about improving the quality of learning for all. It will value and develop individuality rather than conformity, and it places importance on each member of the class, regardless of their potential to achieve to the same levels of other children of their age (p 50).

Differentiation in practice

The current National Curriculum (NC) sets out learning objectives which children are required to achieve. While these are subject to change in the new curriculum, the principles concerned with adapting levels and objectives remain. Glazzard et al. (2010) recommend that teachers select from earlier or later stages of the NC in order to provide achievable objectives. He suggests that children with SEN may be able to work on the same learning objective as their peers, as long as suitable access strategies are provided, or that they may be provided with learning objectives which are linked to the theme the rest of the class are working on but which have been appropriately differentiated (pp 134–135). Similarly, when differentiation is provided for the academically more able pupils, its value should be considered for all pupils. It should be related to planning for all children, and the planned learning outcomes should be related to the general class learning objectives. Ways in which academically more able pupils' work might be differentiated are by

- taking a concept further;

- exploring an idea more broadly;

- interpreting the same task differently;

- learning an additional concept.

For example, consider a literacy lesson where children are being taught how to use descriptive language in response to a picture. The more able children in this group were given a more complex and demanding expectation for their descriptive sentences which included the use of similes, metaphors, connectives, and at least three adjectives in sentences, all correctly punctuated. This was taking a concept further than that required for other learners in the class.

Other ways in which the curriculum can be made accessible to all learners through differentiation are outlined by Evans (2007). These ideas move away from the notion of differentiation by ability and provide some practical ways in which Corbett's three stages of differentiation can be actualised. Evans recommends the following, some of which have been discussed in the previous chapter:

* make sure texts for reading are accessible and strategies are in place to support the less confident reader;

* enlarge print if necessary or use coloured paper or overlays;

* use visual prompts of symbols as reminder or to support understanding;

* use alternative means of recording work which do not involve writing, such as spoken word, images, sorting and labelling, images and scribing;

* make full use of ICT and appropriate software to support learning;

* break down the work into small and more manageable chunks;

* use a multi-sensory approach;

* provide or manage support from peers or other adults;

* allow extra time for the completion of tasks or pre-teach pupils before the lesson to provide maximum opportunity for progress within the lesson;

* provide supporting resources such as spelling banks, number lines and other equipment.

Making the curriculum inclusive can be aided significantly by how the TA is deployed in the classroom. As already outlined in Chapter 12, it is crucial for the teacher to share the planning and expectations of learning with the TA and to ensure that the TA is able to accomplish the given task. Consider a TA in the class working with the academically more able pupils with the brief *to support their writing*. These pupils would be unlikely to extend their learning to their potential as the brief is too vague. The children would be able to access the curriculum, but none would have the opportunity to access an extended curriculum more appropriately matched to their potential.

Better practice is demonstrated in the following example. A trainee teacher shared her planning with the TA and made clear the expected outcomes of the children's learning and how the TA should advance this. There was a child with additional needs in the class but the trainee rejected the idea of the velcro model of support for the individual needs of this child, choosing to work with her personally through targeted questioning, additional resources and providing peer support as required. The trainee also provided the TA with a set of sticky notes to provide quick but specific feedback on the children's progress in the lesson. This enabled the trainee to know how to plan for the following lesson and whether any particular children would benefit from reinforcement of a concept or a different approach.

This flexible approach is consistent with the findings of Farrell and Balshaw (2002, p 48), who consider that working in this way does not draw attention to children with SEN as the TA is seen to work with a range of pupils. It also means that the teacher is responsible for making the curriculum accessible for all of the children in the class, rather than expecting the TA to spontaneously adapt a previously unseen piece of work to allow a child to complete it. The emphasis therefore remains firmly on providing an inclusive curriculum in order to provide the best means possible to advance all children's learning.

Critical questions

Consider a class where you have observed another teacher.

» *How did the teacher provide differentiation?*

» *Which of Corbett's stages of differentiation have you observed?*

» *What is your own experience of providing differentiation?*

» *How might you develop your practice further in order to move towards Corbett's stage 3 of differentiation?*

Consider the class in the first scenario.

» *What practical methods of differentiation do you think could be used to make the curriculum accessible to all learners?*

» *How would you use a TA to support an inclusive curriculum in this class?*

Personalised learning

The document *Personalised Learning: A Practical Guide* was published by the previous government with the intention of engaging and supporting all pupils in their learning (DCSF, 2008). Personalised learning involves building on pupils' prior learning and responding appropriately to children's own voices about how they learn. However, as the document states, *the key challenge for personalisation in the classroom is how to cater simultaneously for all the different needs in one class* (p 9).

The DCSF (2008) recognises that teachers have in the past differentiated by task or outcome. Teachers also differentiate by age and ability; however, other forms of differentiation are being put forward, such as staging the work by how support is offered, by open-tasking (ie setting mixed-ability tasks which challenge all pupils) and by extension or enhancement activities. This approach is considered to be more inclusive as it provides ample opportunity for reasonable adjustments to be made for children with SEN. It also provides opportunity for differentiation by interests, preferences or priorities. It is known as *quality first* teaching (DCSF, 2008, p 9). The DCSF recognises that while *many aspects of personalised learning are individualised ... many needs can be met in the classroom context without resorting to one-to-one remediation* (2008, p 11).

A key element of personalised learning is assessment, and formative assessment in particular. McIntyre (2000) suggests that this is a *much less contentious idea than differentiation by ability* (p 104) as it actively involves the child as well as the teacher in assessing their work and providing appropriate next steps. According to research by Black and Wiliam (1998), formative assessment does improve learning. Formative assessment is part of Assessment for Learning (AfL), other elements of which include:

- objective-led lessons;
- oral and written feedback;
- peer and self-assessment;
- curricular target setting;
- questioning and dialogue. (Ofsted, 2008)

According to the Ofsted impact study, AfL is part of effective planning. It promotes understanding of goals and criteria, helps learners to know how to improve and develops the capacity for self and peer assessment (p 7). As such, it can be seen as a key driver to improve standards.

In the schools that took part in the impact study, where AfL was most successful it was found that teachers used carefully phrased questions which were pitched appropriately for the needs of all learners. They used mini-plenaries in their lessons to redirect the focus of learning, to deal with misconceptions and to showcase children's learning. Teachers made full use of talk partners, using open-ended questions for discussion. They also encouraged pupil feedback to explain issues to others. Additionally, teachers kept a close eye on the progress of the children and were aware of how to develop next steps. They were not afraid to move on from work when it was understood or to deviate from the lesson plan if required for reinforcement of learning. Their use of oral feedback was effective and they gave detailed and constructive written feedback about how to improve. Alongside this, they gave pupils the opportunity to act on advice given, to reflect and respond.

Critical questions

» *Look at this list of AfL strategies. Tick if you have seen these strategies used when you have been in school and if you have used these strategies yourself.*

AfL strategy	Observed others use it	Have used it personally
Carefully phrased questions		
Mini-plenaries		
Talk partners		
Open-ended questions		
Pupil feedback/explanations		
Deviation from lesson plan		
Effective oral feedback		
Detailed and constructive written feedback		
Opportunity to act on feedback		

» *What does this audit of strategies tell you?*

» *What are the most commonly used strategies and why?*

» *Which strategies are least commonly used and why?*

» *Which of these strategies will you try when you are next teaching?*

» *How will these strategies help you to make the curriculum more inclusive for all learners?*

Learning differently

Within a class of children there will be many different learning preferences. There will be those who prefer to work alone, those who feel more confident when in a group, those who excel in creative work such as art or music, or those who are good at practical work such as sport or design technology. Many of our classrooms are weighted towards literacy and numeracy, largely because these subjects are seen as core subjects and are chosen as a measure for SATs and ultimately school league tables. However, with such an emphasis on literacy and numeracy, children who are low achievers in these subjects may be overlooked and their learning preferences ignored.

Multiple intelligences

The work of Howard Gardner is influential in forwarding the idea of multiple intelligences. He recognised that as human beings it is often considered that we possess one intelligence. However, from his perspective as an educational psychologist, he suggests that we may possess *a set of relatively autonomous intelligences* (Gardner, 2003, p 4). He states that many of the commonly understood concepts of intelligence rely on a combination of linguistic and logical intelligences, but he maintains that a fuller appreciation of human beings can take place if a range of intelligences, such as spatial, bodily-kinaesthetic, musical, interpersonal and intrapersonal, are also acknowledged. He observes that these intelligences can be found in everyone, but are subject to genetic and experiential influences which affect the profile of strengths and limitations. Gardner states that while this psychological theory does not have any direct educational implications, *it makes sense to take this fact into account in devising an educational system* (2003, p 5). Therefore it is reasonable to suggest that providing educational opportunities for children that take into account a range of different intelligences can be of great benefit to learners of all kinds and facilitate their access to the curriculum. It acknowledges that language skills are only one kind of intelligence and appreciates that the recognition of other intelligences can provide a flexible and creative approach for diverse learners.

Learning styles

The most common and easiest to implement learning approaches are visual, auditory and kinaesthetic (VAK). Visual learners look for visual diagrams and clues, the use of videos, charts, pictures, diagrams and maps and writing notes for frequent scanning and review. Auditory learners like to sound out words in reading, they prefer verbal instructions, the use of audio equipment, working in groups, discussion and rehearsing information in order to retain it.

Kinaesthetic learners learn by being able to move around, taking risks in learning, role play, making study plans and learning facts by writing them out several times (Reid, 2005, p 121).

More recently, VAK has been criticised as it can be seen as pigeon-holing children into one particular style of learning and assumes they are not able to learn by other styles or approaches or, indeed, to change their learning preferences. Children have been known to announce themselves as being a particular kind of learner and refused to attempt work which requires a different learning approach. Coffield et al. (2004) produced a report on learning styles which showed that evidence to support the effectiveness of learning styles is subjective, often promoted by advocates of one particular approach (p 61).

In considering the notion of VAK, it is important to acknowledge that almost all children learn through vision by the use of charts, diagrams and pictures rather than *word-dominated books* (Franklin, 2006, p 84). Additionally, the use of the auditory dimension in the classroom is essential to the learning process. However, Franklin considers that some pupils identified as kinaesthetic learners may also be seen as being *non-academic*, as such children may be good at sports and practical tasks but low achievers academically (2006, p 84). She is sceptical about the use of VAK to stereotype children as certain kinds of learners and where learning is seen as a capacity rather than a process (p 83). All children are different with different strengths, abilities and difficulties; however, Franklin maintains that a skilful teacher will choose to understand the learning processes rather than label children. She endorses the idea of using effective visual images, providing opportunities for interaction and thinking aloud to stimulate learning for all children rather than only for those considered to be able in one particular learning style (p 84). It is by providing a range of different approaches to learning, including the visual, auditory and kinaesthetic, and incorporating these within your planning and teaching strategies that you are likely to make the curriculum more accessible to the vast majority of pupils.

Critical questions

You are teaching the children to prepare a healthy snack. You have access to cookers and appropriate equipment.

» *How would children with each of the different learning styles described above approach this activity?*

» *Fill in the chart below with your ideas.*

Visual learner	Auditory learner	Kinaesthetic learner
Watch while someone else made the snack	Listen to the explanation	
Follow a recipe step by step		
Look at pictures of what it should look like		

Alternatives to written work

When working with children, it is important to realise that although written methods of recording are frequently used as evidence of the child's learning, all too often it is simply a measure of how well the child can write or communicate through the written word. It may not be a measure of their knowledge or understanding of the concept being taught. For some children, such as those with dyspraxia or dyslexia, the requirement to write about what they have learned provides a barrier and may lead the teacher to believe they have not understood, whereas, in fact, they are just not able to communicate the extent of their learning in written form. To provide an inclusive curriculum you must consider how you require children to demonstrate and record learning. The following are ways in which children can use alternative methods of recording their work:

* flow charts or spidergrams;

* oral presentations;

* making posters or displays, drawing, diagrams, taking photographs;

* using a highlighter, number fans, matching activities, sorting;

* asking another person to scribe;

* role play, the use of video, digital recordings.

Such creative methods are of value to all children and should not just be used for those for whom writing presents a challenge.

A pupil identified as having significant dyslexia found writing a frustrating labour. However, she had an excellent memory for the spoken word. This was put to good use by giving her access to a voice recorder, which would play instructions, reminders and relevant subject knowledge, but also allowed her to record her own responses. Through this means she was able to achieve at expected levels (and higher than expected in some curriculum areas), since the barrier to accessing the curriculum, ie writing, had been removed.

SCENARIO

Britney is 10 years old. She is adopted and so her birth history is not known; however, she appears to have some physical difficulties on the right side of her body. Her right arm and leg are particularly affected. It is thought she may have sustained some brain damage through oxygen deprivation at birth. She walks in a way consistent with someone with mild cerebral palsy and the way she holds her hand reinforces this notion. As a result, she is not able to use her right hand for fine motor skills such as writing or holding equipment such as scissors or a knife. Her handwriting style is clumsy and slow and the presentation of her work is often poor. She rarely manages more than two sentences in any one lesson. It is thought that she may have right-hand dominance, but because of the cerebral palsy-type difficulties has to use her left hand for writing. She wears glasses due to having a squint.

She is very articulate and confident and has a good understanding of what is taught in class. She is a good reader and enjoys practical work which does not involve writing. Some consider she has rather a strident personality and she does tend to override others at times. She is an able musician and plays the horn in the school brass band and orchestra. She is a good swimmer, but finds other kinds of sport very difficult, particularly those requiring a significant degree of co-ordination. As a result, she tends to be reluctant to take part, often seeming to forget her PE kit and complaining during sessions.

Critical questions

Think about Britney.

» *What areas of the curriculum does she excel in?*

» *What curriculum areas present barriers to learning for Britney?*

» *What intelligences does Britney show?*

» *What learning styles do you think Britney might prefer and why?*

» *How could you use Britney's strengths and preferences to enable her to access all areas of the curriculum more fully?*

» *What alternatives to written recording might Britney be able to use?*

» *Britney is taking part in a maths lesson where the children are looking at the programme of study on data. They are expected to draw, read and interpret line graphs and use these to solve problems. Given what you know about Britney, how would you make this lesson accessible for her and guarantee progress in learning?*

Summary

In considering how to make the curriculum inclusive for all learners, it is easy to be overwhelmed by the many and varied approaches that could be employed. Removing barriers to accessing the curriculum for all learners may seem daunting; however, it is important to remember that many of the strategies that are good for individuals are good for all learners. Corbett's notion of a connective pedagogy, which connects the pupil's learning style with how they learn most effectively and ultimately to the curriculum, provides an understanding of differentiation which is not ability-dependent, but promotes effective learning and values difference. The consideration of Gardner's multiple intelligences, along with different learning styles, provides scope for differentiation according to interest, preference or priorities. Together with a consideration of alternatives to written recording, these ideas provide you with manageable steps towards a more inclusive and accessible curriculum for all learners.

Critical reflections

» *Think about a school where you have worked as a trainee teacher. How inclusive would you consider the curriculum to be for all learners? Justify your response with evidence from practice.*

» *What three things will you do as a beginner teacher to make sure the curriculum is accessible to all learners?*

» *How will you make sure the TA in your class is able to promote effective learning for the children with whom she or he works?*

» *What methods of AfL will you introduce in your first class and how will you use this to bring about improvements in children's learning?*

Taking it further

Books and journals

Clarke, S. (2001) *Unlocking Formative Assessment; Practical Strategies for Enhancing Pupil's Learning in the Primary Classroom* London: Hodder and Stoughton Educational.

> This very readable book provides many practical strategies that can be used to develop children's knowledge and use of formative assessment. It links justification for the use of such strategies with how they can be made practical in the classroom.

Web-based material

Primary: Teaching children good communication skills – Rhyl Primary School:

www.education.gov.uk/schools/careers/traininganddevelopment/b00201451/sen-skills/nqt-pillars/pillar6 (last accessed 4 October 2013).

> This video shows how one group of children are taught good communication skills so that they can engage in peer assessment more effectively.

What are P scales? www.education.gov.uk/schools/teachingandlearning/assessment/a00203453/about-the-p-scales (last accessed 4 October 2013).

> This link will take you to the DfE website and to a document which explains what P scales are and how they can support inclusive practice as well as tracking and target setting. The document also contains other links to further information about P scales.

References

Armstrong, F. (2011) Inclusive Education: School Cultures, Teaching and Learning, in Richards, G. and Armstrong, F. (eds) *Teaching and Learning in Inclusive and Diverse Classrooms: Key Issues for New Teachers*. Oxon: Routledge.

Black, P.J. and Wiliam, D. (1998) *Inside the Black Box: Raising Standards Through Classroom Assessment*. London: GL Assessment.

Carter-Wall, C. and Whitfield, G. (2012) *The Role of Aspirations, Attitudes and Behaviour in Closing the Educational Attainment Gap*. York: Joseph Rowntree Foundation. Online: www.jrf.org.uk/sites/files/jrf/education-achievement-poverty-summary.pdf (last accessed 4 October 2013).

Cassen, R. and Kingdon, G. (2007) *Tackling Low Educational Achievement*. York: Joseph Rowntree Foundation. Online: www.jrf.org.uk/sites/files/jrf/2095.pdf (last accessed 4 October 2013).

Coffield, F., Moseley, D., Hall, E. and Ecclestone, K. (2004) *Should We Be Using Learning Styles? What Research Has to Say to Practice*. London: Learning and Skills Research Centre.

Corbett, J. (2001) *Supporting Inclusive Education: A Connective Pedagogy*. London: RoutledgeFalmer.

Department for Children, Schools and Families (DCSF) (2008) *Personalised Learning: A Practical Guide*. Online: http://webarchive.nationalarchives.gov.uk/20130401151715/https://www.education.gov.uk/publications/eOrderingDownload/00844-2008DOM-EN.pdf (last accessed 4 October 2013).

Department for Education (DfE) (2010) *The Importance of Teaching*, White Paper Equalities Impact Assessment. Online: www.education.gov.uk/publications/eOrderingDownload/CM-7980-Impact_equalities.pdf (last accessed 4 October 2013).

Department for Education (DfE) (2012a) *Teachers' Standards*. Online: http://media.education.gov. uk/assets/files/pdf/t/teachers%20standards%20information.pdf (last accessed 4 October 2013).

Department for Education (DfE) (2012b) *Academically More Able Pupils*. Online: www.education.gov. uk/schools/pupilsupport/inclusionandlearnersupport/a00205083/academically-more-able-pupils (last accessed 4 October 2013).

Department for Education (DfE) (2013) *The National Curriculum in England: Framework Document*. Online: www.gov.uk/government/uploads/system/uploads/attachment_data/file/210969/ NC_framework_document_-_FINAL.pdf (last accessed 4 October 2013).

Department for Education and Skills (DfES) (2001) *Special Educational Needs Code of Practice*. London: The Stationery Office.

Department for Education and Skills (DfES) (2004) *Removing Barriers to Achievement: The Government's Strategy for SEN*. Nottingham: DfES Publications.

Evans, L. (2007) *Inclusion*. Oxon: Routledge.

Farrell, P. and Balshaw, M. (2002) Can Teaching Assistants Make Special Education Inclusive?, in Farrell, P. and Ainscow, M. (eds) (2002) *Making Special Education Inclusive*. London: David Fulton.

Franklin, S. (2006) 'VAKing Out' Learning Styles – Why the Notion of 'Learning Styles' is Unhelpful to Teachers. *Education 3–13: International Journal of Primary, Elementary and Early Years Education*, 34(1): 81–87.

Gardner, H. (2003) Multiple Intelligences After Twenty Years, invited address, American Educational Research Association. Online: www.consorzionettuno.it/materiali/B/697/773/16/Testi/ Gardner/Gardner_multiple_intelligent.pdf (last accessed 4 October 2013).

Glazzard, J., Hughes, A., Netherwood, A., Neve, L. and Stokoe, J. (2010) *Achieving QTS Teaching Primary Special Educational Needs*. London: Sage.

Lewis, A. and Norwich, B. (2001) A Critical Review of Systematic Evidence Concerning Distinctive Pedagogy for Pupils with Difficulties in Learning. *Journal of Research in Special Educational Needs*, 1(1).

McIntyre, D. (2000) Has Classroom Teaching Served Its Day?, in Nind, M., Rix, J., Sheehy, K. and Simmons, K. (eds) (2005) *Inclusive Education: Diverse Perspectives*. London: David Fulton.

Ofsted (2008) *Assessment for Learning: The Impact of National Strategy Support*. Online: www.ofsted. gov.uk/resources/assessment-for-learning-impact-of-national-strategy-support (last accessed 4 October 2013).

Pound, L. (2008) *How Children Learn: from Montessori to Vygotsky: Educational Theories and Approaches Made Easy*. London: Step Forward Publishing.

Reid, G. (2005) *Learning Styles and Inclusion*. London: Paul Chapman.

Appendix

Department for Education

Teachers' Standards

PREAMBLE

Teachers make the education of their pupils their first concern, and are accountable for achieving the highest possible standards in work and conduct. Teachers act with honesty and integrity; have strong subject knowledge, keep their knowledge and skills as teachers up-to-date and are self-critical; forge positive professional relationships; and work with parents in the best interests of their pupils.

PART ONE: TEACHING

A teacher must:

1 Set high expectations which inspire, motivate and challenge pupils

- establish a safe and stimulating environment for pupils, rooted in mutual respect
- set goals that stretch and challenge pupils of all backgrounds, abilities and dispositions
- demonstrate consistently the positive attitudes, values and behaviour which are expected of pupils.

2 Promote good progress and outcomes by pupils

- be accountable for pupils' attainment, progress and outcomes
- be aware of pupils' capabilities and their prior knowledge, and plan teaching to build on these
- guide pupils to reflect on the progress they have made and their emerging needs
- demonstrate knowledge and understanding of how pupils learn and how this impacts on teaching
- encourage pupils to take a responsible and conscientious attitude to their own work and study.

3 Demonstrate good subject and curriculum knowledge

- have a secure knowledge of the relevant subject(s) and curriculum areas, foster and maintain pupils' interest in the subject, and address misunderstandings
- demonstrate a critical understanding of developments in the subject and curriculum areas, and promote the value of scholarship
- demonstrate an understanding of and take responsibility for promoting high standards of literacy, articulacy and the correct use of standard English, whatever the teacher's specialist subject
- if teaching early reading, demonstrate a clear understanding of systematic synthetic phonics
- if teaching early mathematics, demonstrate a clear understanding of appropriate teaching strategies.

4 Plan and teach well structured lessons

- impart knowledge and develop understanding through effective use of lesson time
- promote a love of learning and children's intellectual curiosity
- set homework and plan other out-of-class activities to consolidate and extend the knowledge and understanding pupils have acquired
- reflect systematically on the effectiveness of lessons and approaches to teaching
- contribute to the design and provision of an engaging curriculum within the relevant subject area(s).

5 Adapt teaching to respond to the strengths and needs of all pupils

- know when and how to differentiate appropriately, using approaches which enable pupils to be taught effectively
- have a secure understanding of how a range of factors can inhibit pupils' ability to learn, and how best to overcome these
- demonstrate an awareness of the physical, social and intellectual development of children, and know how to adapt teaching to support pupils' education at different stages of development
- have a clear understanding of the needs of all pupils, including those with special educational needs; those of high ability; those with English as an additional language; those with disabilities; and be able to use and evaluate distinctive teaching approaches to engage and support them.

6 Make accurate and productive use of assessment

- know and understand how to assess the relevant subject and curriculum areas, including statutory assessment requirements
- make use of formative and summative assessment to secure pupils' progress
- use relevant data to monitor progress, set targets, and plan subsequent lessons
- give pupils regular feedback, both orally and through accurate marking, and encourage pupils to respond to the feedback.

7 Manage behaviour effectively to ensure a good and safe learning environment

- have clear rules and routines for behaviour in classrooms, and take responsibility for promoting good and courteous behaviour both in classrooms and around the school, in accordance with the school's behaviour policy
- have high expectations of behaviour, and establish a framework for discipline with a range of strategies, using praise, sanctions and rewards consistently and fairly
- manage classes effectively, using approaches which are appropriate to pupils' needs in order to involve and motivate them
- maintain good relationships with pupils, exercise appropriate authority, and act decisively when necessary.

8 Fulfil wider professional responsibilities

- make a positive contribution to the wider life and ethos of the school
- develop effective professional relationships with colleagues, knowing how and when to draw on advice and specialist support
- deploy support staff effectively
- take responsibility for improving teaching through appropriate professional development, responding to advice and feedback from colleagues
- communicate effectively with parents with regard to pupils' achievements and well-being.

PART TWO: PERSONAL AND PROFESSIONAL CONDUCT

A teacher is expected to demonstrate consistently high standards of personal and professional conduct. The following statements define the behaviour and attitudes which set the required standard for conduct throughout a teacher's career.

- Teachers uphold public trust in the profession and maintain high standards of ethics and behaviour, within and outside school, by:
  o treating pupils with dignity, building relationships rooted in mutual respect, and at all times observing proper boundaries appropriate to a teacher's professional position
  o having regard for the need to safeguard pupils' well-being, in accordance with statutory provisions
  o showing tolerance of and respect for the rights of others
  o not undermining fundamental British values, including democracy, the rule of law, individual liberty and mutual respect, and tolerance of those with different faiths and beliefs
  o ensuring that personal beliefs are not expressed in ways which exploit pupils' vulnerability or might lead them to break the law.

- Teachers must have proper and professional regard for the ethos, policies and practices of the school in which they teach, and maintain high standards in their own attendance and punctuality.

- Teachers must have an understanding of, and always act within, the statutory frameworks which set out their professional duties and responsibilities.

Index